ODOO 17 ACCOUNTING BOOK

Preface

Welcome to the comprehensive guidebook on Odoo 17 Accounting, crafted exclusively to empower users, consultants, and business owners with the proficiency to navigate the intricacies of accounting management seamlessly within the Odoo ecosystem. Authored by Cybrosys Technologies, this book serves as your definitive roadmap through the dynamic landscape of Odoo's accounting module, equipped with step-by-step instructions and illustrative screenshots.

In today's dynamic business environment, efficient financial management is paramount to the success of any organization. Odoo introduces innovative features and improvements with each new version release, cementing its position as a leader in the ERP software market. One of the key strengths of Odoo lies in its ability to seamlessly integrate with other modules and third-party applications, allowing businesses to create customized solutions tailored to their specific requirements. Whether it's integrating the accounting module with inventory management for seamless stock valuation or connecting it with CRM for unified customer management, Odoo offers endless possibilities for optimization.

Odoo stands as a beacon of innovation in the realm of enterprise resource planning, offering a versatile, open-source solution that revolutionizes business processes across industries. With its modular architecture, Odoo offers a plethora of integrated applications tailored to meet the diverse needs of modern enterprises. At its core, Odoo fosters efficiency, scalability, and innovation, enabling organizations to thrive in a rapidly evolving market landscape. At the heart of Odoo lies its robust Accounting module, a powerhouse of tools and features meticulously designed to streamline financial operations with precision and agility. Businesses can streamline their accounting processes, gain real-time insights, and make appropriate decisions to drive growth and profitability using the Accounting module in Odoo. With Odoo 17 Accounting, users are empowered with an arsenal of functionalities aimed at optimizing every aspect of accounting management, from invoicing and expense tracking to financial reporting and reconciliation.

What this book covers:

This guidebook leaves no stone unturned as it delves into the depths of Odoo 17 Accounting, offering comprehensive insights into each tool and feature. From configuring your chart of accounts to mastering advanced reporting techniques, each chapter is tailored to equip you with the knowledge and skills necessary to harness the full potential of Odoo's accounting capabilities. In the pages that follow, you'll find a wealth of knowledge and practical insights aimed at demystifying the complexities of Odoo's accounting module, accompanied by step-by-step instructions and illustrative screenshots for a clear and concise understanding.

Who this book is for:

Whether you're a novice exploring the realms of Odoo for the first time or a seasoned professional seeking to elevate your accounting prowess, this book caters to individuals of all proficiency levels. Business owners striving to optimize their accounting management procedures will find invaluable guidance within these pages, alongside consultants eager to leverage Odoo's technological prowess to drive operational excellence. Additionally, educators and students interested in learning about modern accounting practices within the context of an ERP system will find this book to be a valuable resource.

Embark on a transformative journey through Odoo 17 Accounting, guided by the expertise of Cybrosys Technologies. This book is designed to be your companion on the journey to mastering Odoo 17 Accounting, whether you're a beginner looking to grasp the fundamentals or an experienced user seeking advanced techniques. Let this book serve as your compass, illuminating the path toward efficiency, accuracy, and success in the realm of accounting management.

Table of Contents

Chapter 1
Get Started with Accounting Basics

Get Started with Accounting Basics

The process of reporting, documenting, illustrating, and summarizing financial data is referred to as accounting. An organization or business cannot function without accounting. It serves as the primary point of contact for all types of commercial dealings. Accounting has been refreshed over the years as a contained system for maintaining financial records and supporting an accountant's responsibilities. However, the continually changing business climate in the present day necessitates that business owners and accountants reevaluate their roles and duties. Accounting involves more than just creating financial reports and keeping track of books.

Significance of Accounting

Accounting, which is the systematic and thorough recording of a company's financial activities, is essential to its operation, including managing statutory compliance and tracking income-expenditure relationships. Additionally, gathering quantitative financial data is beneficial. The owners, management, investors, and even governments will gain from the accounting system. A company that succeeds needs a solid and well-established accounting and bookkeeping system.

The bookkeeping procedure serves as the foundation of the accounting system, which monitors a company's financial health. At the end of each fiscal year, statistics and information are reported in the form of a financial statement. Accounting is essential for assessing business performance effectively. Comparing accounts with prior years is simple. By maintaining a strong book of accounts, the accounting system also enables you to keep a careful eye on the cash flow. The account-keeping system also makes filing simple and ensures that you never break the law. In addition to all of these advantages, accounting data makes it simple to create a budget that will support a given business strategy. So that you can budget for your future ambitions in an efficient and productive manner. An organization can benefit from proper accounting by receiving the numerous financial reports needed to manage day-to-day operations.

The management of the budget, one of the most crucial components of an organization, will be incredibly easy if the accounting system is reliable. Making the proper company decisions will be aided by the accurate data you obtain from the financial accounts, which will lead to efficient administration and increased profitability.

Double Entry Bookkeeping System

A method of recording transactions in accounting is called double-entry bookkeeping. In this approach, the input is recorded as at least two accounts—debit and credit. The recorded debit and credit amounts in this system must be equal. This means that the total of the reported credits and debits must match. In order to register the transaction on both sides, the system will assist you. In this system, if a transaction takes place and has an effect on one account, an equivalent effect also takes place in the other account. The credit value will be recorded alongside the equivalent debit amount. The chart of accounts for the business will also include a list of the credited and debited accounts.

Let's use a sale that is confirmed for 50 dollars as an example to follow. Both the Income Account and the Receivable Account will be affected. As a result of the sale, the revenue of the company rises. Consequently, the income grows, and $50 is credited to the income account. As Assets grow, the receivable account is debited by $50. Whether an account should be credited or debited depends on the type of account.

The Hierarchy of Accounting

The cornerstone of future growth is finance. Therefore, as a business ruler, you should be concerned with the business or the firm's accounting hierarchy. Without taking the size and type of the business into consideration, the accounting hierarchy is quite significant.

All transactional information is correctly put into the corresponding ledgers in the general accounting system. The nature of a transaction determines how its information is recorded on both sides (the credit and debit sides of accounts). A hierarchy is then followed for general accounting.

Natures

Asset, Liability, Income, and Expense are the four categories of nature.

Natures	Increasing	Decreasing
Income & Liability	Credit	Debit
Expense & Asset	Debit	Credit

Some kinds of accounting systems refer to the accepted patterns of liability and income while adding "Equity" as an additional nature. The profit and loss reports are impacted by all account groupings that fall within the category of income and expenses.

Account Groups

Account Groups are formed by grouping together related ledger accounts. The hierarchy of ledger accounts is supposed to be demonstrated by these account groups. The generation of relevant reports will greatly benefit from this structure of ledger accounts. Regular, Payable, Receivable, and Liquidity account groups are the most frequently utilized account types in Odoo17. These defined groupings are used to describe each of these account ledgers.

SI.NO	Account Name	Nature	Group Under	Affect in Reports
1	Receivable	Asset	Receivable	Balance Sheet
2	Bank and Cash	Asset	Liquidity	Balance Sheet
3	Current Assets	Asset	Regular	Balance Sheet
4	Non-Current Assets	Asset	Regular	Balance Sheet
5	Prepayments	Asset	Regular	Balance Sheet
6	Fixed Assets	Asset	Regular	Balance Sheet
7	Payable	Liability	Payable	Balance sheet
8	Credit Card	Liability	Liquidity	Balance sheet
9	Current Liabilities	Liability	Regular	Balance sheet
10	Non-Current liabilities	Liability	Regular	Balance sheet
11	Income	Income	Regular	Profit & Loss
12	Other Income	Income	Regular	Profit & Loss
13	Expenses	Expense	Regular	Profit & Loss
14	Depreciation	Expense	Regular	Profit & Loss
15	Cost of Revenue	Expense	Regular	Profit & Loss
16	Equity	Equity	Regular	Balance sheet
17	Current Year Earnings	Equity	Regular	Balance sheet

Let's examine each of them independently.

1. Account Receivable (Debtors)

The sum of money necessary for paying for goods or services that have been received but have not yet been paid by the customer is known as an Account Receivable. The debtors are another name for the Account Receivable. These accounts are particularly practical for keeping track of all customer receivables. The receivables will fall under the Assets when we take their nature into account. When taking into account a sale, the receivable accounts are debited based on the increasing number of receivables.

2. Bank and Cash

Every organization's bank and cash account will fall under the Bank and Cash type because it is an Asset by definition. As an illustration, let's say a company decides to make a cash payment rather than a credit purchase and takes into account the amount that is taken out of the bank account. Due to the asset's decrease, the bank account will be credited.

3. Current Assets

Cash and other assets that are planned to be converted to cash within a year are considered Current Assets. So, registering short-term assets will be facilitated by using this account type. This category can include assets like inventory, short-term investments, prepaid expenses, etc. This category includes the bank deposits, loans, and advances provided to the employees.

General accounts include Stock Valuation Accounts, Stock Input and Output Accounts, Deferred Expense Accounts, and numerous others. Because they are assets by nature, Odoo's "Current Assets" ledgers and entries of this sort have an impact on the balance sheet.

4. Non-Current Assets

Non-current assets are regarded as assets that the company purchases or invests in. That investment's quantity does not, however, reverse within an accounting year. As a result, this investment type will produce returns for a considerable amount of time and cannot simply be converted into cash. The following are some examples of this kind of asset: properties, automobiles, insurance, etc. It is impossible to determine the total value within the accounting year. The balance sheet includes a list of each one of them.

5. Prepayments

Prepaid expenses serve as an example of prepayments. Although the goods and services in this instance have already been paid for, they have not yet been received or used. As an illustration, Odoo saw prepaid or deferred expenses as belonging to this category.

For instance, suppose there was insurance with a $30,000 annual payment. The company won't be able to include the entire expense in the current-year profit and loss report. The sum must be spread out over a full year by the organization. As a result, $2500 will be used each month, and the expense will be recorded. The payment will be of the type "Asset," and the asset value will drop annually. Therefore, as the expense steadily reduces, the payment account will be credited and the expense account debited.

6. Fixed Assets

The Fixed Assets account type is highly convenient for recording all fixed asset transactions, including those involving equipment, vehicles, real estate, buildings, furniture, and many more. All the goods that the firm or business intends to use for a long time can be included. Additionally, fixed assets fall under the Assets category. As a result, when we make a purchase, the fixed asset will grow, the fixed asset account will be debited, and the fixed assets will be recorded on the balance sheet.

7. Payables

Creditors is another name for the Payables account category. It is the total amount owed by an organization to anyone or any individual. The payables accounts are appropriate for keeping track of all amounts owed to vendors or suppliers. The payable account is additionally credited as the category of responsibility on a vendor bill.

8. Credit Cards

Another category of account is the credit card, and this account's characteristic is liability. The balance sheet includes information about the credit card. In the case of credit cards, the amount of money spent using the card for any purpose, such as making a purchase or paying for other expenses, will result in certain debts, which we need to repay within a certain amount of time, usually less than or close to two months.

9. Current Liabilities

Short-term liabilities are Current Liabilities, those that must be paid off within a year. The Current Liability Account Type can be listed under the following headings. Among them are overdrafts at the bank, quick loans, taxes and duties, salaries that must be paid, payroll taxes, accruing costs, income taxes, and many other things.

10. Non-current liabilities

Non-current liabilities, also known as long-period debts or financial commitments, are long-term obligations that are shown on the balance sheet and are due in a year or more. Non-current liabilities include things like pension benefit obligations, long-term loans, deferred tax liabilities, and long-term leasing obligations.

11. Income & Other Income

When a company wants to show its income or revenue, the Income & Other Income account type is quite helpful. The nature of the account is income, which will be included in the profit and loss reports. The company's primary source of income is from the sale of its goods and services. And any other income is not considered to be a direct source of revenue. Interest payments, rent payments, and other sources of revenue are a few examples.

12. Expenses

The account types known as expense accounts are used to keep track of every aspect of how much an organization spends on regular expenses over the course of a certain accounting period. This form of expense account comprises delivery costs, income tax costs, costs associated with the creation of goods and services, salary costs, advertising costs, maintenance costs, marketing costs, rent costs, etc. Since expenses are the nature of the Expense accounts type, they will be included in the income statement/profit and loss report.

13. Depreciation

The amount that an organization's assets are depreciated for a particular period is generally referred to as the Depreciation account type. This account type is typically used to track the depreciation of fixed assets. There will occasionally be some depreciation in the case of fixed assets, and each period will undoubtedly see a decline in their value. Depreciation of this kind will, therefore, be linear or regressive. At the time an asset is created, it will also have a book value and a salvage value. The initial cost is represented by the book value. Salvage value is the amount that an organization will receive when selling a fixed asset after all depreciation has been accounted for. Furthermore, based on the depreciation method used, the expense will be spread out over a specific time period as opposed to being added all at once to the current year. The expense account is credited, while the depreciation accounts debit.

14. Cost Of Revenue

The direct costs associated with the company's goods and services are closely correlated with the cost of revenue. This means that it represents the full cost of producing and providing a good or service to customers. It is more comfortable to depict the direct cost linked with the goods and services since it is immediately related to the income statement. It comprises the price of producing the goods and shipping it to the buyers. Cost of revenue is an expense by definition, and as such, this account type will have an effect on gross profit.

15. Equity

The equity account type can be thought of as the financial representation of a company's intellectual property. It displays the sum of money that the employers contributed to beginning operations. Equity can result from a business receiving payments from its owners or from the residual income it generates. In other words, equity is the amount of assets remaining after all liabilities have been paid in full and are recorded on the balance sheet. This account type includes common stock, contributed surplus, treasury stock, common and preference stocks, other sizable earnings, etc. Equity will fall under the category of Asset type when we think about its nature. The equity will be equal to the amount of money invested. Therefore, any investment will result in an increase in equity. The extra equity will then be credited to the capital account.

16. Current year earnings

The equity-based account type known as "Current Year Yearning" is used to reflect the net profit and loss for the current fiscal year on the balance sheet. The earnings for the current year will also be impacted by sales or any other transaction that has an impact on the income and expense account. The balance sheet will also include a mention of this.

Account Ledger

An account or record that can handle bookkeeping entries for balance sheet and income statement transactions, like opening and closing balance in debit or credit, is known as a ledger. This sort of book or digital record includes detailed transaction information and bookkeeping entries, such as bank or cash transactions, stock value, customer billing, vendor invoice records, salary expenses, and many more. The ledgers provide all the necessary data needed to create financial statements.

Every transaction has a reference number that will help them understand the justifications and steps involved in carrying out that particular transaction.

The following are the many account ledgers available in Odoo 16:
1. Income account
2. Expense account
3. Stock input account
4. Stock output account
5. Stock valuation account
6. Price difference account
7. Account Receivable
8. Account Payable
9. Fixed Asset Account
10. Depreciation Account
11. Revenue Account
12. Deferred revenue account
13. Expense account
14. Deferred Expense Account
15. Bank Suspense Account
16. Outstanding Receipts Account
17. Outstanding Payments Account
18. Internal Transfer Accounts
19. Cash Discount Loss Account
20. Cash Discount Gain Account
21. Foreign Exchange Gain Account
22. Foreign Exchange Loss Account

Journals

Journals are key and essential records containing important data and information about a business's transactions according to the date on which the transaction was completed. Account Names, Date, Amount, and even whether the transaction is recorded as a debit or credit are all shown in great detail.

You may see pre-configured journals that are appropriate for practically all sectors using Odoo16 Accounting. Additionally, if necessary, the platform lets you define new journals. Five different types of journals are available on the Odoo16 platform to display similar types of transactions in a single journal. The five journal types in Odoo16 can be listed as follows when we list them.

- Sales
- Purchase
- Bank
- Cash
- Miscellaneous.

Sales Journal

Every single sales-related transaction is documented in the sales journal type. You can set up various sales journals according to your needs using the Odoo platform. You can record transaction details for sales from wholesale and retail separately, for instance, if that is what is necessary. The customer invoices will be recorded here.

Purchase Journal

To compile all transactions related to purchases, use the Purchase journal record. Different buy journals can be made to post received vendor bills, just like with sales journals.

Bank Journal

The Bank Journal keeps detailed records of every bank transaction. You may successfully track customer bank payments, vendor bank payments, and any other transaction recorded by your associated bank account by posting your bank statements.

Cash Journal

Now, we can document all cash transactions in a cash journal. This type of journal can record daily cash transactions and petty cash transactions, and it can also keep track of information about cash payments from customers.

Miscellaneous Journal

The final form of the journal is a Miscellaneous journal, which is excellent for recording transactions that are not covered by the four journals we previously discussed (Sales, Purchase, Bank, and Cash). The journal type can take into account many other entries that don't fit into the other four journal types, such as inventory value, inventory changes, exchange difference, opening balance, and many others. Even for a salary or all of your corrections, posting a journal type entry is quite convenient. There are no advanced settings available in the Miscellaneous journals.

These five journal kinds can each have a sequence number set up on the Odoo17 platform for convenience.

Types of Accounting in Odoo 17

Odoo 17 primarily concentrates on three kinds of accounting practices. Accounting can be divided into two categories: "Anglo-Saxon accounting" and "Continental Accounting."

Odoo launched Storno Accounting, which employs negative credit/debit values for reverse entries.

Continental Accounting

The Odoo system and continental accounting, which is the most widely practiced accounting, and Odoo17 strongly support these ideas. This accounting practice is available both in the Enterprise and Community edition of Odoo 17. When making a purchase, this accounting will have an influence on the expense account. As soon as a product is found in stock, the expense of that item is therefore taken into account. Continental accounting is used by the Odoo17 platform by default. The stock can also be manually or automatically validated. The stock is unaffected if it is done manually, but the information must be manually posted at the end of each month or year.

Select the "Automated" inventory valuation technique if the stock valuations must be recorded as the stock is taken in and taken out. Numerous beneficial effects of Continental accounting's long history can be seen in your company's accounting. Consequently, we may examine how various transactions or procedures in continental accounting are impacted by the ledgers.

Transactions in Continental Accounting

The financial activity that has a direct impact on a company's financial situation and financial statements is known as an accounting transaction. Basically, we may include any kind of money exchange under this category. These transactions are handled differently by different organizations or companies. So that we can examine some of the fundamental accounting transactions.

1. **Purchase Process**

The financial transactions that are necessary for the business to buy the goods or services needed to generate sales are referred to as purchases. All transactions related to purchases are referred to as "purchase journals" on the Odoo17 platform. The purchase voucher contains a record of all these transactions related to purchases. It is the transaction handled by the seller of a good or service bought, and it could even be a good or service bought, as well as any other asset bought. An entire series of transactions, including purchase order, material receipt, rejection out, purchase invoice, and purchase return, are included in a purchase.

Purchase Order: An official document produced by a buyer committing to pay the seller for the sale of a specific good or service that will be provided in the future is known as a purchase order. For the required sum, a buy order can be made for any products or services from a vendor. The beginning of a purchase order does not immediately affect the ledgers for either stock or accounts.

Material Receipt: The next operation is called Material receipt, and it deals with details like product quantities and lot numbers in regard to the goods that are intended for the employees' on-site job. The inventory item must be received and added to the inventory if the supplier supplies the product. The inventory will be updated with the quantities. Therefore, only the stock accounts are impacted by Material Receipt.

The "Stock Valuation Account" and "Stock Input Account" in the Odoo17 platform are impacted when the product is received.

Accounts	Nature	Increasing Or Decreasing	Credit Or Debit
Stock valuation account	Asset	Increasing	Debit
Stock Input account	Liability	Increasing	Credit

Rejection Out (Purchase Return): The organization frequently returns the products it has purchased even before making the payment. It might be for any cause. The product will be rejected if it becomes damaged. Similar to how there will be several factors involved in the rejection. The stock will consequently reverse. In this instance, only the stock will be impacted; the accounts won't change. The stock value will likewise drop as a result.

Accounts	Nature	Increasing Or Decreasing	Credit Or Debit
Stock valuation account	Asset	Decreasing	Credit
Stock Input account	Liability	Decreasing	Debit

Purchase Bill Creation: The payable account and the expense account will be impacted if you create a bill for the purchase order. Due to the fact that the payable account's nature is "Liability," it will be credited. On the other hand, because the expense account is an "expense" account, it is debited.

Accounts	Nature	Increasing Or Decreasing	Credit Or Debit
Account Payable	Liability	Increasing	Credit
Expense Account	Expense	Increasing	Debit

Registering Payment: The payable account and the outstanding receipt account are both impacted when you generate a payment. The liability will be reduced if the payment has been made. Consequently, a debit will be made from the payable account. In the bank and cash journals of Odoo 17, a temporary account called outstanding payments is used to store unreconciled inputs. The kind of outstanding payment is "Asset." Therefore, the outstanding payment account is credited as the assets decrease.

Accounts	Nature	Increasing Or Decreasing	Credit Or Debit
Accounts payable	Liability	Decreasing	Debit
Outstanding Payments	Liability	Increasing	Credit

Reconciling: The sum will be transferred to the bank account after it is compared or reconciled to the bank statement. As a result, the account for outstanding payments is debited, and the bank is given credit.

Accounts	Nature	Increasing Or Decreasing	Credit Or Debit
Outstanding Payments	Liability	Decreasing	Debit
Bank Account	Asset	Decreasing	Credit

The term "purchase return" refers to when a customer returns a product to a seller for a refund, store credit, or any other reason based on the seller's duty. The occasional return of a purchase will also happen. For instance, if the buyer is dissatisfied with the product, if they purchased it in error, if the merchant sent them the incorrect product, or even if they purchased more products than they actually needed. When a purchase is returned, the stock is reduced, and the paid amount needs to be refunded because it occurs after the invoice. Therefore, both the stock accounts and the accounts will be impacted by the purchase return. Reverse journal entries that are appropriate should be created to make up for this.

The table below lists each purchase transaction's journal entries in detail.

Operation	Accounts Affected	Debit	Credit
Purchase order	No Accounts Affected		
Material Receipt	Stock Valuation Account	XX	
	Stock Interim Account		XX
Purchase Bill	Expense Account	XX	
	Account Payable		XX
Registering Payment	Account Payable	XX	
	Outstanding Payments		XX
Reconciling	Outstanding Payments	XX	
	Bank Account		XX

2. **Sales Process**

Sales transactions include any sale, contract, or other transfers that include the disposal of goods, services, or other assets, both tangible and intangible. Here, we may talk about how the Odoo17 platform can help you handle sales transactions, the operations that go along with them, and how that affects the journal entries. Operations like Sales Orders, Delivery Notes, Rejection IN (Sales Return), Sales Invoices, and Invoice payment are all part of a sales transaction. We might start by examining the following operations of sales transactions.

Sales Order: A sale order is essentially a document created by the seller to gather details regarding the goods or services the customer has requested. Every detail is included in the sales order, including information on the product or service, the price, the quantity, the terms and conditions, and many other things. The selling order is, therefore, solely intended for the creation of orders since it has no effect on inventories or accounts.

Delivery Note: An element connected to the shipment or delivery of goods is a delivery note. This will include the specifics of the goods, how many there are, and how much they cost. Dispatch Note and Goods Received Note are other names for the Delivery Note. The stock value reduces as a confirmed order is fulfilled from the inventory and delivered to the customer.

Two accounts, the "Stock Valuation Account" and the "Stock Output Account," are impacted by the delivery of goods to customers.

Accounts	Nature	Increasing Or Decreasing	Credit Or Debit
Stock valuation account	Asset	Decreasing	Credit
Stock Output account	Liability	Decreasing	Debit

Rejection IN (Sales Return): Numerous times, buyers return products even after being billed. Adjustments are made to stock and accounts as a result of this form of sales return. They will also have reverse journal entries created for them. For keeping track of the products that customers have rejected or returned, a Rejection IN is a very helpful feature. If the goods are returned prior to billing, just the stock will be impacted; the accounts are unaffected. Additionally, the stock value rises when the product is added back to the inventory.

Accounts	Nature	Increasing Or Decreasing	Credit Or Debit
Stock valuation account	Asset	Increasing	Debit
Stock Output account	Liability	Increasing	Credit

Sales Invoice Creation: A type of accounting document called a sales invoice is sent to a buyer by a vendor of products or services. Everything will be mentioned, including the service provided, the product provided, the price the buyer must pay, the mode of payment, and more. It is necessary for bigger transactions and is a legally binding agreement between the company and the customers.

Both the Receivables Account and the Income Account will be impacted in this situation. The Account Receivable is labeled as an "Asset," and the Income Account is labeled "Income" when we analyze the characteristics of these accounts. In this instance, the revenue is rising while the asset is decreasing. As a result, the Income Account is debited, and the Account Receivable is credited.

Accounts	Nature	Increasing Or Decreasing	Credit Or Debit
Income Account	Income	Increasing	Credit
Account Receivable	Asset	Increasing	Debit

Registering Payment: On payment registration, a temporary account called Outstanding Receipts is used. Due to payment registration, a journal entry is produced with Accounts Receivable and Outstanding Receipts.

Accounts	Nature	Increasing Or Decreasing	Credit Or Debit
Accounts Receivable	Asset	Decreasing	Credit
Outstanding Receipts	Asset	Increasing	Debit

Reconciliation: After reconciliation, the sum will be transferred to the bank account after it is compared to the bank statement. As a result, the bank is debited, and the account for outstanding receipts is credited.

Accounts	Nature	Increasing Or Decreasing	Credit Or Debit
Outstanding Receipts	Asset	Decreasing	Credit
Bank account	Asset	Increasing	Debit

You can see a breakdown of all the sales transactions' journal entries by looking at the table below.

Operation	Accounts Affected	Debit	Credit
Sales order	No Accounts affected		
Delivery Note	Stock valuation account		XX
	Stock Output account	XX	
Customer Invoice	Income Account		XX
	Account Receivable	XX	
Registering Payment	Accounts Receivable		XX
	Outstanding Receipts	XX	
Reconciling	Outstanding Receipts		XX

	Bank Account	XX	

Finally, using the double-entry bookkeeping method, the total of the credits will equal the total of the debits.

Anglo-Saxon Accounting

For tiny areas, such as those found in the United States, United Kingdom, Ireland, Canada, Australia, and many other nations, Anglo-Saxon Accounting is applicable. Odoo17 only offers Anglo-Saxon accounting in the enterprise edition. There are numerous contrasts between the two accounting systems, Continental and Anglo-Saxon. We talked about how a purchase affects the expense account in Continental Accounting. However, in Anglo-Saxon accounting, after executing a sale order has an impact on the expense account.

You must enable Anglosaxon accounting from the Odoo Accounting Configuration Settings if you wish to use all of its features, and you should activate the developer mode. The cost distinctions between Account and Stock account properties when the inventory valuation is automated is another important aspect of the Anglo-Saxon accounting system. To track the price difference between the vendor bill and the purchase cost, use the price difference account.

Transactions in Anglo-Saxon Accounting

1. Purchase Process

In some cases, the expense won't register when it is made. The purchases could be made in bulk and consumed over a lengthy period of time. Therefore, including them as an expense in financial entries will have a bigger effect on the company's profit and loss. It is, therefore, common practice to record acquired products as assets and costs at the moment of use in order to handle those scenarios. Ledgers contain the cost of spent assets.

We will start by making a product purchase.

Purchase Order: Purchase orders do not impact any accounting ledgers; they just produce a valid document for receiving products or services from the vendor.

Purchase Receipt: After the goods' receipt has been acknowledged, the arriving assets must be added to stock. As a result, both stock input accounts and stock valuation accounts are impacted by stock.

Accounts	Nature	Increasing Or Decreasing	Credit Or Debit
Stock valuation account	Asset	Increasing	Debit
Stock Input account	Asset	Decreasing	Credit

When stock is received and recorded in the "Stock input account," it is thought of as an asset until it is sold or consumed at which point it becomes a liability. So, it might be either assets or liabilities. [Liability = -Assets] as either the liability or the asset changes.

Purchase Return: There is occasionally a chance that the purchased item can be returned because of a quality problem or product damage. As a result, stock accounts are reversed, and the stock move is exactly the opposite of the incoming.

Accounts	Nature	Increasing Or Decreasing	Credit Or Debit
Stock Valuation Account	Asset	Decreasing	Credit
Stock Input Account	Asset	Increasing	Debit

Purchase Bill: Posting the purchase bill follows completion of the purchase receipt. As was already indicated, in Anglo-Saxon, the direct expense will be recorded as an asset rather than at the time of purchase. As a result, once a bill is generated, "Account Payable" and "Stock interim accounts" are impacted. The amount to be paid to the vendor is noted in Account Payable. As a result, when a bill is generated, the amount owed to the vendor rises, increasing the company's liability and crediting the Account Payable.

Accounts	Nature	Increasing Or Decreasing	Credit Or Debit
Account Payable	Liability	Increasing	Credit
Tax Account	Asset	Increasing	Debit
Stock Input account	Asset	Increasing	Debit

Register Payment: Making a payment or sending money to the vendor is known as registering it. 'Account Payable' and 'Outstanding Payment Accounts' are impacted by this process. The company's liability decreases as a result of payments made to the vendor. The company's payable liabilities are recorded in account payable. As a result, Account Payable, which by definition is a liability, is debited when the liability diminishes.

Accounts	Nature	Increasing Or Decreasing	Credit Or Debit
Accounts Payable	Liability	Decreasing	Debit
Outstanding Payments	Liability	Increasing	Credit

The Outstanding Payment account serves as a middleman for holding unreconciled outbound payments alongside cash and bank journals. Rather than using the Account Payable, these outstanding payment accounts are used to reconcile with the bank statement. As a result, whenever a payment is registered, the "Outstanding Payments" account is credited.

Reconciliation: The bank statement and vendor payment must match because that is the next step. The 'Outstanding Payment' and 'Bank' accounts are thus impacted by reconciliation.

Accounts	Nature	Increasing Or Decreasing	Credit Or Debit
Outstanding Payments	Liability	Decreasing	Debit
Bank Account	Asset	Decreasing	Credit

During this procedure, it will be noted that the vendor has finally received payment from the bank account. As a result, the asset in "Bank" decreases, which credits "Bank," and the liability in "Outstanding Payment" reduces, which debits "Outstanding Payment."

The table below displays the total journal entries made during the buying process.

Operation	Accounts Affected	Debit	Credit
Purchase order	No Accounts Affected		
Material Receipt	Stock Valuation Account	XX	
	Stock Input Account		XX
Purchase Bill	Stock Input Account	XX	
	Account Payable		XX
	Tax Account	XX	
Registering Payment	Account Payable	XX	
	Outstanding Payments		XX
Reconciling	Outstanding Payments	XX	
	Bank Account		XX

2. Sales Process

The sales transaction entails a number of procedures, including the establishment of the order, the handling of the product delivery to the customer, the generation of the invoice, as well as its payment and reconciliation.

Sale Order: A sales order is made when a customer specifies the goods and services they need, the quantity they need, the confirmed pricing, etc. There is no impact on any accounts.

Delivery Note: After an order is accepted, the items must be delivered to the consumer. The attributes of the stock account will change once delivery has been authenticated. The stock that was supplied to the customer is tracked in the "Stock Output Account." A "Stock Output Account" is an expense by nature, and in this case, the expense value rises and is debited. Additionally, the value of all the stock or assets in the warehouse declines and is recorded in the "Stock Valuation Account." So, a credit is made to the stock valuation account.

Accounts	Nature	Increasing Or Decreasing	Credit Or Debit
Stock Valuation Account	Asset	Decreasing	Credit
Stock Output Account	Expenses	Increasing	Debit

Sales Return: Take into account a customer returning goods for any reason. In this manner, the stock is likewise inverted.

Accounts	Nature	Increasing Or Decreasing	Credit Or Debit
Stock Valuation Account	Asset	Increasing	Debit
Stock Output Account	Expenses	Decreasing	Credit

Sales Invoice: The 'Income Account' and 'Account Receivable' are impacted when creating a sales invoice for a customer. While "Account Receivable" refers to assets, "Income Account" refers to income. Thus, as assets grow and income rises, the "Income Account" is credited, and the "Account Receivable" is debited. Additionally, two other ledgers—the "Stock Output Account" and the "Expense" Account—are also impacted because, according to Anglo-Saxon accounting, the expense is impacted as soon as the acquired item is used up or sold out.

Accounts	Nature	Increasing Or Decreasing	Credit Or Debit
Income Account	Income	Increasing	Credit

Account Receivable	Asset	Increasing	Debit
Tax Account	Liability	Increasing	Credit
Stock Output Account	Expenses	Decreasing	Credit
Expense Account	Expenses	Increasing	Debit

Payment Registering: The 'Account Receivable' and 'Outstanding Receipts' accounts are impacted once payment has been received from the customer and has been registered in Odoo17.

Accounts	Nature	Increasing Or Decreasing	Credit Or Debit
Accounts Receivable	Asset	Decreasing	Credit
Outstanding Receipts	Asset	Increasing	Debit

The amount that has to be collected from the customer is recorded in the receivable accounts. 'Account receivable' is an asset by definition. As the client pays, assets are depleted and credited. Following a temporary storage period in the "Outstanding Receipts" account, the incoming funds were later reconciled with the "Bank." Assets are the basis for the Outstanding Receipts account, which is debited as the asset value rises.

Reconciliation: When a payment is compared to a bank statement, the asset in the bank grows, which results in a debit to the bank. Additionally, there is the parallel outstanding receipts account, where assets decline and are credited.

Accounts	Nature	Increasing Or Decreasing	Credit Or Debit
Outstanding Receipts	Asset	Decreasing	Credit
Bank account	Asset	Increasing	Debit

Sales Return: Products returned have an impact on stock, and if the invoice has been paid, the refund must be recorded with a credit note.

The entire journal entry is listed in the next page.

Operation	Accounts Affected	Debit	Credit
Sales order	No Accounts affected		
	Stock valuation account		XX

Delivery Note	Stock Output account	XX	
Customer Invoice	Income Account		XX
	Account Receivable	XX	
	Tax Account		XX
	Stock Output Account		XX
	Expense Account	XX	
Registering Payment	Accounts Receivable		XX
	Outstanding Receipts	XX	
Reconciling	Outstanding Receipts		XX
	Bank Account	XX	

Storno Accounting

Storno is the Italian word for "cancellation" or "writing off." Therefore, under this technique of accounting, the original journal entries will be reversed using negative credit or debit amounts that have been recorded in your account. A bookkeeper can remove a file that has inaccurate accounting information about the recorded amount with the use of this procedure.

Reconciliation

Reconciliation is an accounting procedure that properly compares two different types of records to determine whether they are accurate and consistent. To find any discrepancies between them, reconciliation is the best way. This technique is useful for demonstrating the consistency, accuracy, and completeness of the accounts in the general ledger.

It will be helpful to explain the variance between two financial records or account balances in the context of account reconciliation. In other words, the method enables you to guarantee that the amount deducted from an account equals the amount actually spent. The balances at the end of each accounting period can be easily verified using this suitable procedure. The timing of payments and deposits may legitimately contribute to minor types of variations. The unauthorized differences will, nevertheless, be successfully found. Your records can be reconciled on a daily, monthly, or annual basis.

You may view both Payment Matching and Bank Reconciliation on the Odoo17 platform. Entry matching and reconciliation are accomplished using these two techniques. Let's go over each of them below.

Payment Matching

The strategy used in the Payment Matching method is to compare the invoice or bill that was created with customer or vendor payments. Let's use the creation and registration of a customer invoice as an example. Automatic payment matching will take place when the customer payment is included, it should be done through register payment from the invoice, however, payments match the invoice.

Bank Reconciliation

The bank reconciliation process is highly helpful in assisting the user in comparing the information from a person's or an organization's cash account to bank facts. A company can determine whether there are any discrepancies in the account using the bank reconciliation and the comparing approach. An organization will be able to quickly take corrective action if any variations are discovered, thanks to these sophisticated advantages.

The purpose of bank reconciliation is to compare the bank statement with the system payment entries recorded in Odoo. The customer invoice and the customer payment are matched, just like in the example above. The following step is to compare the bank statements. The invoice will have a corresponding entry in the bank statement. Bank reconciliation is the phrase used now for comparing financial records to bank statements.

Accounting Methods

As we previously covered, the Accounting module of the Odoo17 platform uses the double-entry bookkeeping system, which makes it very simple to maintain every journal entry's automated balance. Therefore, the total of the credit will always equal the total of the debits. Accounting Methods are divided into two divisions based on when revenues and costs are recorded.

- Cash Basis
- Accrual Basis

Therefore, there are two different ways to record tax information on accounting transactions: cash basis accounting and accrual basis accounting. The main distinction between these two approaches is how and when the tax is recorded. Let's examine these two approaches.

Accrual Basis

The default accounting approach, known as the accrual basis, records tax information on revenues and costs as soon as they are generated. This method, which is included in Odoo17, is useful for immediately entering taxes in accounting ledgers and tax returns.

Cash Basis

Tax on revenue or expenses is reported using the cash basis method after receiving payment in cash from clients or after paying suppliers in cash. In this instance, the revenue tax is only recorded at the time when the payments are received. Additionally, expenses are only reported after suppliers or employees have been paid. From the Accounting Configuration Settings, the Cash Basis option can be enabled. Taxes that can be generated in conjunction with an invoice or payment using the same technique will also be impacted by cash-based accounting.

Terms used in Accounting

The following can help you understand some basic accounting terms:

1. **Entity:** A well-defined economic unit called an "accounting entity" that separates the accounting of specific transactions from other divisions or accounting entities. From the standpoint of accounting, an organizational structure with distinct goals, procedures, and records might be considered an accounting entity, eg: company.

2. **Transactions:** A transaction is a business operation that affects an organization's financial operations on a financial basis. When purchasing a product, making a sale, or incurring any type of expense, money will be transferred, and this transaction will have an impact on the accounting records.

3. **Capital:** The financial resources that financiers put in businesses with the intention of using them to finance operations can be simply defined as capital. It can be used to pay for ongoing expenses as well as to finance upcoming growth.

4. **Stock:** The term "stock" is frequently used to refer to the quantity of easily available goods that are kept in a store or warehouse and are prepared for purchase or delivery.

5. **Goods:** Goods are made, materialized commodities that are in constant demand on the market.

6. **Creditors:** The term "creditors" or "receivables" refers to a person or business that owes money under a credit arrangement. Through a loan arrangement or contract, the creditor typically offers the opposing party credit to take up money.

7. **Debtors:** The people or organizations who owe money to their suppliers are known as debtors or payables. The person who borrows money from a creditor is said to be a debtor.

8. **Liabilities:** The company's debt is referred to as liabilities. The bank loans, unpaid debts, mortgages, and any other financial obligations the business has. Current liabilities and non-current liabilities are the two types of liabilities. Short-term liabilities include current liabilities. This group includes overdue bills, payroll taxes, accrued expenses, loans, advances, etc. Long-term obligations, such as long-term loans, long-term leases, deferred tax liabilities, and other items, are included in the non-current liabilities.

9. **Assets:** Assets are any resources that a company or organization has access to in terms of financial accounting. Anything that has the potential to produce good economic value

and is used over the long term qualifies. The asset may fall within the categories of Fixed asset or Current asset. The category of fixed assets includes items like furniture, automobiles, land, machinery, buildings, and other equipment. Current Assets are important in business since they relate to an organization's ability to pay its short-term liabilities and short-term liquidity. Additionally, it is easily modifiable. Cash, accounts receivable, stock inventory, prepaid obligations, cash equivalents, and many more items are examples of current assets.

10. **Revenue/Income:** Revenue or income is the total amount of money made by selling goods or rendering services related to an organization's core business operations. It is, in essence, an organization's whole revenue or profit. In accounting, the income is displayed on the income statement's top line.

11. **Expenses:** Expenses are the operational costs incurred to generate income for a business from an accounting standpoint. The expense account will be charged for the costs.

12. **Profit:** The term "profit" refers to a financial gain, more particularly, the difference between the gain and the cost of purchasing, operating, or creating a good or service.

13. **Loss:** Loss is the term used to describe the financial costs incurred by a business while generating revenue. Profit and loss are shown by the difference between revenue and outgoing costs.

14. **Equity:** Equity is the amount of money a business owner invests in or owns. The actual amount of firm equity is shown by the balance sheet's difference between assets and liabilities.

15. **Bookkeeping:** The act of maintaining financial records for a business is referred to as bookkeeping. At the conclusion of the fiscal year, it establishes precise and organized financial reports.

16. **Stakeholders:** Stakeholders are the people or organizations who consistently have an interest in or concern for the entity. Employees of an organization can be thought of as stakeholders with a stake in its expansion.

17. **Shareholders:** Owners of an organization's shares are known as shareholders. A stakeholder may or may not be a shareholder, while a shareholder is always a stakeholder.

18. **Sales:** The exchange of goods and services for cash is referred to as sales.

19. **Purchase:** The act of purchasing products or assets is a form of business. Purchases can be made using cash or credit.

20. **Ledger:** The account or record used to maintain bookkeeping entries or transaction entries for balance sheet and income statement transactions is known as the accounting ledger.

21. **Journal:** The account that records every aspect of a business's financial dealings is called a journal. It can be used to transfer information to other accounting records and for future account reconciliation. Odoo17 uses five different sorts of journals: sales, buy, cash, bank, and others.

22. **Journal Entries:** A journal entry is a group of accounting records for a business's transactions. It also includes the ledgers that have an impact on the credit and debit

sides of the transaction, together with the reference number, accounting date, and journal entries related to the transaction.

The Odoo17 Accounting module evolved into a more reliable and cozier tool for managing the financial management parts of the business by pursuing new and improved capabilities.

Chapter 2
Get Started with Accounting Basics

Get Started with Accounting Basics

Odoo is an advanced enterprise resource planning (ERP) solution that provides complete control over your company thanks to the platform's innovative and well-defined features. Odoo is one of the top ERP solutions now available on the market and is favored over alternative business management solutions by many commercial organizations due to its dependability, operational preparation, and sophisticated control and administration skills of your firm.

This chapter will go through the following topics:

- Brief introduction of the Odoo software
- Localization features of the Odoo platform, installation, and hosting methods
- The modules' customizable parameters for accounting

Let's go over each component individually.

Odoo ERP: An Overview

With the introduction of components of digitization and global connectivity, corporate operations management has switched to business management software solutions. Today, there are a number of items on the market that are marketed as "business management solutions," allowing consumers to access their cutting-edge operational capabilities. Enterprise and resource planning software is a well-known category of business management technologies that have gained widespread use. The theory of total company control was well-established even before ERP solutions were developed. Additionally, with the introduction of digitization, the idea was translated into a software model, paving the way for the company management solutions that are offered today.

Odoo is one of the well-known full-featured Enterprise Resource Planning (ERP) systems. Fabien Pinckaers, who currently serves as the company's CEO, founded it in the first decade of the new century as Tiny ERP. When the platform evolved into an open-source platform, it was renamed Open ERP. Odoo version 8 was released, which was the basis of the current platform available for Odoo. Since 2014, Odoo has released an updated version every year. The latest version, version 17, is the most advanced and fastest Odoo yet.

The upcoming release of Odoo 18, the latest version, is scheduled to be released in the fourth quarter of the year during the Odoo Experience Meeting 2024.

Although it started as a humble business, Odoo has grown into one of the most well-known companies around the world. Odoo has more than 2,550 partners who are able to build and deploy other required Odoo services. With its flagship product, Odoo, which bears the company's name, the company expanded globally. With its infrastructure and capabilities used in over 100 countries and over 7 million users worldwide. Its open-source infrastructure design, which has allowed many developers to participate, is one of the main factors contributing to its immense popularity worldwide. This has also led to the system being a customizable software solution that helps companies define the platform for their operations as needed.

Another aspect is Odoo's design, which is modular in nature and provides you with dedicated user modules. Each standalone module that is available by default adds more functionality to the application. Covering Accounting, Sales, Purchasing, CRM, Inventory, Field Services, Marketing Automation, SMS Marketing, Email Marketing, Projects, Planning, and more, these standalone modules are functional tools that are application-specific. In addition, these modules are interconnected so that you can use one centralized work function. Connection functions can be customized with the many options included in each module to give you complete control over the data flow.

Since Odoo is an open-source business management software, it is supported by the Odoo community. The Odoo community consists of all the people who use and support Odoo, including all official Odoo partners, consultants, and developers. To get related services to Odoo, you should contact the authorized partners of Odoo and choose the best among them. As the best Odoo partner, Cybrosys Technologies can provide you with comprehensive and expert service for your Odoo needs.

The Odoo Apps Store has a number of apps created by the Odoo community, as Odoo does not provide custom features, and it takes time to build them on the platform. The applications created here perform the unique tasks described in the application and can be installed and used on your platform. The application must be downloaded according to the version of the Odoo platform you are currently using, as some applications may not work with all versions of Odoo. Odoo is available in two different versions: a commercial version and a community version. On the other hand, the community version of Odoo can be considered as the basic version of the software and can be used with minimal features. On the other hand, Odoo Enterprise Edition is the most advanced version of the software, allowing extensive development, customization, and integration of unique Odoo applications.

You now have a clear understanding of the Odoo platform. Let's move on to the next part, where we will talk about the installation and hosting of components of the Odoo platform.

Odoo Installation and Hosting

As mentioned earlier, the Odoo platform comes in two variants: a community version and an enterprise version. Both community and enterprise editions are available for installation in on-premise, cloud-based, and online versions of the feature based on the activities you need to perform to run the business. With Odoo, you can choose one of these hosting options for the Odoo platform. There are three main ways to host Odoo: First is the web version of Odoo, which you access with a unique login and access to the platform and is used to manage your business. In addition, Odoo online is only available in the enterprise version. Therefore, you will not be able to use this version of Odoo immediately after installation. Editing of Odoo Online's functionality is also limited, but you can customize the options offered by each module. The existing Studio module allows you to make further changes and create new applications, but only in the established way of working in Odoo Online.

Another is cloud-based hosting, where Odoo platforms can be configured to run on a cloud platform, which can be on-premise or on a dedicated or shared server, depending on your needs. And now Odoo can be used to manage a company where Odoo provides a server. These are the options you need to set up Odoo hosting and manage your business. Let's move on to the next section, which will help you understand the installation aspects of Odoo and how to set up a specific database for Odoo.

Odoo can be installed and used on both Windows and Linux-based platforms, allowing users to run their business using Odoo on two well-known operating systems. If Odoo is installed on a Linux-based machine, the configuration file can be downloaded from the Odoo official website. For Windows, you can download Odoo from the official website by selecting the Odoo version you need and the corresponding Windows version.

Let's proceed with a thorough understanding of both installation factors.

How to Install Odoo in a Linux-based (Ubuntu) System?

Odoo can be used with Linux if properly configured based on the operating system and version of Odoo. You can set up Odoo on your Linux-based computer using the methods below.
Step 1: First, update your server and system to the latest available feature version.

```
sudo apt-get update
```

```
sudo apt-get upgrade
```

Step 2: The next step is to set up and secure a dedicated server for operations after the servers are upgraded.

```
sudo apt-get install openssh-server fail2ban
```

Step 3: After the server is configured, you need to create a new Odoo user to act as an administrator and monitor operations.

```
sudo adduser --system --home=/opt/odoo --group odoo
```

Step 4: You can configure the Odoo platform on your Linux-based system using PostgreSQL. First, install Postgres with the following Python code:

```
sudo apt-get install -y python3-pip
```

You should now switch from PostgreSQL to Postgres, which will allow you to create and further manage your Odoo database:

```
sudo apt-get install postgresql
```

Once Postgres is installed, log in to Postgres to create a new user for our Instance.

```
sudo su - postgres
```

Now, if you are using Odoo 17 to **install,** you should create an Odoo 17 user:

createuser --createdb --username postgres --no-createrole --no-superuser --pwprompt odoo17

To gain access to advanced optional features, the newly created user in Odoo 17 should be configured as the root user, giving them system administrators:

psql

ALTER USER odoo17 WITH SUPERUSER;

Finally, exit out from the psql and Postgres:

`\q`

`exit`

Step 5: Next, we need to install the Odoo dependencies on the dependencies specified for the platform.

`sudo apt-get install -y python3-pip`

Install Odoo platform dependency packages and libraries:

`sudo apt-get install python-dev python3-dev libxml2-dev libxslt1-dev`

`zlib1g-dev libsasl2-dev libldap2-dev build-essential libssl-dev libffi-dev libmysqlclient-dev`

`libjpeg-dev libpq-dev libjpeg8-dev liblcms2-dev libblas-dev libatlas-base-dev`

Finally, you should verify the installation with the newly installed dependencies:

`sudo apt-get install -y npm`

`sudo ln -s /usr/bin/nodejs /usr/bin/node`

`sudo npm install -g less less-plugin-clean-css`

`sudo apt-get install -y node-less`

Step 6: Next, Github should be cloned:

Initially install the Github in the server and then clone it:

`sudo apt-get install git`

Don't forget to edit the system user before cloning, because according to Odoo it can't be done afterwards:

`sudo su - odoo -s /bin/bash`

You should perform the cloning form repository and respective branch of Github:

git clone https://www.github.com/odoo/odoo --depth 1 --branch 17.0

--single-branch.

At last exit from the cloning and continue with the installation of Odoo:

`exit`

Step 7: The next step is to install all required Python packages: First, you need to install and configure the packages with pip3:

`sudo pip3 install -r /opt/odoo/requirements.txt`

Next, you need to download and install wkhtmltopdf for Odoo platform to support PDF report function:

```
Sudo wget:
```

```
https://github.com/wkhtmltopdf/wkhtmltopdf/releases/download/0.12.5/wkhtmltox_0.12.5-1.bionic_amd64.deb
```

```
sudo dpkg -i wkhtmltox_0.12.5-1.bionic_amd64.deb
```

```
sudo apt install -f
```

Step 8: Last but not least, you need to configure Odoo and related services.

Create a configuration file for platform features in the Odoo folder that can be copied to a specific location:

```
sudo cp /opt/odoo/debian/odoo.conf /etc/odoo.conf
```

Add all the required details to the file:

```
sudo nano /etc/odoo.conf
```

Update the configuration file:

```
[options]
```

```
; This is the password that allows database operations:
```

```
admin_passwd = admin
```

```
db_host = False
```

```
db_port = False
```

```
db_user = odoo17
```

```
db_password = False
```

```
addons_path = /opt/odoo/addons
```

```
logfile = /var/log/odoo/odoo.log
```

Define and set up the access rights to files:

```
sudo chown odoo: /etc/odoo.conf
```

```
ssudo chmod 640 /etc/odoo.conf
```

Next, create a directory of logs for the operations in Odoo:

```
sudo mkdir /var/log/odoo
```

Define and configure Odoo user access to the specified folder:

```
sudo chown odoo:root /var/log/odoo
```

Next, configure the required Odoo services:

```
sudo nano /etc/systemd/system/odoo.service
```

Now you need to put the snippet defined below in the file:

```
[Unit]

Description=Odoo

Documentation=http://www.odoo.com

[Service]

# Ubuntu/Debian convention:

Type=simple

User=odoo

ExecStart=/opt/odoo/odoo-bin -c /etc/odoo.conf

[Install]

WantedBy=default.target
```

Next, you need to assign the root user to the file you created:

```
sudo chmod 755 /etc/systemd/system/odoo.service
```

```
sudo chown root: /etc/systemd/system/odoo.service
```

Step 8: Finally, you need to run Odoo. First, launch the Odoo platform with the following command:

```
sudo systemctl start odoo.service
```

Next, you need to check the status of the platform:

```
sudo systemctl status odoo.service
```

If the status shows that it is active, use the following URL to access the platform.

```
"http://:8069"
```

Additionally, the log file can be checked with the command:

```
sudo tail -f /var/log/odoo/odoo.log
```

After booting your computer, run the following command to start Odoo services:

```
sudo systemctl enable odoo.service
```

Your Odoo platform is effectively implemented and ready to run on a Linux-based system if you follow the steps above.

Now let's take a look at how to install the Odoo platform on Windows-based computers or devices.

How to Install Odoo in a Windows-Based System?

The Odoo platform can be installed as easily as Windows-based systems without any configuration codes. The steps listed below can be used to install the Odoo platform on Windows systems.

The Windows installation file can be downloaded from the Odoo website as shown in the following image.

The download URL is below:

https://www.odoo.com/page/download

Now you need to double-click the downloaded file to install it. This will launch a pop-up window similar to the image below.

Next, edit the PostgreSQL configuration information in the window as shown below:

Next, you need to specify the destination folder where Odoo will be installed and configured.

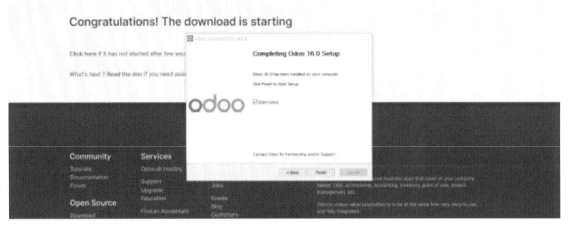

Finally, you need to start the application and then configure it to use the database as described in the next section.

Once the installation is complete, you can start using Odoo for your needs. The following section describes the functions related to database configuration.

Creating Your Database

So far, we have talked about hosting and installation elements. Let's continue by looking at the components of creating a database for your company's operations. Once you have received a valid subscription, you can start creating a database on your Odoo platform. If you don't have an Odoo account yet, you can create one in the next window that appears, as shown in the screenshot below.

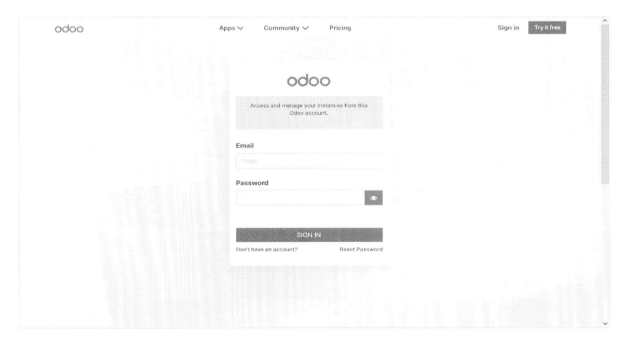

The next step after creating accounts is to create a database for your business. Once the Odoo accounts are created, you can make this selection in the database creation window. First, you need to enter the master password, database name, email address, password, phone number, language, and country in the database creation box shown below. Due to Odoo's localization feature, which is described in more detail in this chapter, the Odoo platform database is configured based on the country you specify.

The ability to define demo data in the database is another important item located in the database creation menu. This information is provided by Odoo itself to help you understand the various aspects of operations management. All types of introductory information can be removed or modified according to your needs.

As soon as the database settings are done, you can continue, and the database panel will appear. One thing to remember is that the database is configured according to the country you select, which increases the localization of some module support services facilities. Another thing to remember is that you do not have to enable the Demo Data option if you are using an Odoo platform that you have configured for real-time operational management of your business. There is no module or application installed in the database, and you can only see the application module and related settings, as shown in the following image.

When you select the Apps module, all the applications available on the platform will be displayed for you to choose and install according to your needs. Screenshot of the Application module is shown in the following image.

Let's take a closer look at the applications offered under the accounting categories as shown in the attached image since the book focuses on the Accounting module of the Odoo platform.

Depending on your business requirements, you can implement invoicing, accounting, consolidation, various payment acquisitions, and localization modules.

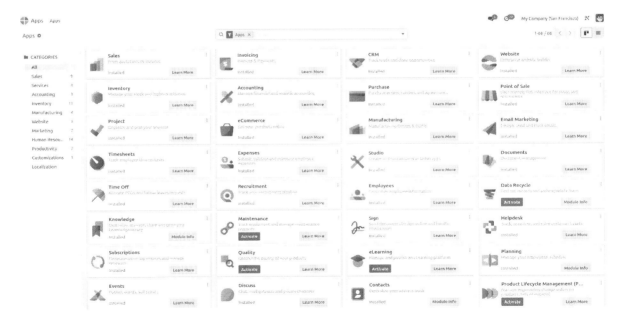

As shown in the following image, once the application is installed, it will appear as an icon on the database panel. By selecting the icon, you can select any module, and the main Odoo panel for that module will be displayed.

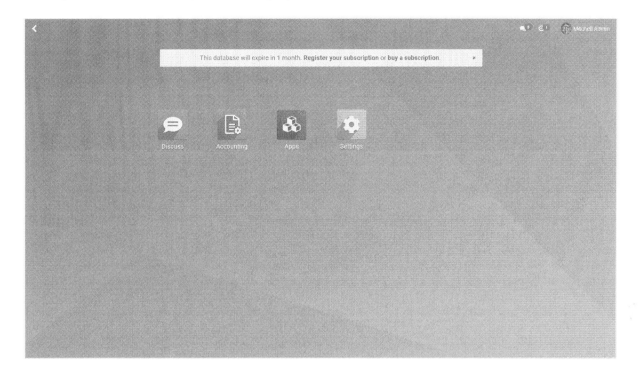

When we first configured the database using the Demo Data option, the modules display predefined demo data as shown in the following screenshot. Because the installed module has a special functional connection with the support module, in some situations, the support module of Odoo functions is automatically installed when the module is installed.

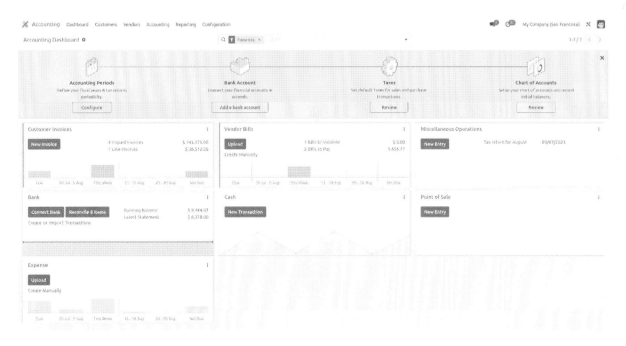

Depending on your usage needs, you can configure your Odoo system database in different ways. The approaches discussed above allow you to configure the database according to your needs. So far, we have talked about installation, hosting, and further changes to the Odoo database. Let's move on to the next section to learn more about Odoo's localization features.

Localization, the Best Feature of Odoo

Odoo is a highly developed and user-friendly enterprise resource planning system that is currently used as enterprise management software around the world. Odoo has been widely adopted by various business establishments due to its dedicated infrastructure and operational capabilities. Local features that Odoo advertises or claims to be features can be considered as the most important and best features of Odoo as they allow business organizations to operate according to their location and country of operation.

With the localization function of the Odoo platform, you can set taxes according to the country where you do business. Based on the location, the Odoo accounting module helps you define various taxes, including sales tax, purchase tax, service tax, GST, VAT, cess, and many more. Odoo's accounting module has a separate menu window where these settings can be configured. The currency in which the business is conducted is another factor considered as an aspect of localization. The Odoo platform helps you set the base currency based on the country selected in the Odoo configuration.

In addition, Odoo allows the use of multiple currencies in business operations, which contributes to the smooth operation of international companies. Additionally, invoicing and invoicing are based on regional or national practices, and companies operating there should be able to adapt to this method. On the Odoo platform, you can define various billing restrictions and functions and save them as templates for later use. The localization function is also in other Odoo modules, for example, the purchase management module, where product descriptions and purchases can be made according to the requirements of the law and with the permission of the relevant authorities. Similar elements can be observed in Odoo's sales module, where companies operating in the region must comply with regional standards and regulations. Odoo's buy and sell modules include unique configuration menus and options that allow you to localize these features.

The platform's support for multiple languages is an additional part of Odoo's localization component, which is useful for international companies. Any language can be added to Odoo processes, and the language settings can be quickly adjusted according to your needs. Based on the peculiarities of the localization of the region, HR management must also be functional. On the Odoo platform, the recruitment procedure and other HR functions can be defined according to the guidelines of the regional administration. In Odoo, you can set other features such as working hours, working days, paid days off, and holidays. Now that we are clear about the localization aspect of the Odoo platform let's understand the customizable options available in the accounting module of the Odoo platform.

Configurable Options in the Accounting Module

The accounting module of the Odoo platform offers comprehensive operational management of the financial side of any company's activities. Many elements of financial management and accounting can be customized because Odoo is a customizable program. In addition, the Accounting module of the Odoo platform has a configuration menu with several configurable default values. All Odoo modules have a configuration menu that allows users to fully configure the functional management and performance of each module.

You can enable and disable this using the checkbox as part of the configurable options provided. You also have options to define an action from which you can select an entity from a drop-down menu. Each of these alternative types is defined based on a specific functional need. By building the platform, you have the opportunity to add unique features, which you can do with the help of experienced Odoo developers. Installation of various third-party Odoo applications from the Odoo application store provides customizable options for the specified modules to define functions. Additionally, you can change the default modules available through the Studio module. You can also create custom modules using the Odoo studio module with customizable options, just like any other default module.

In the Settings tab, you can choose from a long list of configuration options for the compute module. These options allow you to precisely define the functions of financial management and accounting. Additionally, these are the default options that come with both the Community and Enterprise versions of Odoo. However, the functional features of the community version are limited, while the commercial versions are significantly more advanced. We will continue to learn more about how each option works in the following sections as we navigate to the Accounting module settings page.

Accounting Import

The accounting import section allows you to handle the initial configuration, such as setting up the Chart of Account, and you can also import the Chart of account, open balances, contact addresses and journal information. It is basically implemented to bring the necessary data into Odoo quickly and easily from an external resource instead of entering it manually.

The manual view option directs you to the chart of accounts, where we can also set initial debits and credits, or even import the initial balance from the favorite import record option. We can check the opening balance here even if the opening balance has been posted.

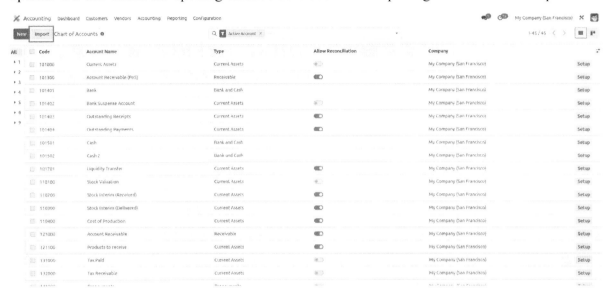

The next Import option takes you to the accounting import guide, where you can import contact details, charts of accounts, and journals.

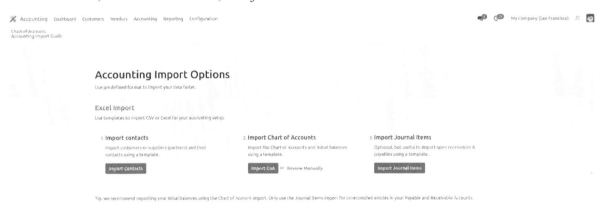

Using a predefined template will help you import data faster. CSV or Excel templates can be used to import accounting data. Import contact information can be used to import partner information (both customer and supplier). You can import the chart of accounts and opening balances. Import journals allow you to import journals into Odoo. This is optional but useful for importing open receivables and payments using a template. Odoo recommends that you import your opening balance using Chart of Accounts Import and only use Journal Import for unreconciled entries in your Payable and Receivable Accounts.

Define the Taxes Based on the Region

In the Taxes tab of the Settings module, set operational taxes for the operational aspects of your business. If no special tax is charged on the product, the taxes mentioned below apply to both buying and selling activities and are considered in the activity. Now let's see what options are available in the Tax Setup section of the Accounting module settings menu.

Default Taxes

Initially, in the Taxes section, you can set default taxes to use the platform to manage your business. All local transactions defined on the platform are subject to these taxes. Here, you can select the VAT and Purchase tax options from the drop-down menu. You can set taxes in the Taxes menu item in the Settings menu of the accounting module; here, you simply set the corresponding rates according to your needs. The Settings tab of the Default Tax Settings menu of the Accounting module can be seen in the following screenshots.

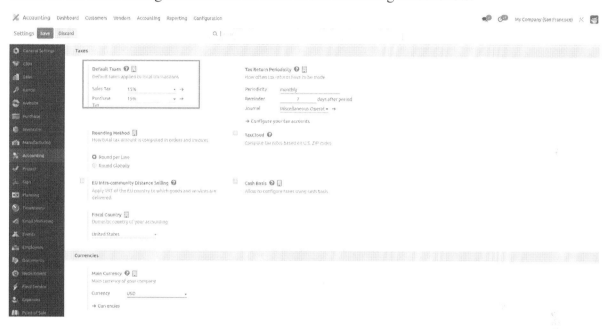

Tax Return Periodicity

The tax collected must be returned to the authority at specified intervals; the time may depend on the procedures of authorities and/or companies. The frequency of return depends on the competent authorities and can be once a month, once a quarter, once a year or once a year. In the Tax return periodicity menu, you can change the settings related to the return, which indicate how often the returns must be sent. The cycle can be set under the menu to occur once a year, semi-annually, every four months, once every three months, every two months or once a month. In addition, you can set a reminder that can be set for days after the period.

In addition, the work platform has already created journals defined in the menu, which are used to record collected taxes.

You can also set up tax accounts by selecting Set Up Tax Accounts, which will take you to the Tax Groups box, where you can set up tax account information. Defined taxes are displayed here and you can select one of them to create a tax account. As you can see in the image below, you can define the Tax Prepayment Account, Tax Utilization Account (payable), and Tax Utilization Account (receivable) from the Tax Groups menu.

Rounding Method

The Rounding elements of the taxes received, which can be based on the two settings available by default in Odoo, is another feature that can be configured from the Taxes menu. Round per line or Round Globally are both acceptable. In general, you can choose between these two solutions depending on your work needs.

The "**Round per Line**" option in Odoo accounting allows for more exact and targeted rounding for particular goods or services inside a document by ensuring that rounding is applied independently to each line item. When distinct items in the same document require different rounding, this method can be helpful.

When "**Round Globally**" is selected in Odoo accounting, rounding is done consistently to the total amount of a document, guaranteeing uniformity across all line items. By treating the document as a whole rather than rounding each line item separately, this strategy streamlines the rounding process.

TaxCloud

The TaxCloud computation will compute the taxes on sales, purchases, and any other commercial operations for a company operating in the United States based on the ZIP codes. The TaxCloud setup, one of the Odoo platform's localization components, will be based on US ZIP codes. The TaxCloud option, as seen in the image above, may be enabled or removed in the Taxes settings menu. You may also define the API ID, API Key, and Default Category, all of which are customizable. You may discover more about the credential components by selecting the "how to get credentials" option, which will take you to the TaxCloud settings page.

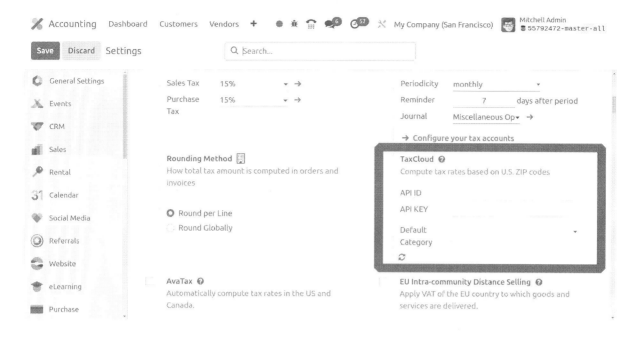

AvaTax

Odoo 17 supports AvaTax integration, allowing users to map taxes based on tax registrations and regions. AvaTax is a tax engine that assists with tax compliance.

Businesses can use Avalara AvaTax, an integrated third-party application, to determine sales tax amounts on their invoices according to a customer's location. To make tax compliance simple for clients, Avalara provides pre-built connections and custom integrations with popular accounting, ERP, e-commerce, and other business applications.

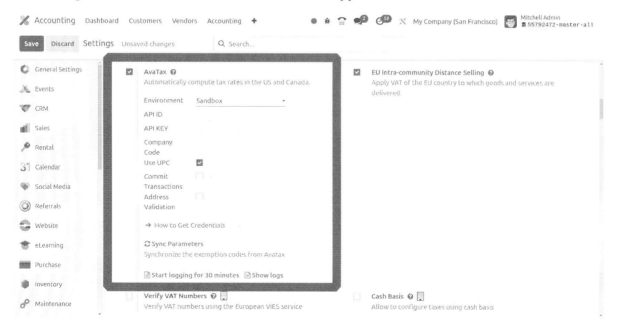

EU Intra-community Distance Selling

EU intra-community distance selling is the sale of products and services across borders to consumers (B2C) in member states of the European Union by vendors who are registered for VAT implications. The transaction is carried out remotely, usually by phone, mail order, internet platforms, or other modes of communication.

Distance selling within the EU is governed by particular VAT laws and regulations. VAT must be charged by the vendor at the rate that applies in the buyer's nation. This still stands valid, even if the vendor is based outside of the European Union.

By establishing and configuring new fiscal positions and taxes depending on the nation in which your business is located, the EU Intra-community Distance Selling feature assists you in adhering to this legislation. Select EU Intra-community Distance Selling under Accounting ‣ Configuration ‣ Settings ‣ Taxes, then click Save to activate it.

If you sell products based on digital technology in the country where your business operates, you must meet the EU VAT requirements for digital products. You can enable or disable EU VAT for digital products using EU-based Odoo, which treats it as a localization component. In addition, you can select the country of fiscal activity from the drop-down menu to tax your Odoo-related activities in the selected country.

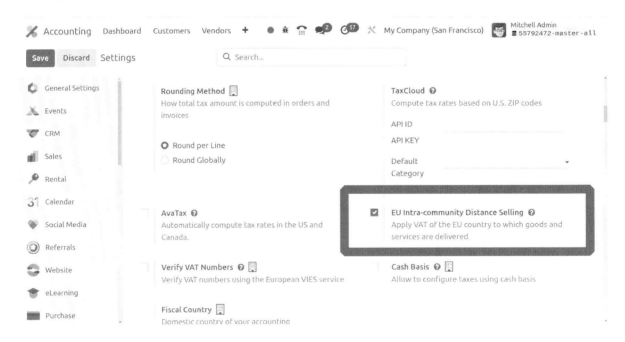

Fiscal Country

Fiscal country determines your company's home country, and that determines what the tax laws mean for your business. This is critical information for determining the tax rates and rules applicable to a company's financial transactions.

Each country has its own accounting practices regarding taxes, chart of accounts, journals, requesting tax points, etc. At first, when setting up a company in Odoo, we must mention the country of our company accordingly. We decide which accounting localization we should use.

As you mention your company country in the company details currency, it will be automatically updated according to the company country. The tax country in settings will then be updated to your company's home country, such as the United States.

The company's base currency is automatically updated accordingly. When creating a new company, a fiscal localization must be defined in the accounting configuration to install the accounting package defined in the Fiscal Localization section for each country.

Once this package is added and saved, all default charts of accounts, taxes, journals, tax rates, etc., are automatically installed in the database and do not need to be configured separately. In addition, if you want to add or change the installed information, it is also possible to edit them, but only before making any accounting entries.

Cash Basis

Using the Cash Basis option under the Taxes menu, you may handle the tax procedures on cash payments received. This feature may be enabled or disabled depending on corporate policy. Let's move on to the following section of the settings, which is focused on currency management, to understand the next operational menu.

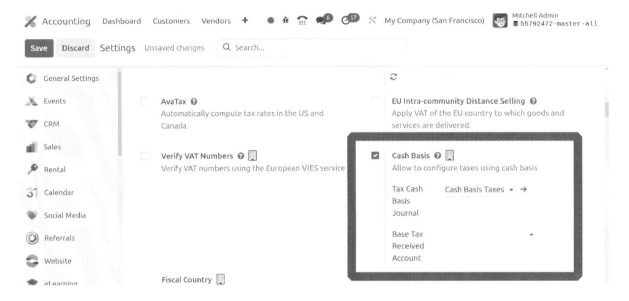

Currency Management

You can configure your company's currency operations with Odoo using the Currencies option in the Settings tab of the accounting module. In this menu, you can set the main currency of the company's operations. The option drop-down menu allows you to select a currency. All available currencies are defined on this page. The currency in which the business is defined also acts as the primary unit of account, and you can use other currencies to operate your business.

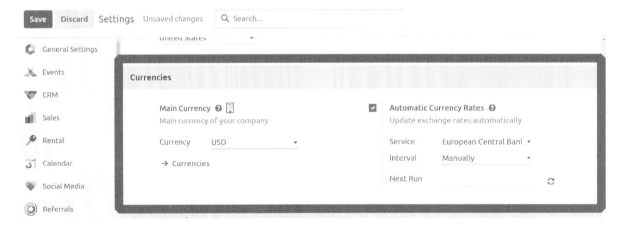

Also, if your country acts as an international tag, you need to manage each location's currency correctly. Thanks to this, you can configure the Multi-Currency option of the Odoo platform, which allows you to save bets in any currency in the world and automatically adjust exchange rates.

To help with automated currency rate updates, select **Automatic Currency Rates**. This can be completed manually, every day, every month, or every year during specific times.

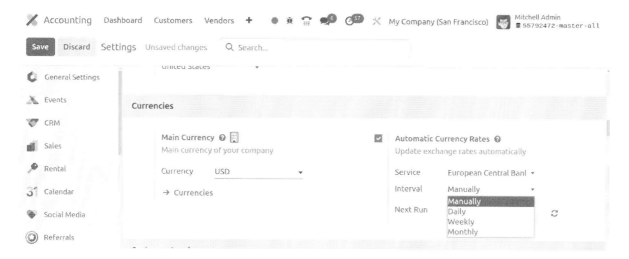

Let's move on to the next section of the menu, Invoice Management, accessible from the Settings tab of the accounting module.

Complete and Effective Invoice Management

Sending customer invoices with control elements helps your ability to fully and successfully manage the invoicing process. The default configuration option found in the Customer Invoices section must first be configured. The setting is possible in the default billing settings and in the Send and Print settings. Print, Email Sent, and Send by Mail are the three invoice-sending options that can be configured. If there are, they will appear in the Send Invoice field for you to select.

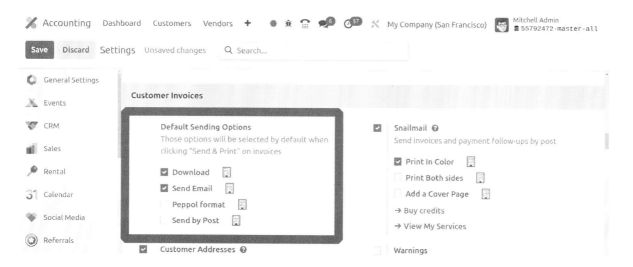

In addition, the subtotal tax display of the generated invoice line can be set to either Tax Excluded or Tax Included, depending on the operational needs of the company or the rules issued by the authorities.

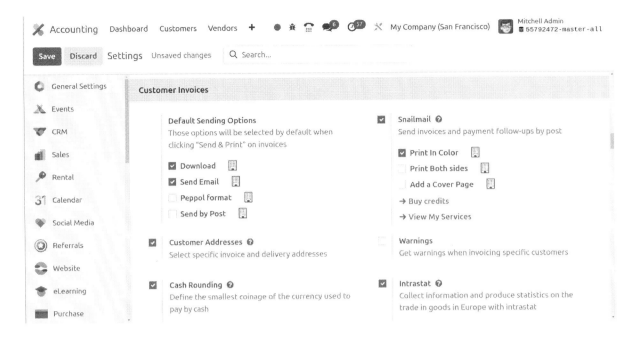

Another localization option that allows you to send invoices directly by mail is snail mail. You can set up direct customer invoices by enabling Snailmail under Customer invoices. Snail Mail's default settings include the option to print in color, print on both sides and add a cover page. The platform also has a Buy Credits option in the Settings menu, which will take you to a website where you can buy Odoo Credits for Snail Mail since the functionality of the service is integrated according to the cost of credits.

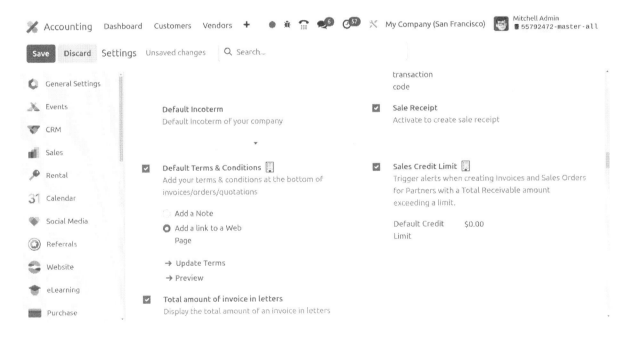

You can also enable or disable several other settings in the Customer invoices section, including default terms displayed on the invoice, warnings, cash rounding, Intrastat, default incoterm, and sales receipt. Let's take a closer look at these options.

Warnings

By enabling the warning option, you may set warnings for certain customers identified in the Odoo platform. These warning messages will appear once the invoices have been created. Furthermore, these alerts may be tailored to your needs in order to inform operators based on the consumer. As a consequence, you will be able to cancel the transaction and create an invoice for that client.

Cash Rounding

The invoice pricing will be adjusted to the nearest whole figure since it is unlikely that a customer would get precise change or that the counter will have enough coins to finish their transaction during retail time operations. With Odoo, you can customize the Cash Rounding procedure to meet your individual requirements and the currency in use. If you enable the cash rounding option, a cash rounding menu icon will appear, allowing you to specify cash rounding.

Customer Addresses

With Odoo Sales, you can specify multiple shipping and billing addresses. For some customers, it is very useful to specify specific billing and shipping addresses. Not all have the same delivery location as the billing location. In Odoo 17, this feature allows customers to add a separate shipping address.

Line Subtotals Tax Display

The subtotal row of the invoice is the total sum of the quantity of the purchased quantity of product. The average amount shown on the invoice can be either Tax-Included or Tax-Excluded.

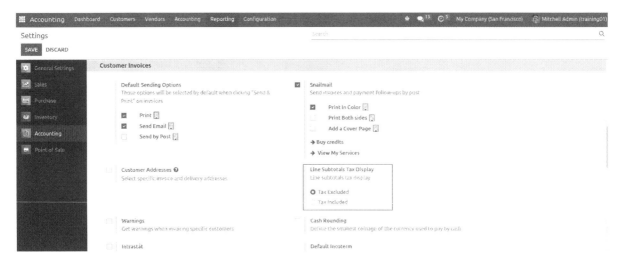

If tax excluded is selected to show subtotal tax on the line, the subtotal on the invoice line is tax excluded.

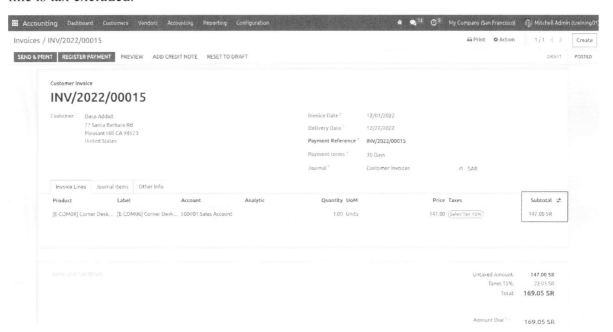

If Taxes are selected as the tax display for the Subtotal line, the subtotal is displayed as an amount with taxes in the calculation line.

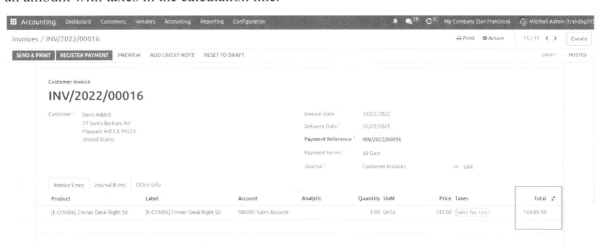

Intrastat

The setup of Intrastat, which may be done here by enabling the option, is another part of localization in terms of Odoo's business operations in Europe. When you enable the option, you will get a drop-down menu where you may select the default incoterm to be used.

Default Incoterm

In addition to the ability to define it, the default incoterm may be adjusted in the Odoo Accounting module settings. There is also a drop-down box where you may pick the default Incoterm.

Sales Receipt

If the Sales Receipt option is turned on, a receipt can be created for the sale of the product after the sale. As a result, the same number of products are sold, invoiced, and shipped.

All configuration options are available in the customer invoice management section of the accounting module. Let's move on to the next section, which includes configuration options for managing customer payments.

Sales Credit Limit

The maximum amount of credit available to the customer is called a credit limit. It is used to reduce the loss that the company incurs if the customer refuses to pay. The size of the credit limit is decided by the finance department. In the accounting settings, we can set a sales credit limit that can be applied to each partner as a company policy.

In Odoo 17, you can also set a maximum credit limit for certain partners. So, if this function is turned on, we can set a credit limit for the partner using the partner form, and it is also possible to see the requirements of the partner.

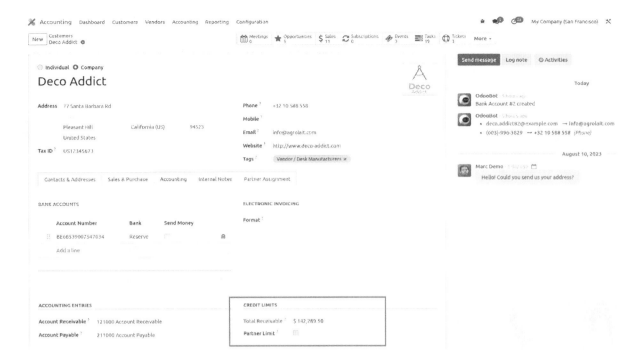

If a partner's receivable amount exceeds the partner's limit, future bills will show a warning that the partner has reached their credit limit.

Default Terms & Conditions

Writing thorough and correct terms and conditions on sales invoices entails a plethora of minute but critical data, such as detailing the company's details, the description of the goods or services being offered, and any applicable taxes or discounts.

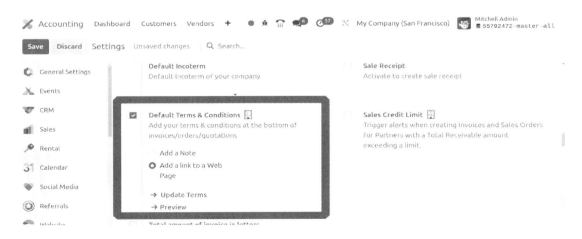

So, under terms & conditions, the default terms and conditions may be added, which will display as notes or as a link in the Invoices/Sales Orders/Quotations.

Total Amount of Invoice in Letters

The Accounting module for Odoo 17 now has a new function that allows you to print the total amount of invoices in the letter. Enable this from the settings of the Accounting module under the Customer Invoice section as shown below.

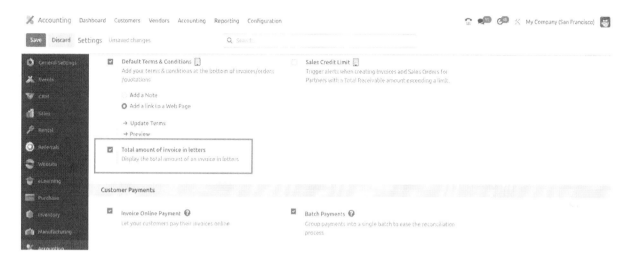

After enabling this feature, let's create an Invoice for a customer and confirm it. Once the invoice is confirmed, take the print of the invoice, which will show the Total amount of the invoice in letters as shown below.

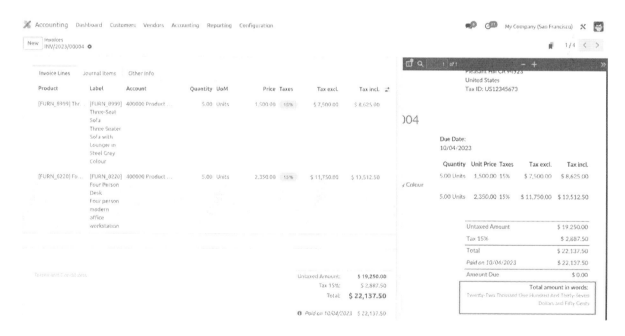

Streamline the Customer Payments

The management of customer payments is of primary importance in the financial operations of any company, and the configuration menu of the Odoo accounting module offers various configuration options for this purpose. You can enable online payment of customer invoices by enabling features such as online bill payments. In addition, the installment payment option can be activated, which allows the consumer to pay several bills at the same time. A useful localization option for European countries is SEPA Direct Debit (SDD), which enables fast collection of payments from customers using Euro-SEPA services. The options for managing customer payments found in the Settings menu of the accounting module are shown in the image below.

With Odoo, you can process several payments at once with efficiency and less manual labor by using the **Batch Payment** option. It makes it simple for companies to organize and carry out payments for several bills or invoices in a streamlined and integrated way.

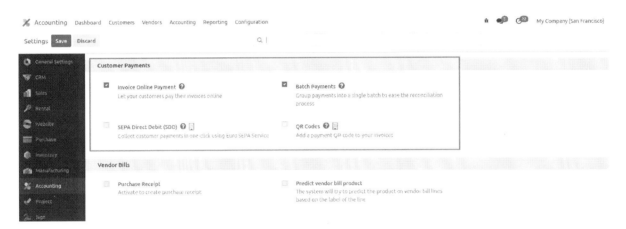

If you enable QR codes, you can add a QR code to your invoices that consumers can scan to pay. With all these options, you can correctly define and process customer payments. So far, we've talked about creating customer invoices and managing payments. Let's move on to the next part, where we will discuss Vendor bills management.

Vendor Bills Configuration Tools

Odoo's accounting module makes it easy to manage vendor invoices for purchased goods. To effectively manage vendor bills, you need to set the right options in the accounting module's configuration menu. The advanced option of the Odoo Platform accounting module helps you proactively understand vendor bills based on previous supplier invoices.

The menu has options for digitizing invoices, such as Do not digitize invoices, Digitize invoices only on request and Digitize all invoices automatically. If you need to digitize an invoice, you will need to purchase some credits, which you can do by selecting one of the Purchase Credits options. You can also get just one invoice line per tax with the OCR Single Invoice Line Per Tax option. In addition, the possibility of creating purchase receipts for product procurement procedures can be implemented.

These are the several configuration options that are offered under the Vendor Bills. Let's move on to the administration options for Vendor Payments found in the settings menu.

Full Control of Vendor Bill Payment

The advanced vendor payment management capabilities offered by Odoo's accounting module are useful for the company's accounting management capabilities. You can edit this by enabling checks and selecting Check Layout from the drop-down menu. Additionally, you can configure the Control Top Margin and Control Left Margin settings and enable Multi-Page Control Loop.

In addition, companies in European countries have the option of SEPA Bank Transfer (SCT), which allows them to pay their invoices with one click using Euro-SEPA services. Let's move on to the next section to learn more about the options related to banking and cash management in the configuration menu of the Odoo accounting module.

Managing the Finances with Bank and Cash Management

The bank and cash management options found in the configuration menu of the accounting module provide comprehensive insight into the efficiency of operations. By describing the transfer account and using it, you can set up transfers between banks under the menu. In addition, you can enable automatic import, which automatically imports bank statements. If you want to import bank statements into a CSV file, you can also enable the CVS import option. By enabling the QIF import function, you can import bank statements in QIF format.

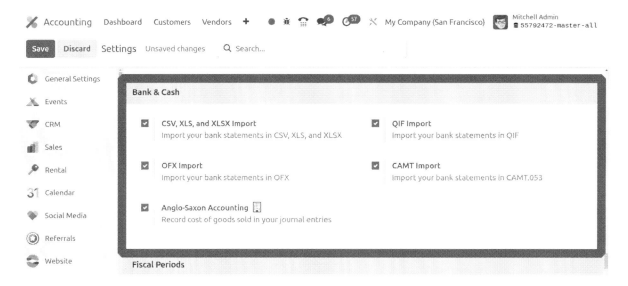

Additionally, you have the option to enable QFX Import and CAMT Import to import bank statements in these formats. The default accounts used for different operations can be defined in the Default Accounts section. When you set up and use an internal transfer account, you can set up Interbank transfers from the menu.

The Default Accounts section defines the default accounts used for various accounting operations, including Profit Accounts, Loss Accounts, Bank Suspense Accounts, Outstanding Receipts Accounts, Outstanding payments Accounts, Internal Transfer Accounts, Cash Discount Accounts, Cash Discount Loss Accounts, Deferred Expenses Account, Deferred Revenue Account, Income Account, Expenses Account etc. Each account is used for specific functions.

Profit and loss statements are used to reflect the exchange rate difference that occurred during the transaction. A change in the exchange rate results in either a loss or a profit for the company, and these losses or profits are reflected in the income statement depending on the scenario. The journal entry corresponding to the exchange rate difference is entered in the mixed journal specified in the Journal field.

A Bank Suspense Account is a temporary account used in Odoo to settle bank statement transactions where the exact account is uncertain. Basically, they are used to show the amounts on the bank statement up to the reconciliation date since the exact match is not known. Transactions in the escrow can then be periodically monitored and transferred to the correct accounts when they have been reconciled or paid.

The Outstanding Receipts Account and Outstanding Payments Account are temporary accounts that will keep unreconciled entries. These accounts are used to avoid situations where accounts receivable and accounts payable are directly related to reconciliation. Once the reconciliation is done, the amount is transferred to the bank. An internal transfer account is an intermediate account for interbank transfers.

Next comes the Cash Discount Gain Account and Cash Discount Loss Account, which are used to reflect the discounts or rebates given in the accounting transaction which are posted to the respective accounts. Let us now further understand the aspects of defining fiscal periods in the Odoo accounting module in the next section.

Odoo v17 includes a significant modification in the setting of automatic stock valuation, as well as the addition of a new configuration to incorporate the "Cost of Production" account. This will help to provide transparent stock movement and value as part of the Cost of Production account ledger, from raw material consumption through finished goods stock valuation. To add the account, enable the feature from the settings of the accounting module under the Stock Valuation section, as shown below.

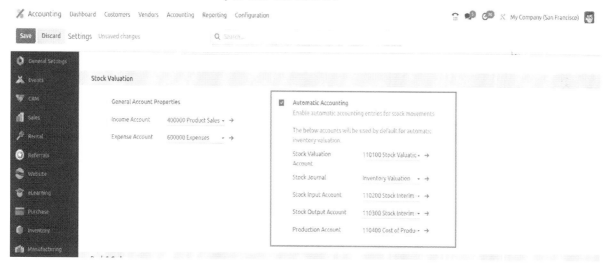

Configurable Fiscal Periods and Positions

In Odoo's accounting module, you can set the accounting period during which your company operates. You can specify a fiscal period by specifying the last day and month in the Fiscal Period tab. You enable the option if the fiscal activities are carried out based on fiscal years. Additionally, you can set an invoicing threshold by selecting a date from the calendar when you set the invoicing switch threshold. Any date that is entered as the Invoicing Threshold made prior to that date is placed in canceled status. In addition, the income component and the reporting component are removed, and you start the operation.

A valuable feature of Odoo during development is the threshold setting to delete all test data from invoices, vendor bills, and related revenue associated with them. In other words, once the test actions are completed and the threshold is set, the platform returns to its new form, ensuring that all test actions remain undone. Let's move on to the next section, where we will discuss the analytical accounting and budget management of the accounting module.

The Odoo 17 Accounting application now has a new feature called the Dynamic report. This tool allows you to effortlessly navigate through reports and uncover what is hidden behind the numbers.

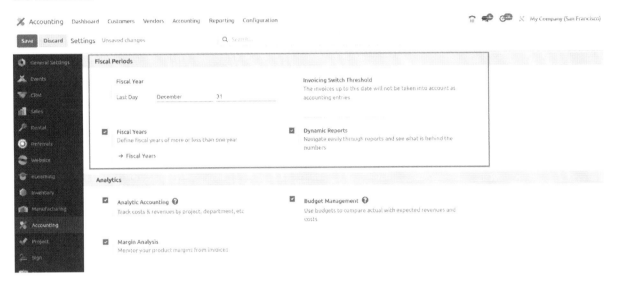

Analytical Accounting and Budget Management

With Odoo's Analytic accounting tools, you can grow in the financial management tasks of your company. All analytical accounting setup options can be configured from the Analytics menu in the Analytics module's Settings tab. Using the menu option, you can enable and disable the analytical accounting component of your company's activities. Analysis identifiers can also be applied according to the needs of operations, which simplifies the classification of analysis accounts and related processes.

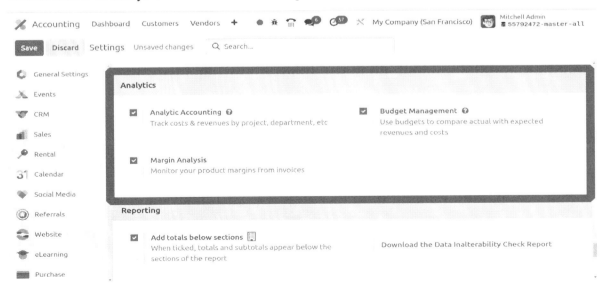

In addition, the budget management options ensure that you have adequate control over the activities related to the financial budget as well as the free funds of the company. By activating the Margin Analysis option, you can also track the product margins from invoices. The options available in the Analytical Accounting settings are displayed in the Settings menu of the Accounting module. As we move forward, we will learn more about the configuration options for generating analytics reports.

Create Informative Reports

In the Reporting and Analysis section, there are two options for generating reports. To get started, you can enable the Add Totals feature under the sections below that describe the sum of the parts of the report. In addition, you can select the Download Data Audit Report option from this menu, which will download the report to your computer.

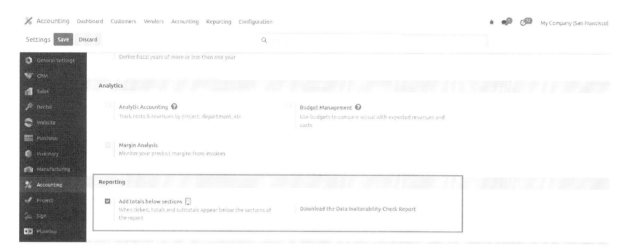

Depending on the usage requirements, there are many customizable options available in the configuration menu of the accounting module of the Odoo platform. You can quickly change them to get the operational control you need over your company's finances.

At the beginning of this chapter, we covered the basics of Odoo and its installation and hosting features. The localization feature of the platform is then discussed, followed by the installation functions of the Odoo accounting module. This chapter has covered in detail every option in the configuration panel of the accounting module.

In the next chapter, we will focus in detail on the configuration tools available in the compute module.

Configurable Options in the Accounting Module

The Odoo platform's Accounting module will offer total operational management of the financial side of any company's operations. Odoo 17 is a customizable software that allows you to set up different parts of accounting and financial management. In addition, the Accounting module of the Odoo 17 platform has a configuration menu with several configurable default values. All Odoo 17 modules have a configuration menu that allows users to fully configure the functional management and performance of each module.

You can configure the settings by checking the corresponding boxes to enable and disable it. You also have options to define an action from which you can select an entity from a drop-down menu. Each of these alternative types is defined based on a specific functional need. While building the platform, you also have the opportunity to add unique features, which you can do with the help of experienced Odoo developers. Installing various third-party Odoo applications from the Odoo app store provides customizable options for specified modules that allow you to define functionality. Additionally, you can change the default modules available through the Studio module. You can also create custom modules using the Odoo studio module with customizable options, just like any other default module.

The Settings tab of the Accounting Module Settings page provides access to a number of configuration options. These options allow you to precisely define the functions of financial management and accounting. Additionally, these are the default options that come with both the Community and Enterprise versions of Odoo. However, the functional capabilities of the community version are limited, while the commercial version is significantly more advanced. We will continue to learn more about how each option works in the following sections as we navigate to the Accounting module settings page.

Also, if your country acts as a global brand, you need to properly manage the currency of each location. To save bets in any currency in the world, the Odoo platform allows you to set up a multi-currency option.

Let's move on to the next menu, Manage Invoices, in the next section, accessible from the Settings tab in the accounting module.

Storno Accounting

Storno Accounting in Odoo 17 is used to record reversed entries as negative. Both negative credits/debits are shown in red in the financial statements. The original transaction is "zeroed out" for each reversal transaction because they all appear in the same debit or credit column.

Accounting Firm Mode

Another feature in Odoo 17 is the Accounting Firm Mode, which helps to change the sequence of the bill/invoice. A Quick Coding field can be defined and a set of documents defined based on the coding can decide whether it is exchangeable or not. The total (tax inc.) field enables you to add a tax-included value to your invoice document, which will automatically split the service amount and tax in the invoice line. Also, the billing date will be auto-suggested.

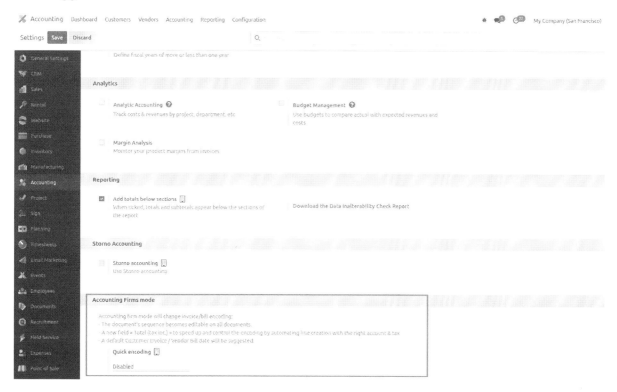

The accounting module of the Odoo platform contains several configurable options that can be expressed as user requirements in the configuration menu. You may quickly customize them to get the necessary operational functional management over your business's finances.

At the beginning of this chapter, we covered the basics of Odoo and its installation and hosting features. The localization feature of the platform is then discussed, followed by the installation functions of the Odoo accounting module. This chapter has covered in detail every option in the configuration panel of the accounting module. In the next chapter, we will focus in detail on the configuration tools available in the accounting module in detail.

Chapter 3
Unraveling Odoo 17 Accounting Module Configuration Tools

Unraveling Odoo 17 Accounting Module Configuration Tools

For companies of all sizes, the Odoo17 Accounting module is a complete software solution. It's intended to give users a simple platform to manage all of their financial activities, from payments and invoicing through bank reconciliations and financial reporting. The Sales, Purchase, and Inventory modules of Odoo17 are integrated with the Accounting module to give a complete picture of a company's financial operations. Users may effortlessly manage their accounts with its wealth of features, keeping track of their earnings and outgoings in real-time. Additionally, the Odoo17 Accounting module has helpful features like integrated tax calculation, multi-currency compatibility, and budgeting tools.

In order to understand their financial data better, consumers also have access to a number of analytics and reports. The significance of accounting, as well as the many fields and tools available in the Settings menu of the Odoo 17 Accounting module, were covered in the first chapter. Let's continue by learning about the configuration tools and menu options in the Odoo 17 Accounting module.

The configurational tools offered by the Odoo17 Accounting module will be covered in this chapter, including:

- Accounting configurations
- Payment Options
- Asset Models
- Analytical Accounting
- Configuring Invoicing
- Configuring bank Payments

Here, every function offered by the Configuration tools will be in-depthly reviewed.

Accounting Configurations

To manage the finances and bookkeeping of your company, you can choose one of the several accounting configurations available in Odoo17. In comparison to other settings, it has the highest priority. You can configure financial records in the system using the accounting configuration tool in Odoo17. You can use it to manage your accounts, set up taxes, set up invoices, and balance your bank accounts. Additionally, it enables you to set up multi-currency accounting, manage budgets, and construct charts of accounts. It can also be used to generate reports and offers a variety of options for controlling payment terms. Before beginning the organization's financial management operations, the accounting settings must be established. Because it affects all of the company's operations, changing the accounting setups after they are set up will be quite challenging. Chart of Accounts and Taxes are the two primary components that need to be set up first under this page. In the parts that follow, we may fully comprehend the configurational features of accounting.

Configuring Chart of Accounts

A company's financial management processes must include the Chart of Accounts. It is a list of all the accounts or ledgers a company utilizes to monitor its income, expenses, assets, liabilities, and equity. The Chart of Accounts normally comprises equity accounts, sales and expense accounts, cost of goods sold, and operating expenses, along with asset accounts like cash, accounts receivable, inventory, and fixed assets. Liability accounts include accounts payable and loans. A crucial component of financial reporting is the chart of accounts, which ensures that financial transactions are reported in the appropriate accounts.

The form of the accounts used in the financial reports is defined by a chart of accounts, which plays a significant role in accounting. It is a crucial tool for monitoring a company's financial health and enables users to evaluate their overall results swiftly. Additionally, it aids in ensuring the truthful and accurate reporting of financial transactions. It will facilitate the simple creation, editing, and viewing of all financial accounts and allow you to manage and customize your financial statements and reports.

Balance sheets, income statements, and other accounts are included in Odoo17's Chart of Accounts, a traditional double-entry bookkeeping system. You can design your own accounts and categories and tailor the system to your own accounting needs, thanks to its adaptability. The system will always ensure that your financial operations' records are accurate and fit for usage in the future. The configuration of the Chart of Accounts is the primary and initial step you take when starting your accounting and financial management using the Odoo17 accounting system. It's just because it serves as the foundation for all future operations. For total oversight of the administration of the financial operations, Odoo17 offers the option to construct a bespoke chart of accounts based on the needs of the organization.

In Odoo, the chart of accounts is relatively easy to define. In the Accounting part of the Configuration tab of the Odoo 17 Accounting module, as seen in the figure below, you only need to pick the Chart of Account menu.

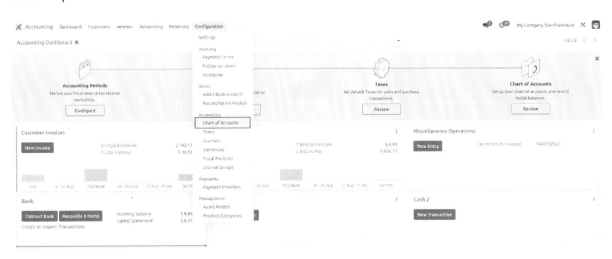

The pre-configured chart of accounts details shown below can all be seen in the Chart of Accounts window.

As seen in the screenshot below, all of the generated Chart of Accounts records are displayed with pertinent information, including Code, Account Name, Type, Account Currency, Company, and other specifics.

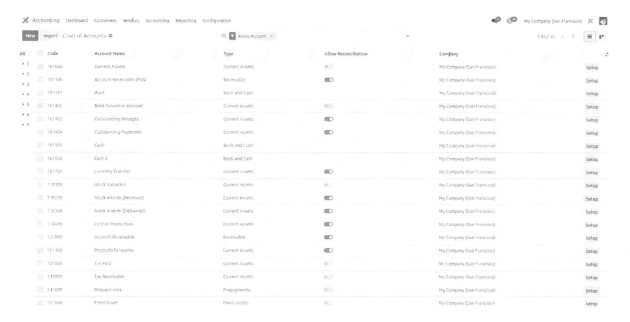

You can also observe a setting that can be turned on or off. You can set up reconciliation for the specific chart of accounts if you enable this option. By choosing the Kanban view menu icon, you can also see the details in the Kanban view since it is a list view. For the purpose of obtaining any specific Chart of Accounts, robust sorting tools such as Filters, Group By, and Search options can be employed. You can define a group of entries using the Group By option based on similarity or other criteria.

You can click the **New** button located in the top left corner of the window to start a new Chart of Account. As seen below, the system will now display a new row in the same window to construct a new chart of accounts.

The allocated field is where you can enter the Account Name. Then, using the dropdown menu, choose the Account Type in the Type area. All of the default types will be shown in the dropdown menu. Asset, Liability, Equity, Profit Loss, Expense, Income, or Other are the possible categories. Additionally, each type of account will have a number of subtypes, as seen in the screenshot below.

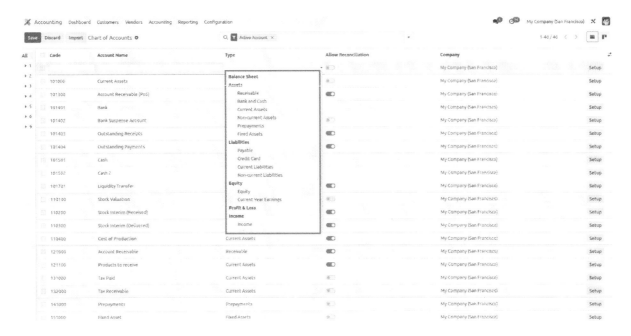

According to your preferences, you can also set or disable the Allow Reconciliation area. Include the Company and the Account Currency as well.

At the beginning of the process, it is easy to define the hierarchy of the Chart of Account operations for the Odoo17 platform. The concerned responsible team can set up the hierarchy of operations for the specific chart of accounts as soon as your business activities are established.

You can see the numbers as they relate to the hierarchy on the very left side of the Chart of Accounts window. You only need to choose the arrow alternatives for that, which are displayed on the window's left side, as seen in the figure below.

Additionally, it will be possible to view the relevant journal entries concerning the Chart of Accounts in the smart button 'Balance,' and this will serve as a precise definition of the financial activities of the Chart of Accounts in the organization. For the appropriate chart of accounts, it is also possible to establish the default tax of activities, which will be extremely helpful for saying that the financial operations carried out are combined with the defined taxes. Additionally, you are free to select and explain the tags for the relevant chart of accounts based on the company's operational region.

Additionally, you can restrict the use of this specific chart of accounts by selecting the 'Deprecated' option. To do this, select the Deprecated option from the Chart of Account menu, as shown in the example below.

The only Chart of Accounts that can see this special feature are the ones that are currently in use. You cannot immediately stop using and operating with a Chart of Account if you are compelled to do so since it contains all of the financial information for the operations that were in use and will be very valuable in the future. The Deprecate option can be quite useful in certain circumstances. You can stop its activity in finance management by enabling this option. You will still receive the corresponding chart of account entries and data. However, they won't be operational.

How to Create a New Chart of Accounts?

With the Odoo 17 Accounting module, you merely need to select the CREATE button, which is located on the Chart of Accounts panel as we previously described. You can explain the new Chart of Account on the new line that is shown. You can configure the Reconciliation option after entering the Code, Account Name, and Chart of Account Type. The SETUP option is then available under each of the Chart of Accounts that are indicated in the provided image.

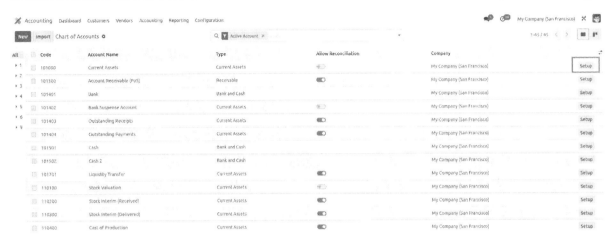

The SETUP menu item directs you to a different window where you can configure the relevant Chart of Account. The window in question is shown in the screenshot below.

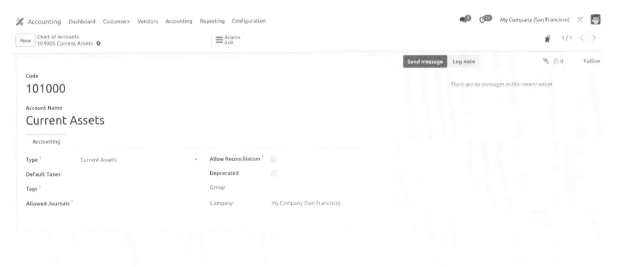

You can define the necessary details in this Chart of Account setting window. It will display the previously specified information, including Code, Account Name, and Account Type. Additionally, settings are available on the Accounting and Automation tabs.

You can specify the Account Type under the Accounting tab. The account type is used for informational purposes to provide legal reports created for individual countries, to establish the guidelines for ending a fiscal year, and to produce opening entries. Then, there is the Default Taxes option, which we just mentioned. Then, you can list the optional tags you need to apply for custom reporting in the Tags area. You can now list the journals in which this account may be used in the Allowed Journals section. This account can be used in any journal if it is left blank. The Account Currency is then an option for you to mention. So that you can force this account's entire journal to use this particular currency. Entries may use any currency if there is no specified currency. If this account permits the matching of journal items to invoices and payments, you can then enable the Allow Reconciliation field. You also have the Deprecated option, which was previously covered.

The Chart of Account can also be edited; simply move the cursor over the appropriate fields to make it editable, and an upload icon will show up at the top to save your changes.

Additionally, the 'New' button is now visible in the form view's upper right corner, which simplifies the process of creating a chart of accounts. Additionally, the 'Balance' smart tab displays the balance amount in that account, which is derived from several journal entries.

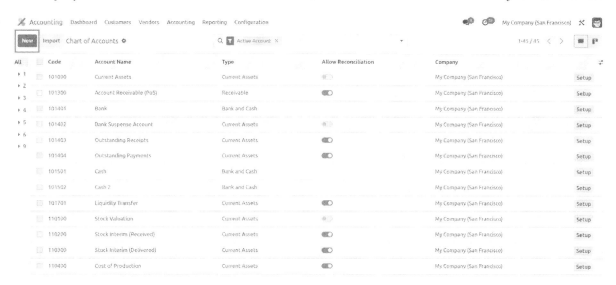

According to the needs of the business operation, you can import or construct a variety of Charts of Accounts using the Odoo 17 Accounting module. You can use this facility to quickly and easily summarize each finance management's accounting processes. The option to import records is simple to locate. The 'import records' option is available next to the New button, which allows you to import Chart of Accounts information in CSV or xlsx format.

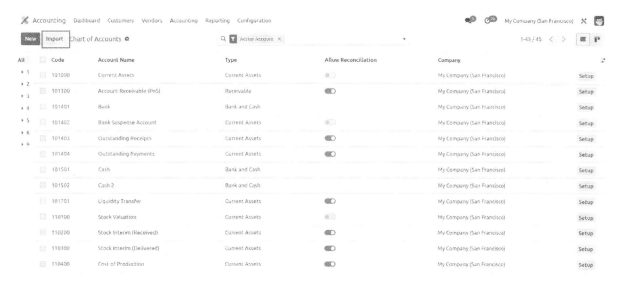

Let's move on to the following session, establishing Taxes, where we may explore the various aspects of establishing taxes on business activities based on the region. Up to this point, we have been talking about the Chart of Accounts option.

Configuring Taxes

To guarantee that the company complies with local rules, taxes are a crucial component of the business process that must be managed correctly. Taxes can be set up in the Accounting application of Odoo 17 Accounting. This section will walk you through the process of configuring taxes in Odoo 17. Due to the fact that taxes are an expense that must be disclosed on financial statements, they play a crucial part in accounting. Understanding the various tax rules and regulations is necessary for accounting for taxes. You also need to be able to accurately record, submit, and pay taxes to the appropriate tax authorities. Both accounting and tax knowledge are combined in tax accounting.

Tax returns must be prepared, the correct tax liability must be determined, and returns must be filed with the correct tax authorities. In addition, it entails the recording of tax-related transactions, including payments, credits, and deductions. Additionally, the creation of financial statements to reveal a person's or a company's tax liability.

The amount that needs to be deducted from employee wages for taxes is also determined using tax accounting. Tax accounting is also used to figure out how much money should be deducted from employee paychecks for benefits and other deductions. It also entails creating tax budgets and projections that can be utilized by a business or individual to plan their tax obligations and cash flow. To ensure that a business or individual complies with the relevant tax rules and regulations, tax planning is crucial. It is, however, a complicated topic that necessitates a full knowledge of the numerous tax laws and rules. Tax preparation, filing, and payment help can be obtained from qualified accountants and tax preparers. The process of preparing, filing, and computing taxes can also be automated using software tools like Odoo17 Accounting.

Taxes are regarded as a debt owed by the client to the service provider in exchange for a favor. When submitting taxes, the organizations must pay the same amount to the government or other authorities. All nations operate their taxes in a variety of ways, with varying percentages, and it solely depends on the local governing bodies in each nation. Because of this, the accounting management tool you use in your company needs to have the ability to configure specific taxes for various operations, and the Odoo17 Accounting software excels at this.

For defining all tax kinds for their sales, purchases, and services offered, the Odoo 17 Accounting platform is very convenient, and it can be defined based on the nation in which the firm works. One of the localization tools that the Odoo17 platform provides may provide this capability.

You can use the following procedures to arrange taxes for your business activity.

Navigate to the Accounting module and select the "Configuration" menu from the left-hand menu list. As illustrated in the image below, select the 'Taxes' menu under the Accounting part of the Configuration menu.

To add a new tax, use the NEW button in the Taxes window. Additionally, as seen in the picture below, the Taxes window will show all of the previously configured taxes' specifics. The present taxes can also be changed. The crucial information about the configured taxes, including Tax Name, Tax Type, Tax Scope, Label on Invoices, and Company, will be shown in the window. In addition to these choices, you may view a boolean field called Active to enable or disable the particular tax.

Therefore, it is extremely easy to build tax computation for the applicable taxes that are already defined utilizing the Odoo17 platform. Additionally, the platform provides a number of default tax computations, including Fixed, Percentage of Price, Percentage of Price Tax Included, Group of Taxes, and Percentage of Price.

Fixed Tax Computation: The automated tax calculation method known as Fixed Tax Computation in Odoo17 Accounting enables the calculation of taxes based on a preset set of guidelines and tax rates. Taxes, sales, and purchase calculations, as well as payroll and other financial operations, can all be done using this system. Businesses that need to swiftly and precisely calculate taxes and have a lot of transactions can benefit from this solution. Businesses that need to keep accurate records for tax compliance might benefit from fixed tax computation in Odoo17.

Group of Taxes: You may set up and manage various tax rates using the Group of Taxes Computation tool in Odoo17 Accounting. You can also group taxes and apply them to transactions. Users can make various tax groups, allocate taxes to them, and then apply those taxes to their transactions. This makes it easier to guarantee that all taxes are calculated accurately and consistently.

Percentage of Price: It depends on the kind of taxes being used in the Percentage of Price Tax Computation. For illustration, a conventional VAT rate might be 20%, but a custom duty rate might be 10%. Different sorts of transactions may be subject to a certain tax at a specific rate. It will be based on the predetermined fixed percentage of the total amount.

Percentage of Price Tax Included: Finally, the setup of the tax regulations affects how the Percentage of Price Tax Included computation is calculated. The percentage of tax that is included in the price will be determined automatically when the tax rules are configured, depending on the applicable tax rate. The tax configuration options in Odoo17 Accounting contain the proportion of the price tax included in the computation. The award sum will include the tax amount.

Returning to the Taxes window, you can view the different fields that must be filled out to establish a tax in the Taxes Creation window. Below is a screenshot of the creation form. First, you can enter the tax name in the Tax Name area here in the window. The Tax Type can then be mentioned. Using the dropdown menu, you can choose between Sales, Purchase, or None. Where the tax is selectable is determined by this Tax Type. The 'None' selection indicates that the tax is ineffective on its own. However, a group can still use it.

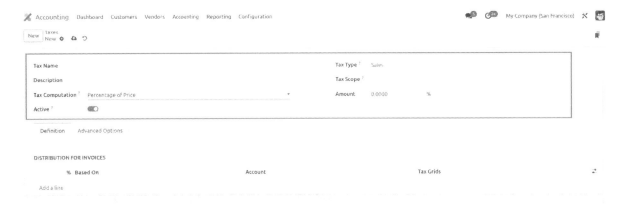

You can fill up the Tax Scope form after selecting the appropriate option in this field. Either services or goods may be chosen. You can limit the application of taxes to a certain product category, such as services or goods, by using this parameter. Then, in the Amount area, you can include the tax amount in percentage.

Additionally, you can use the dropdown to select the Tax Computation. Options like Group of Taxes, Fixed, Percentage of Price, Percentage of Price Tax Included, and Python Code are available in the drop-down menu. You can specify the Definition tab based on the chosen option. The option to set the Tax active's boolean field to false will, therefore, allow you to conceal the tax without actually eliminating it.

Additionally, under the Definition tab, you may define the definition of the tax on the many aspects of business operations. The Distribution of Invoices should be described in the DISTRIBUTION FOR INVOICES part of any tax computations other than the Group of Taxes. Where you can use the 'Add a Line' option to describe the Tax definition, the '% based on', the Account on which to post the Tax Amount, and the Tax Grids.

With the aid of creating a line, it is also possible to delete the current definition and create a new one. The DISTRIBUTION FOR REFUNDS can likewise be defined using the same approach.

Furthermore, additional fields like Label on Invoices, Tax Group of the defined tax, and many more were available under the Advanced Options tab in the Taxes creation window. You can enable or uncheck the 'Include in Analytic Cost' option. The amount calculated by this tax will be assigned to the same analytic account as the invoice line if you enable this option. The 'Include in Analytic Cost' option is only accessible if Analytic Accounting is turned on.

The Company and the Country for whom this tax is applicable can then be specified in the corresponding fields.

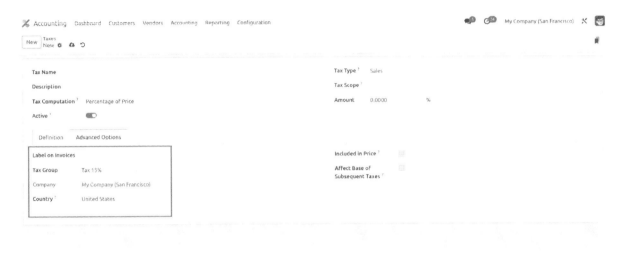

If the price you use on the goods and invoices includes the tax amount, you may also check the box next to the option "Included in Price." You also have a field called "Effect Base of Subsequent Taxes" that, if enabled, will cause taxes higher in the series than this one to be affected. The 'Base Affected By Previous Taxes' field is another option that you have, and it can be turned on or off. If you make this field active, taxes at lower positions in the sequence might attempt to affect this one.

The Tax Exigibility field, which has the options 'Based on Invoice' and 'Based on Payment', is the last one. The tax is due as soon as the invoice is validated if you choose Based on Invoice. If the tax exigibility is based on payment, it must be paid as soon as the invoice payment is received.

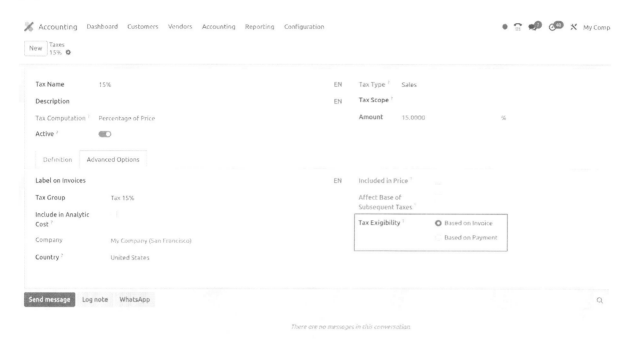

The screenshot above highlights the creation widow of the taxes for the advanced options. Only after enabling cash basis in the configuration settings will the Tax Exigibility field appear there.

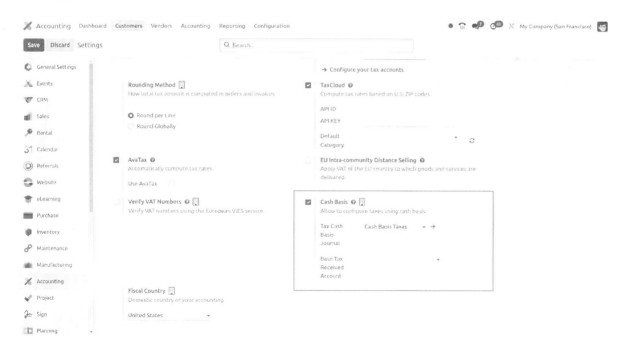

Everything pertaining to the Tax Configuration is included here. If a tax configuration is successful, you can use it in business activities. With the help of this function, you may specify all sales taxes, purchase taxes, and service taxes, which can then be applied to every good and service in accordance with the specifications.

Cash Basis Tax Configuration

When using a cash basis tax setup, revenue is recorded when funds are received, and expenses are recorded when funds are dispersed. Businesses that have a lot of expenses but little sales benefit from this form of accounting. This is one of the crucial elements to consider when your company operates with cash. Taxes are recorded when the payment is finished, not when the goods or service is delivered, or the invoice is validated, according to how Cash Basis is defined in Odoo17. You can use this feature to record and report your taxes using a cash basis rather than an accrual basis. Smaller companies that must immediately disclose their taxes or companies that must adhere to certain rules may find this handy. Odoo 17 Accounting will record your taxes as you pay them under the Cash basis tax setup, providing you with a more precise and up-to-date picture of your financial condition. This can assist you in making better tax payment plans and ensuring that you pay your taxes on time.

You must first activate the Cash Basis option from the Configuration Settings window of the Odoo Accounting platform in order to make the Cash Basis Taxation feature available on your Odoo17 platform. As seen in the figure below, the 'Taxes' area is located here in Settings.

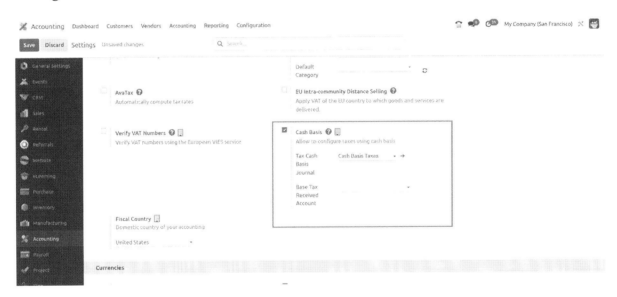

The Base Tax Received Account and the Tax Cash Basis Journal should be defined if you want to configure taxes on a cash basis. Therefore, during reconciliation, it will make an entry for such taxes on the specified account.

Only you, as we indicated earlier, will be able to specify the tax due in the Tax configuration window once you activate the option from Settings. This indicates that the option labeled Tax Exigibility will appear in the Advanced Options tab when configuring taxes, as seen below.

The tax structure and financial management of a business will take a blow if this alternative is chosen in order to comply with local or state regulations.

The tax on the good or service will therefore, be credited to the temporary tax account upon reconciliation once the Cash Basis Tax has been established. The Tax Received Account will be credited with the equivalent sum.

Everything regarding the arrangement of taxes is now pretty clear, so let's move on to the following section, where we'll talk about Tax Group.

Tax Group

To categorize various taxes, tax groups are utilized in the advanced Options of tax setup.

There are several tax types, such as VAT, CESS, Retention Taxes, GST, etc., depending on the nation. Odoo17's tax configuration and application to invoices and bills result in a calculation of the total that includes the tax amount.

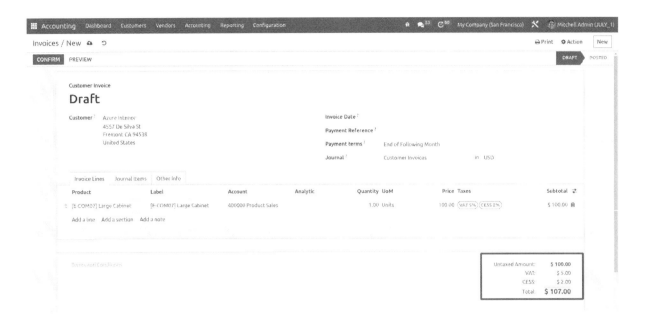

Multiple taxes may be charged to an invoice in specific circumstances. So, we can use a tax group to identify each tax specifically. Therefore, individual taxes are shown in the tax report and invoice.

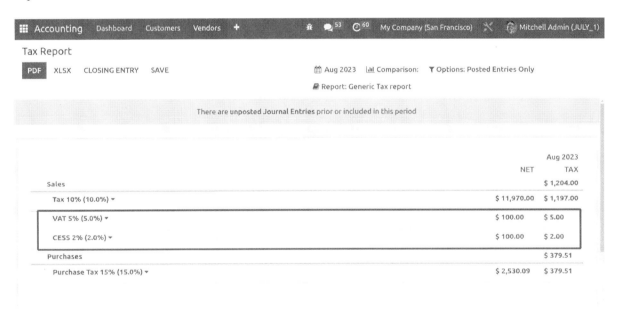

Now that we have a clear understanding of Tax, let's move on to the journals in the following section.

Configuring Journals

All financial transactions are recorded in the accounting system using journal entries, which are the first phase of the accounting cycle. The term "journal entry" refers to a simple accounting record of a business transaction that includes information about the transaction's specifics, including the date, amount, account impacted, and a brief description. The double-entry accounting system, which mandates that every financial transaction be documented in at least two accounts, relies heavily on journal entries.

Journals are the records that are used to record accounting transactions in Odoo 17 Accounting. Sales, purchases, receipts, payments, and other transactions that have an impact on the company's financial status are entered in journals. A summary of the company's financial situation at any given time is also included in the journals. Accounts may be reconciled, financial patterns can be examined, and reports can be generated. It will offer a record of the occasion, sum, and goal of every transaction. For certain time frames, such as monthly, quarterly, or yearly, journals can be produced.

Journals, as we all know, are crucial components of accounting operations in any business. They assist in categorizing certain processes and serve as the foundation for financial operations. Every form of business must keep and require journal entries. A strong feature of the Odoo 17 Accounting module enables the construction and administration of custom journals. This option allows you to specify each journal. Odoo17 provides a distinct menu for controlling it, titled Journals, within the Accounting portion of the Configuration menu. Below is a screenshot of the Journals window.

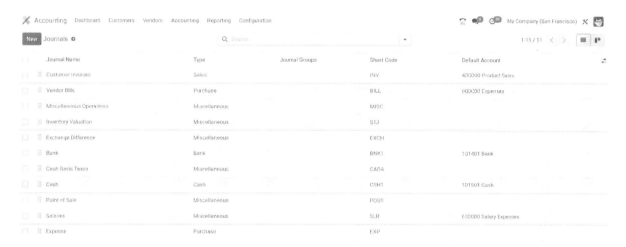

The Journals window gives a **New** option to start a new Journal as well as a clear preview of the previously established Journals. As seen in the image above, the window shows important information about the journals, including the default account, short code, and journal names, types, and groups.

By selecting the appropriate menu icon located in the window's top right corner, you can switch between the Kanban and List views of the window. Along with the search bar, the Filters, and Group By choices can both be customized and defaulted under Favorites that accomplish the necessary functions, including Save Current Search.

From the actions, one will be able to import and export records, with knowledge functionality like 'Insert view in article' and 'Insert in article.' Also, we will be able to add the journals to 'My Dashboard,' and with the spreadsheet feature, one can add details to the spreadsheet using the 'Link menu in spreadsheet' and 'Insert list in spreadsheet.'

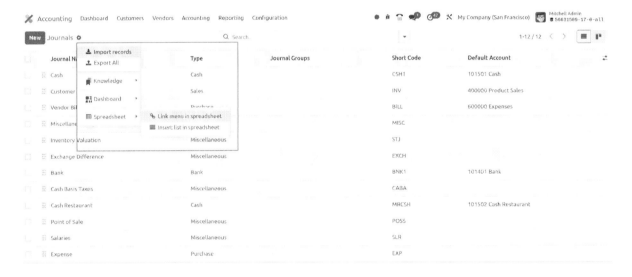

These options are all very helpful for finding the required journal from the longer list of designated journals rapidly. Additionally, the specific Odoo17 module makes it very easy to specify journal Types based on those that are already established as defaults. Additionally, for each journal that is defined, a journal type can be selected. The type of journal can be Miscellaneous, Cash, Bank, Sales, or Purchases.

All sales transactions in a company are recorded in the sales journals in Odoo17 Accounting. Sales orders, delivery, invoices, partner payments, as well as any other connected transactions, may be included in these transactions. Sales journals make it simple to keep track of all sales-related data and can be used to produce many reports, including sales reports and analyses of sales trends, among others.

You can use purchase journals to keep track of every business-related purchase transaction. These journals are employed to keep tabs on the price of the products and services acquired as well as to produce financial statements. The debit and credit sides of the purchase are recorded in the journal entries, and the entries are then posted to the general ledger. The cost of the goods and services, as well as any applicable taxes, are recorded in the purchase journals. The acquisition of inventory, raw materials, and completed goods are all documented in the buy diaries.

As we previously stated, the Purchase journal defines all of the company's purchase operations, just as the Sales journal is used to define all of the sales operations entries. Similar to how the Cash Journal will characterize each cash operations entry in relation to how the business is run with cash payments. Additionally, it is the same as the Bank Journal, where all bank-based transactions are entered.

Any transactions that do not fall under one of the predefined categories of transactions are recorded in a miscellaneous journal entry in Odoo17 Accounting. Discounts, returns, allowances, bank charges, and other erroneous things can all be entered into it. The account balance of any accounts that need modifications outside of the typical accounting period can likewise be changed in this manner. The Odoo17 Accounting's Miscellaneous Journals include:

- General Journal
- Adjustment Journal
- Inventory Adjustment Journal
- Currency Exchange Journal
- Stock Valuation
- Expense Journal
- Miscellaneous Journal Entries
- Tax Journal

You can organize all the entries that don't fit into any other journals in the Miscellaneous journal. Now, select the **New** button in the top left corner of the Journals box to configure a new Journal. You can first mention the Journal Name in the creation form. Then, using the dropdown menu, select the appropriate Journal Type. All of the journals, including Sales, Purchase, Cash, Bank, and Miscellaneous, are represented in the dropdown menu.

You can also define the accounting information, such as the short code and currency, using the Journal Entries menu. You can enter the shorter name you want to display in the Short Code field. This prefix will also be used by default to name the items in this journal. It is quite helpful for ensuring that the credit note entries and invoices begin with the designated code. For instance, if we define a short code as INV, invoice generation will begin with that word before moving on to the sequence number.

The Currency section also specifies the currency that will be used to enter statements. Additionally, the window will display additional fields according to the journal type you have chosen. Default Income Account and Dedicated Credit Not Sequence are additional fields that are available if you choose Sales as the category. You can choose the default one from the dropdown menu or create a new one. If you don't want to share the same sequence for invoices and credit notes created from this journal, you can activate the Dedicated Credit Note Sequence option.

Additionally, the CONTROL ACCESS area of the Advanced Settings tab is where you may choose the Allowed accounts in the corresponding field with the aid of the dropdown menu. You can leave these fields blank if you don't wish to exercise any control. It is possible to enable or disable the "Lock Posted Entries with Hash" box. If you enable this field, the accounting record or invoice is hashed as soon as it is posted and cannot be changed again. This is a great way to guarantee that no invoice created under a certain journal is altered. Once it is posted, it cannot be changed to any other form or returned to draft status.

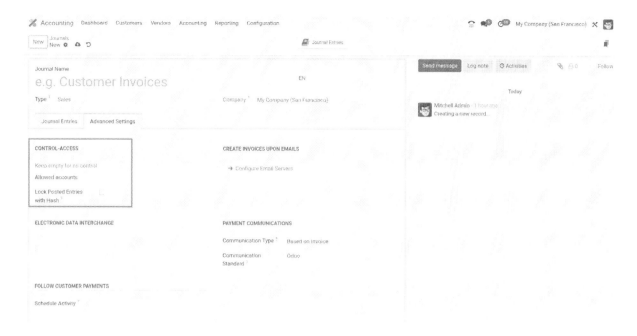

If the Type is Sales, you'll additionally show the extra fields under several headings, such as PAYMENT COMMUNICATIONS, CREATE INVOICES UPON EMAILS, and FOLLOW CUSTOMER PAYMENTS.

Communication Type and Communication Standard fields are included in the PAYMENT COMMUNICATION section. To make it easier for customers to remember to refer to a specific invoice when making a payment, you can define the default communication that will appear on their invoices once they have been validated in the Communication Type area. Open, Based on Customer, and Based on Invoice are the three options available here. You may do the same for the Communication Standard field. For each sort of reference, you can select a different model using this field; the default option is the "Odoo reference."

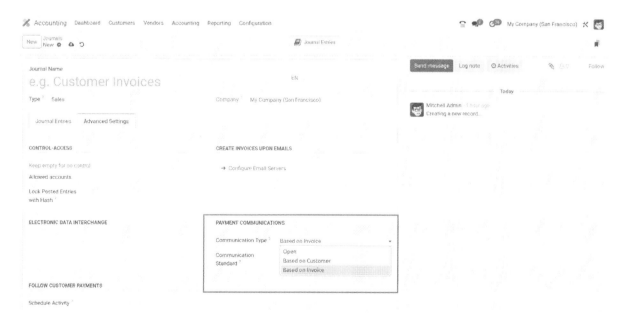

In the CREATE INVOICES UPON EMAILS section, you may also configure Email Servers. It will work well to guarantee that an invoice will be generated if the email is received under the appropriate server domain.

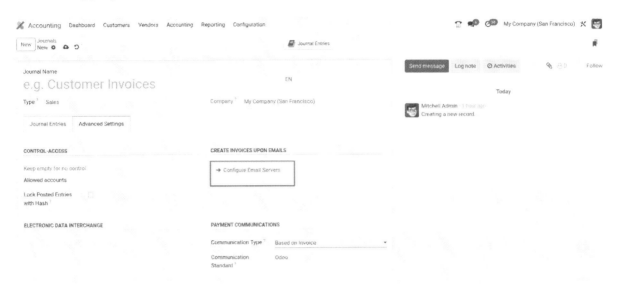

Additionally, you can submit XML or EDI invoices via electronic invoicing by using the section on ELECTRONIC DATA INTERCHANGE. You can do that by turning on the E-Invoice option. If the appropriate localization module for "e-invoicing" is installed, which will be possible with accounting localization, then electronic invoicing will be available. An XML/EDI document will be generated and attached once this capability is enabled, along with invoices and credit notes.

You also have a space for scheduling an activity for the upcoming payments from customers. Any activity you indicate will automatically be scheduled on the due date for payments, which will improve the collection process. The drop-down menu can be used to select an activity.

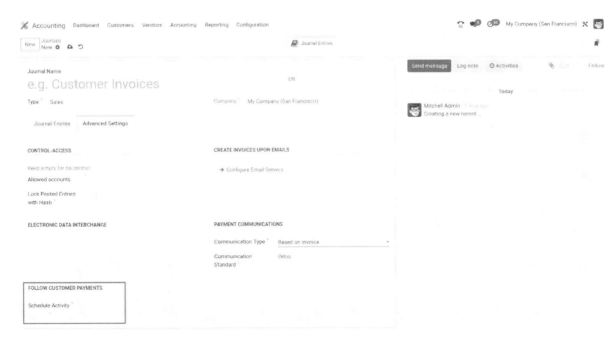

Finally, you have the choice to communicate with readers of the associated journal by sending messages and describing log notes. Other users of your Odoo 17 platform, who may be members of the staff of your business or affiliated members, could be followers. The Log Note option helps you record the changes made by the employees and describes them together with the time and date, while the Send Message option is quite helpful for notifying any pertinent information.

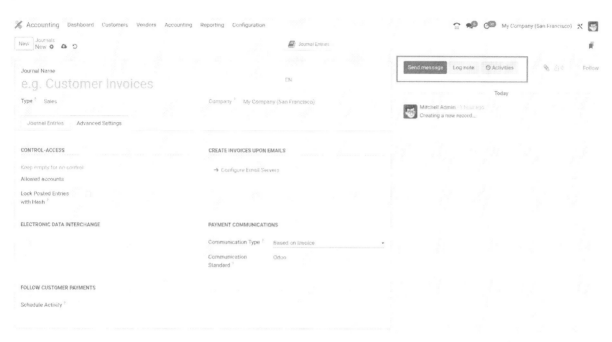

In addition to all of these choices, you can also see the smart tab in the window's upper right corner, as seen in the illustration below. The 'Journal entries' smart tab will display every entry made in that specific journal.

We now understand how to configure the Sales journal type. In Odoo17, the steps for creating the Sales, Purchase, and Miscellaneous journals are all the same. Let's now talk about the Bank journal's configuration processes, which differ from those for Sales, Purchase, and Miscellaneous journal kinds.

The creation window will show the various sections, including Journal Entries, Incoming Payments, Outgoing Payments, and Advanced Settings when you choose Bank as the Journal Type.

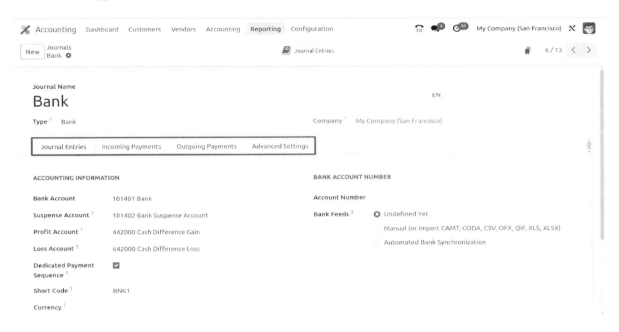

You must provide details about journal entries under the "Journal Entries" tab. As a result, you can provide the ACCOUNTING INFORMATION, including the Bank Account, Suspense Account, Profit Account, Loss Account, Short Code, and Currency information. The Suspense Account serves as a temporary account until the bank statement transactions for each journal activity are reconciled, and is used to post bank statement transactions until the bank account is balanced with the payments.

The Profit Account is also used to record a profit when a cash register's ending balance deviates from the calculation made by the system. When the cash register's closing balance differs from what the computer calculates, it is advantageous to record a loss in the loss account. The Dedicated Payment Sequence option for activating is also shown in this section.

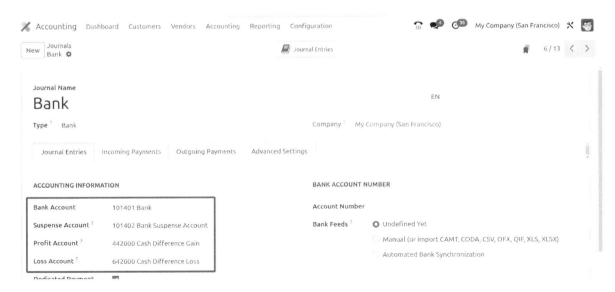

In the 'BANK ACCOUNT NUMBER' section, the Account Number can also be specified in the appropriate field. Additionally, you have the choice to designate Bank Feeds, and the registration of bank statements will be carried out in accordance with your choice. Three options are available here: Automated Bank Synchronization, Import (CAMT, CODA, CSV, OFX, QIF), and Undefined Yet. When you select the Import option, more fields will be displayed, including the QIF Decimal Separator, which is necessary to prevent conversion problems, and the QIF Dates format, where you can select either dd/mm/yy or mm/dd/yy depending on the firm. Split Transactions, the third field, can be turned on to split group payments for CODA files. You can import information from the dashboard using the Import option.

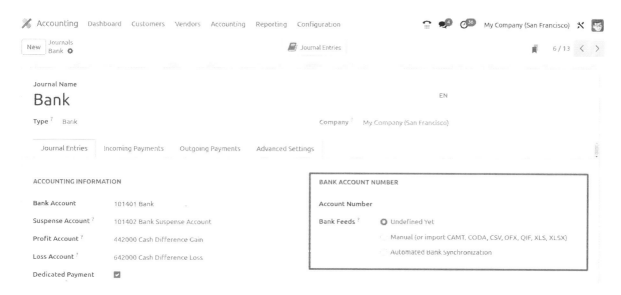

The Odoo 17 platform can be made accessible for directly retrieving the invoice payment information from the bank servers by selecting Automated Bank Synchronization. Additionally, you will have control over the review of the synchronized operations via the Dashboard.

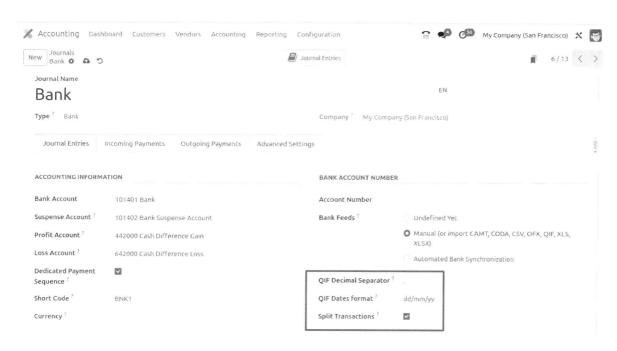

The incoming payment setup details can now be defined under the Incoming Payments tab. Therefore, you can specify the Name and Payment Method using the Add a line option.

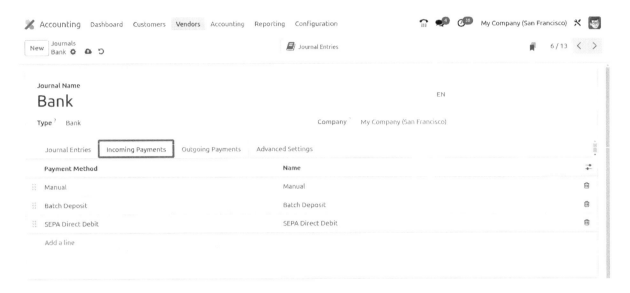

You must set up the outgoing payment methods under the Outgoing Payments tab. The 'Payment Method' and 'Name' can be defined using the Add a Line option because it is almost the same as the Incoming Payments. You can select a method from the drop-down menu and then apply it. If the payment method is brand-new, configuring it won't take much work.

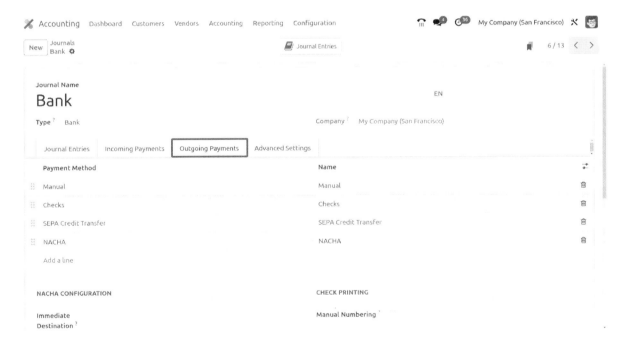

Furthermore, if your pre-printed checks aren't numbered, you can enable the Manual Numbering field found in the CHECK PRINTING section.

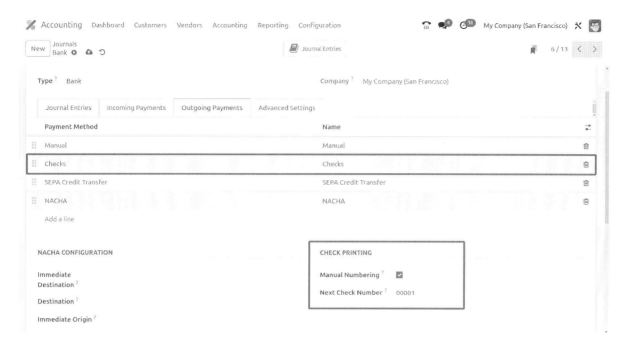

Additionally, there is the NACHA CONFIGURATION, where a number of fields are available, including Immediate Destination, Destination, Immediate Origin, Company Identification, and Originating DFI Identification. The bank will supply all of these facts.

NACHA CONFIGURATION: The term NACHA stands for National Automated Clearing House Association compliant ACH file, which will be produced using US localization. At the appropriate location, information such as the immediate destination, the immediate origin, the company identification, and the origination DFI identifier can be provided. Your bank will frequently inform you when you are authorized to send payments using ACH. With this payment method, you can pay a vendor and create the NACHA file that goes with it.

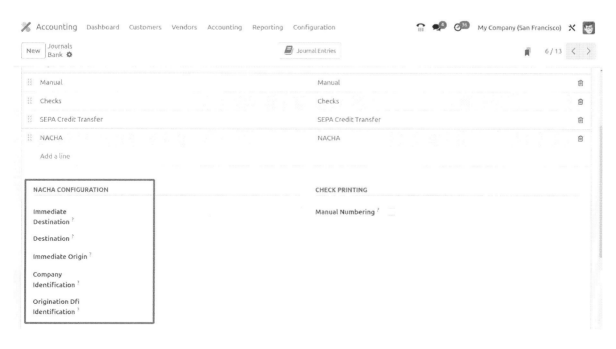

When a customer generates an invoice payment, the funds are not directly credited to the bank account; instead, they are placed in the Outstanding Receipt Account, which is described here. Only the payment will be deposited to the company's bank account following the automatic or manual reconciliation of the bank statement and the payment is done. The amount for the vendor bill will also be generated from Accounts Payable in the case of Purchase Payment, moved to the Outstanding Payments Account, and then when the bank statement reconciliation process is carried out in relation to the vendor bill, the bank will be reconciled with outstanding payment entries rather than the payable account.

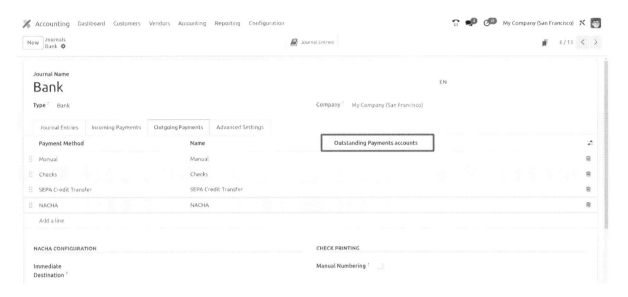

The final option, Advanced Settings, is identical to the Sales, Purchase, and Miscellaneous accounts in the Journals configuration. Therefore, based on the operational requirements, the account operation details for the Cash and Bank journals can be modified.

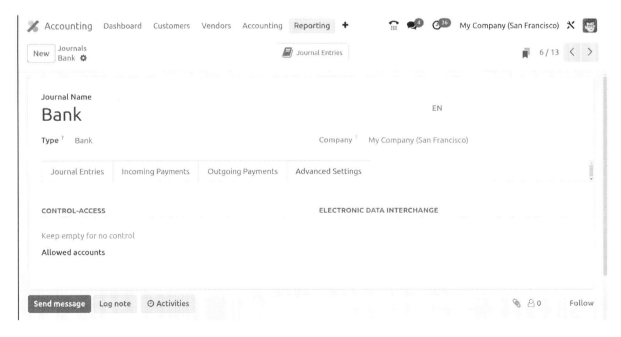

These are the proper methods for creating and editing journals, and these journals can be used to create journal entries for the financial administration of an organization. Now that we have covered every component of journal design, we can examine journal groups, which are important for categorizing journals.

Journal Groups

You will have the opportunity to categorize numerous business operations elements through categorization, which is a crucial aspect of business operations. It will enable you to divide the process into delicate discs. For a company's accounting procedures to run smoothly, you can define several journals using the Odoo17 platform. There is a good probability that entries will be confused when defined in various journals. Thus, a special ability to group the journals was provided by the Odoo17 platform. This cutting-edge function will provide a lot of assistance in categorizing all the configured journals.

Go to the Configuration menu of the Accounting module to access the Journal Groups menu, where you can view all the journal groups that were previously described in the Journal Groups window, as shown below.

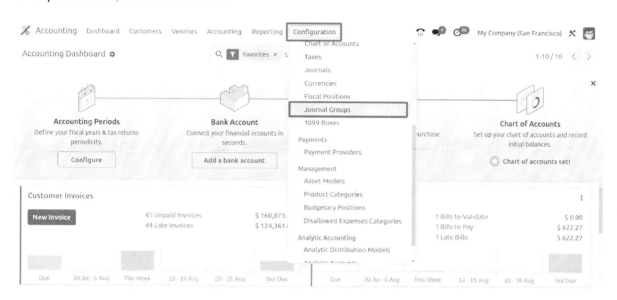

You will enter the window when you select the Journal Groups menu. You can make brand-new Journal Groups by pressing the **New** button. The instant your cursor passes over the New button, a new line for configuring journal groups will appear in the same window.

There, you can list the Excluded Journals and enter the names of the Journal Groups. The Company field can be customized and will be automatically assigned. This window also has access to the many sorting features offered by Odoo17. You can rapidly sort out the necessary groups using the pre-set and configurable filters, as well as the Group By choices.

One of the standout features of the Odoo17 Accounting module that enables you to classify your accounting journals into categories is Journal Grouping. The groups can be used to streamline reporting and more effectively manage accounting data. Users will find it simpler to track and view all of your transactions with the help of this feature. By giving a centralized mechanism to compare the various sorts of transactions, journal grouping also contributes to the accuracy of the financial records. Then, financial data may be more effectively organized and analyzed using these categories.

Journals can be grouped using this functionality based on the company, transaction type, or other factors. Users can now easily look up and access particular journals as needed, thanks to this. Users can arrange journals based on the type of transaction, which aids in keeping their finances organized. Users may quickly discover which journals require reconciliation, which aids in accounting reconciliation.

In reporting, these Journal groupings are used to bundle pertinent data together for display. You can complete the Filtering and Group By requirements for various accounting and journal activities. The Odoo17 platform places a high priority on report generation, and with the use of filtering features, a variety of reports connected to accounts may be acquired in a matter of seconds. To simplify the procedure, you only need to select Journal Types as the filtering criteria.

While defining it, it is also possible to choose the appropriate Chart of Account Types because doing so makes it easier to sort out the requirements for the accounting information in relation to the Chart of Account Types that are being established.

While defining it, the Chart of Account Types can also be chosen for the relevant one; this is advantageous for the filter of the accounting data with regard to the Chart of Account Types that are being defined.

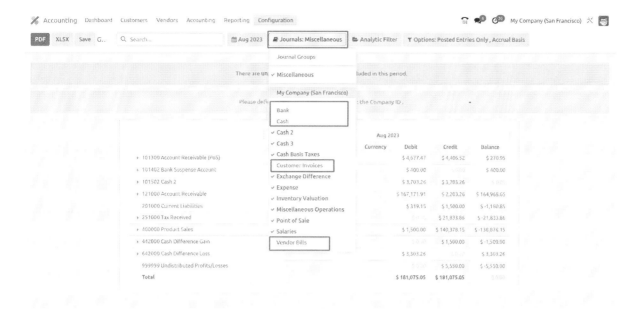

The accounts Customer Invoices, Vendor Bills, Bank, and Cash mentioned in the journal will not be included in the filter of reports since the journal group "Miscellaneous" has been selected in the report. Therefore, for the efficient operation of journal management operations, the Journal Group feature has a considerable impact on the accounting department of any organization.

After thoroughly understanding the capabilities of Journal Groups, let's have a look at the Currency Management tool that is included in the Odoo17 Accounting module in the part that follows.

Currency Management

Users may simply manage numerous currencies in their accounts thanks to the extensive Currency management capability included in the Odoo 17 Accounting module. A currency rate system and an automatic currency conversion method are included in this feature.

Users can specify the exchange rate and choose the preferred rate for each type of currency using the currency rate method. Users can also establish various rates for various kinds of transactions using this approach.

Users can automatically convert any transaction amount from one currency to another using the automated currency conversion method. The mechanism for determining currency rates and the rate established for each type of transaction is used for this. Additionally, it gives you the option to choose the currency symbol that will be used when showing quantities in various currencies. This guarantees that all quantities are shown in the proper currency and that the exchange rates are properly applied. Users can also simply monitor and report on transactions made in various currencies. Getting a clear image of their accounts and transactions in several currencies is quite beneficial.

Multinational corporations will frequently have a large number of clients and suppliers from different countries. Therefore, the great and potent currency management system that we have built into the Odoo17 platform is extremely relevant. The primary reason for this is that various payments, including vendor bills and invoices, must be made in accordance with their respective currencies, and the organization will keep to a specific set of currencies whereby all of the organization's operations are carried out. Therefore, the platform's Currency Management tool is useful for managing multiple currencies.

The Currencies menu may be found in the Odoo 17 Accounting module's Configuration menu, as can be seen in the screenshot below. With only one click, you may access the Currencies pane, as displayed below.

The Important Currencies of Operation in the World list will be displayed in the Dedicated Window. By selecting the Kanban menu icon in the window's upper right corner, you can also open the window in Kanban view. You can view each currency's details in this window, including the Currency Name, the specific currency's symbol, Name, the Last Updated Date, and the Current Rate (as it relates to the base currency set). The "Use on eBay" section to specify the operation is also visible, as is the Active option, which can be activated or disabled in accordance with the wishes of the organization.

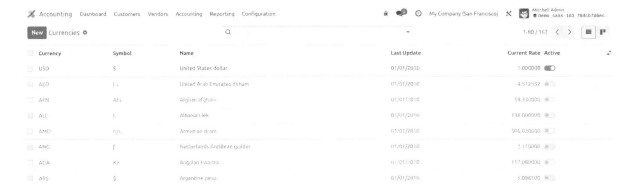

All of the default currency records are selectable, and using the associated options under the Action button, you may carry out various operations including archiving the currency, making a duplicate record, deleting it, or showing currency rates.

If you need to set up a new currency, you can do so by selecting the NEW button in the Currencies window. You will now draw the creation form as it is displayed below.

The Currency area is where you can enter the currency code. The AFIP Code must then be assigned so that it can be utilized for electronic invoicing. The Name, Currency Unit, and Currency Sub unit can be mentioned in the respective fields. The 'Use on eBay' option can also be turned on to make this currency available on eBay. The Active field is similar in that it can be activated or removed depending on the needs.

Finally, you can find the currency rates under the Rates tab. Based on the most recent updates to exchange rates, you can establish new rates for the currency here. Under the Rates tab, you can define the Date, Company Name, Unit per USD, and USD per Unit.

The Automated Currency Rates option is another feature provided by the Odoo17 platform. It can be accessed via the Settings window of the Odoo17 Accounting module. You may find the option under the Currencies area of the Configuration Settings, as seen in the figure below.

You can update exchange rates automatically if you turn on the Automated Currencies Rates option. You must do this by selecting the service provider for the currency rate update from the dropdown list that is presented in the Service field. For instance, it can use the dropdown to select the European Central Bank, the Bank of Canada, the Mexican Bank, etc. according to the location in which your business works. Additionally, you can specify whether the currency will be updated manually, daily, weekly, or monthly. The calendar pop-up under the "Next Run" column allows you to change the update's next date.

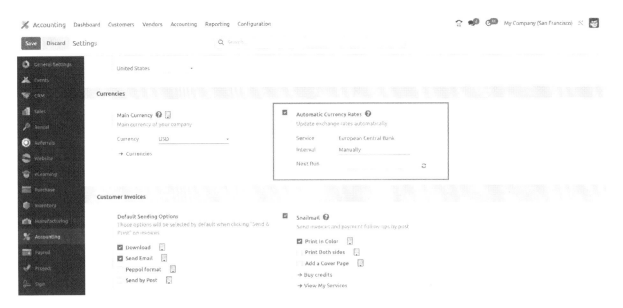

As a result, the Odoo 17 Accounting module provides a unique tool for controlling currency exchange rates. It enables you to quickly update a currency's exchange rate within the system, enabling them to function with other currencies. Users will be able to follow their transactions in several currencies thanks to the module's support for multi-currency transactions. It also offers reports for examining currency exchange rates and monitoring currency performance. The module also gives consumers a variety of options to personalize the settings for their currency exchange rates. They are able to better manage and have more control over their finances as a result.

The Post Exchange difference entries tool, found in the Default Accounts section of the Odoo17 Accounting Settings window, can help you manage currency exchange rates more effectively. The tool's screenshot is displayed below.

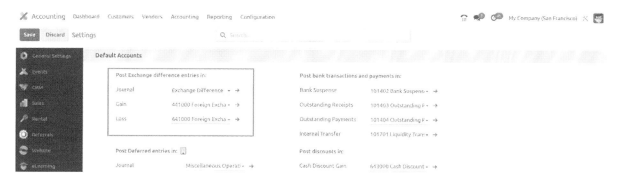

The platform gives users the possibility to define the Journal, the Gain Account, and the Loss Account using this option. In light of this, if the transaction experiences a loss as a result of exchange rate variations, it will be recorded in the Loss Account, which is currently being developed. The Gain Account that you have mentioned here will be credited with the amount if, on the other hand, the transaction gains money due to changes in exchange rates. These developments, along with the platform's capable Multi currency management capability, may help you run professional international commercial operations.

Let's move on to the system's fiscal position management feature now that we are familiar with the multi-currency management features of the Odoo17 Accounting platform.

Fiscal Position

Tax regulations that can be imposed on a customer, supplier, or product are mapped out in the Fiscal Position section of the Odoo 17 Accounting module. Based on their nation, state, and other factors, you can assign different tax laws to clients. This aids in managing the various tax laws in various nations. This is helpful for businesses that provide goods or services to clients abroad. This makes it simple to comply with the tax laws of several nations, which is quite helpful. With the help of this function, you may set up tax regulations differently depending on the area or type of product purchased by the customer. It can be used to specify various tax rates for certain clients or goods. This account management organization is the ideal solution for a company's global financial management. The taxes and the bank accounts specified for the transactions can be automatically adjusted using this tool.

The Accounting part of the Configuration tab in the Odoo17 Accounting software includes a menu called Fiscal Positions that can be accessed.

You may manage all the fiscal position entries in the Fiscal Positions window by using the Fiscal Positions menu as its key. Every predefined Fiscal position will be displayed in the window, as seen in the illustration below.

All of the fields in the window's display are selectable, and you may choose from among the defined fiscal position records to see all of the information for that particular one. If the platform manages additional Fiscal Positions, you can also retrieve the necessary Fiscal Position using the Filters, Group By, and advanced Search tools, and to Save Current Search. The gear wheel icon facilitates Import Records, Link menu in spreadsheet, Insert view in article, Insert link in article, Insert list in spreadsheet, and Add to my dashboard choices.

List view and Kanban view both provide access to the window. The window's Kanban view is provided below. An excellent technique to provide necessary Fiscal Positions is to use the NEW button. The Fiscal Positions creation form is provided below.

The Fiscal Position field is where you can specify the name of the fiscal position. Following that, you may see other fields to set, including Use TaxCloud API, Use AvaTax API, Detect Automatically, and Foreign Tax ID. Depending on the options, each of these fields can be enabled or disabled. To automatically calculate tax rates, you must input your TaxCloud credentials if the Use TaxCloud API option is selected. The Detect Automatically box allows you to automatically apply this financial position to the partner operation's country, country group, cities, or federal state. If you want to apply just to a specific country, you also have the choice to specify the country where you can mention the country.

You can now define the "Tax on Product" and the "Tax to Apply" in the setup window's Tax Mapping tab. In this way, the applicable tax that must be applied to the goods can be stated. Additionally, the matching product tax will be used in accordance with the fiscal position if the fiscal mapping is approved by the Odoo17 system when the partner is allocated for the operation.

Similar to the 'Add a line' option, the Accounting Mapping tab enables you to choose the Account on Product and the Account to use instead. Additionally, you may include the legal remarks that must be printed on the invoices in the given Legal Note line.

The Avatax Invoice Account and Avatax Refund Account, which are the accounts that Avatax will use for invoices and refunds, respectively, can be defined under the Avatax settings tab of the Fiscal Positions creation form. In the space provided, you may also add Legal Notes here.

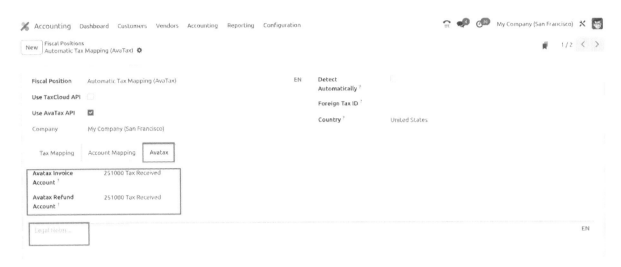

After setting up all of these components, you can apply them to bills and invoices to have the tax and accounts mapped in accordance with the example's established rule.

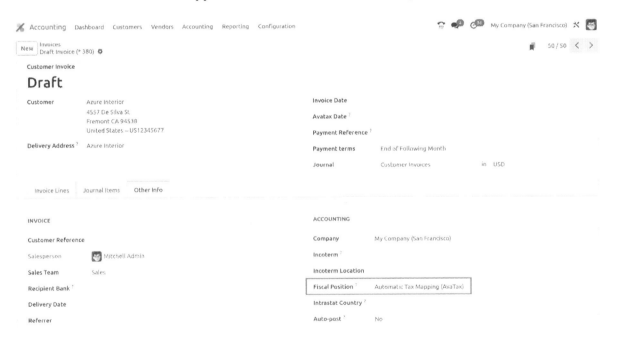

Financial standing for partners is automatically determined based on the specified country group, country, and federal states.

Let's move on to the Online Synchronization feature of the Odoo17 Accounting module now that we are clear on the Fiscal Position menu and its configurable components.

Online Synchronization

Odoo 17's Online Synchronization, a useful feature of accounting is that enables users to maintain their books or records current and in sync with their external accounts. Data from external accounting systems is immediately imported and synced. Users can map their accounts and have transactions like invoices, payments, and journals generated automatically. Users can maintain accurate and balanced books with the feature's double-entry bookkeeping capabilities. To make sure all of your bank account transactions are recorded, you may quickly reconcile them.

This useful tool makes it easy to communicate data with other systems by allowing you to synchronize your Odoo17 Accounting data with an external system and keep your accounting data accurate and up-to-date. By connecting two systems, such as Odoo 17 and an external accounting system, the online synchronization capability operates. The two systems can share data in real time after the connection has been made. This implies that whenever an entry is made in one system, the other will be updated automatically.

You can define choices for how data is transferred between the two systems using this capability. You can decide which fields are excluded from synchronization, for instance. Additionally, you can specify how data is handled when the two systems disagree about how to use it.

The Online Synchronization tool is the most effective approach to keep track of each time your bank account and Odoo 17 are synchronized. You can synchronize your Odoo17 database with your Odoo cloud instance using this. This function is intended to streamline and improve the reliability of data transfers between various databases. The sync functionality transfers data from the Odoo database to the cloud instance on a regular basis, and then downloads updates from the cloud instance. By doing this, it is made sure that both databases are current and that any changes made in one are mirrored in the other.

You must first establish the connection and authentication between their local database and the Odoo cloud instance in order to use the synchronization capability. The Configuration part of the Odoo interface is where this is done. You can reach the Online Synchronization menu via the Configuration tab's Banks section, as seen below.

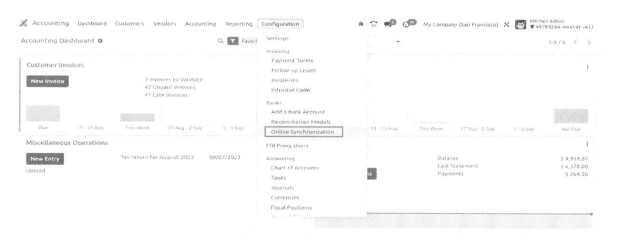

You can set the synchronization parameters, such as frequency and the data to be synced, once a link has been made.

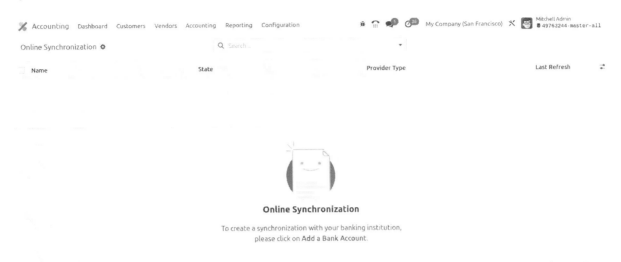

You can add a bank account using the ADD A BANK ACCOUNT menu found in the top left corner of the Online Synchronization window. You will then draw a second window containing descriptions of all the operational banks, as seen below.

You can choose the bank accounts for your business operation from the list you've already outlined. Click the Connect button after selecting the necessary bank to connect to the associated bank account.

The '**Create it**' option, which is visible in the window's bottom right corner, allows you to create a new bank if the one you need is not among those listed. When you click this button, a pop-up menu allowing you to create a new bank account will appear.

You can choose the bank accounts from the list you've already listed for your business operations. Click the Connect button once you've selected the necessary bank to connect to that account. If the bank you need is not listed, you can establish a new one with the help of the "Create it" option shown in the window's bottom right corner. After clicking this button, a pop-up menu will appear where you can open a new bank account.

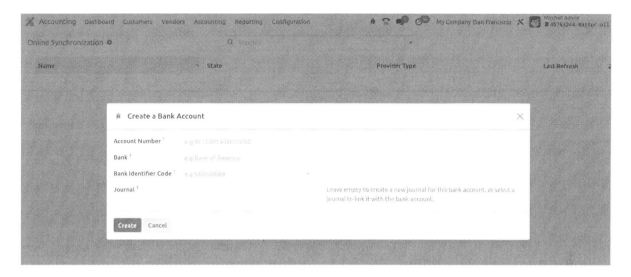

By entering the necessary details, including Account Number, Bank, Bank Identifier Code, and Journal, in this window, you can open a new bank account.

For seamless operation, the very user-friendly Odoo17 instance offers a list of bank accounts that includes practically all well-known banks operating globally. You also have the opportunity to build bespoke bank accounts according to your requirements.

The bank statements will be automatically fetched from the bank server to Odoo17 at a specific interval of time, say every 4 hours or every 12 hours, which may be set in the scheduled action for the online synchronization, once the bank has been set up and connected with Odoo17. Therefore, during online synchronization, it will keep track of all the time spent in sync with the bank, as well as its status (such as whether it is connected, experiencing a problem, or not), and the most recent refresh time and date.

We have so far covered the many elements included in the Accounting Configuration menu as well as the tools explained in the Accounting module's Configuration tab. Let's now go into more detail about the various Payment setting options offered by the Odoo 17 Accounting module.

Everything regarding the configuration of Online Synchronization is now pretty clear, so let's move on to the next section, where we'll talk about how to define horizontal groups.

Defining Horizontal Groups

One of the improved features of the Odoo 17 Accounting module, which formulates specific requirements, is Horizontal Groups. The financial statements can be filtered using these horizontal groups. Only if the developer mode is enabled will this functionality be accessible through the accounting application's configuration menu.

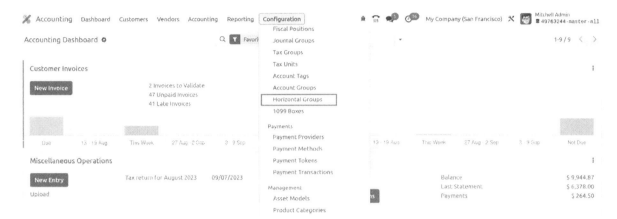

The ability to create horizontal groups is provided by the NEW button in the horizontal groups. When constructing horizontal groups, we can specify which financial reports will contain this horizontal group.

We can enter the domain under the section field.

As a result, the data was filtered according to the domain in the financial reports after applying the horizontal group.

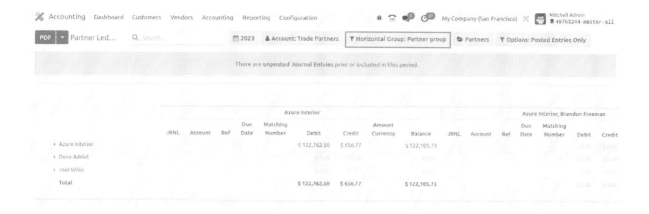

Payment Options

For completing the operational requirements of Accounting operations management, Odoo17 has a variety of configuration tools and methods. The management of Payments and their associated functions can be regarded as one of the core elements of Accounting management operations. The finance department is responsible for collecting all incoming and outgoing funds. You must therefore be prepared with all the cutting-edge features and tools in this digital age in order to specify and accept the payment appropriate for accepting funding from a variety of sources.

The Odoo17 platform prioritizes payment alternatives above all else, and it makes it simple and quick to manage and see payment terms, payment modes, and payment methods. You may quickly set up various payment terms, payment mechanisms, and payment options for all of their clients, vendors, and consumers using the platform. This enables reporting on payment patterns and tracking incoming and outgoing payments. Additionally, it makes it simple to send payment requests and bills fast. It offers a more efficient method of managing and processing payments. This involves setting up and managing payment terms, controlling automated payments, and setting up and managing payment options. Payment options offer a thorough and practical method of managing and processing payments, freeing up time and resources to concentrate on other areas of the company.

The Payment Acquirers, which are the most practical means of accepting payment, are the main component of the Payment choices of configurations provided in the Odoo17 instance. Therefore, we may list the Payment Acquirers that are present in the Odoo17 system in the part that follows.

Payment Providers

The services that allow you to process payments for your clients are known as payment providers. The Odoo 17 Accounting module's Payment Providers feature enables you to accept payments and pay suppliers, customers, or vendors. This streamlines the payment and collection process, lowers manual errors, and guarantees on-time payment. Additional advantages offered by payment providers include integrated accounting, fraud prevention, and automatic reconciliation. It allows connectivity with several banks as well as online payment processors like PayPal and Stripe. Customers can now pay orders or bills online from the Odoo17 website using a safe and secure payment gateway. Through streamlining the payment process and increasing consumer satisfaction, this integration enables speedier payments.

The Payment Providers option is easily accessible in the Odoo17 instance. You may access the Payment Providers menu icon in the Payments section of the Accounting module by selecting the Configuration tab, which is displayed in the image below.

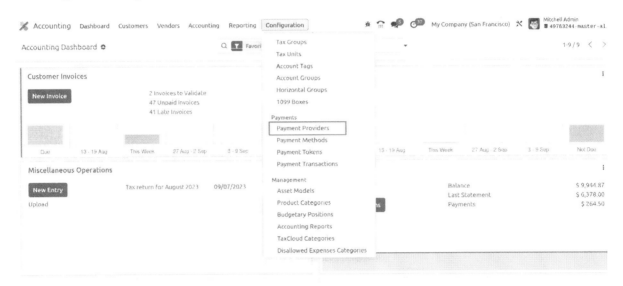

The Payment Providers window, which is accessible from the menu and displays all of the installed and defined payment providers, is a link that can be used to access the menu.

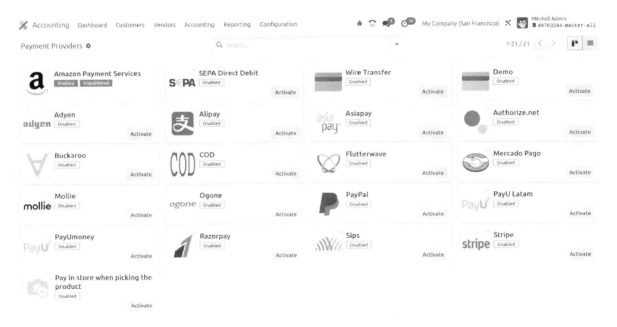

You can see the names and logos of the Payment Providers that are being made operational right here in the window. Additionally, the necessary Payment Providers can be enabled by simply choosing and turning on the appropriate provider. In order to quickly find the appropriate Payment Provider, you also have the opportunity to filter and organize using the different default as well as configurable Filters and Group By options. You can choose from any of these listed Payment Providers to view the configuration information, and you also have the option to modify the information.

You can choose a certain provider to access all of its information. For instance, by clicking on this record, we may read the details of the "SEPA Direct Debit." As seen in the image below, you will see a new window where you may view all of the details.

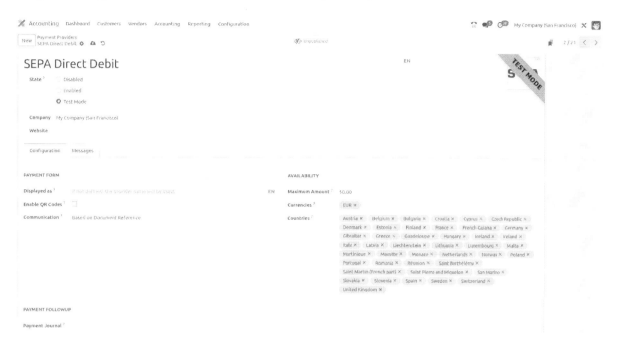

From the Odoo17 platform's App Store, users can access the various Payment Providers intended for the platform's operations. You may access all the accounting-related software that can only be installed from here under the Accounting category.

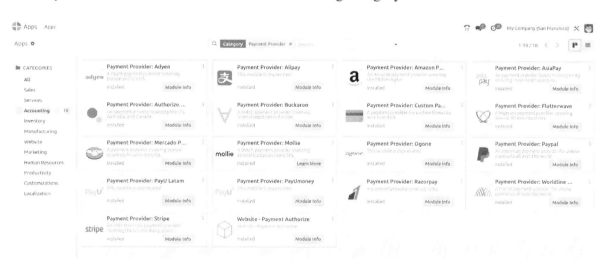

The management options for the Odoo17 Accounting module can then be covered.

Management Options

The supervision of an organization's accounting operation is among the crucial and important components. Your financial operation will become a headache if it is not properly handled with care and attention. Therefore, it is necessary to implement appropriate management controls and procedures. Sufficient administration and regulating options are provided by the top Odoo17 software, which is quite advantageous for smooth accounting-related processes. Its cutting-edge tools and features let you set up everything quickly.

This specialized Odoo17 Accounting application can handle all of the company's financial tasks. The platform's well-designed management features have the ability to completely change how an organization manages its finances. The available management options in the Accounting module's Configuration tab are examined in detail in the section that follows.

Asset Models

Asset management is crucial to the functioning of any organization. It involves managing a company's intangible, physical, and financial assets to maximize their effectiveness and worth. It entails keeping tabs on how the assets are used and maintained, taking proactive steps to lower the risks connected to them, and making sure they are promptly replaced when required. Organizations can use asset management to make educated choices about where to invest in new resources and how to manage those that already exist. Asset management done right may help businesses cut costs, lower liabilities, and foster long-term growth.

The Asset Models in the Odoo 17 Accounting module setup gives you the ability to manage the fixed assets of your business and produce depreciation entries. You can track asset costs, compute depreciation, and produce financial reports thanks to it. You may manage and keep track of the insurance, maintenance, and other relevant information for each asset with this function. It also aids in keeping track of asset costs over the course of their useful lives and the accompanying depreciation costs. Additionally, the asset models offer a mechanism to track the asset's worth through time as well as its present book value. Asset models can also be used to generate reports that detail the asset's past performance as well as its current worth.

The following asset models are definable in the Odoo17 Accounting module:

- **Fixed assets**: Fixed assets are physical items that a company uses for a considerable amount of time and have long-term worth. Land, structures, furniture, and equipment are some examples.
- **Depreciation**: Assets lose value over time due to depreciation. Different depreciation techniques, including Straight lines, declining balances, and based on day per period, can be used to accomplish this.
- **Leasing**: A third-party seller may lease assets to you.

- **Intangible Assets**: Non-physical assets such as patents, copyrights, and trademarks are considered intangible assets. On the balance sheet, these assets are listed as assets that will be depreciated over time.
- **Impaired**: When an asset's fair value drops, it is said to be impaired. This may be the result of several things, like market conditions, competitive forces, or technical obsolescence. The financial statements must reflect the impairment.

You can establish the parameters for how assets are tracked and handled in Odoo17 using the Asset Models feature. You can set the asset value, the depreciation rate, and the depreciation calculation method for an asset using this feature. Users can also configure particular depreciation rules for various asset models, such as various calculation techniques for one type of asset and a various rate for a different type of asset. As a result, Odoo17's asset management options are expanded, and the information is kept current and correct.

The asset models feature's primary goal is to give an organization a simple method for managing and tracking its assets. With the aid of the Assets Models menu, which is accessible through the Management section of the Configuration tab of the module, the dedicated Odoo17 Accounting module frames the asset management processes.

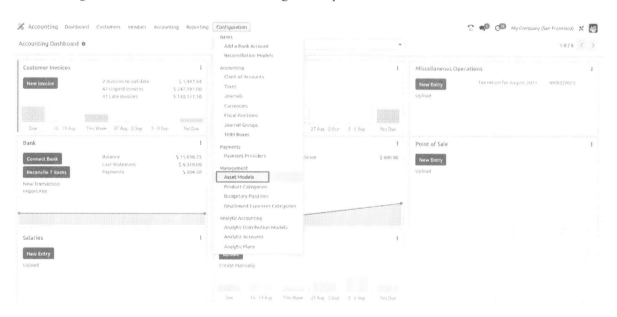

You may access the Assets page by using this menu. On this page, you can view all of the asset models that are currently in use as well as information about them, such as the Asset Name, Fixed Asset Account, Depreciation Account, Method, Number of Depreciations, and Period duration, as shown in the screenshot below.

Select one of the previously configured asset models to view it in more detail. You may find and group the desired asset model from the entire list using the Filter, Group By, and Search options in the interface. By selecting **New**, the new Asset model can be built. The creation form screenshot is shown below.

Enter the asset model's name in the Asset Model name field to define a new asset model. Then, in the designated fields, you can configure the operating components of it. A few fields to determine depreciation features are shown in the DEPRECIATION METHOD section. In order to determine the quantity of depreciation lines, you can select the appropriate method to use. It can be described as either Declining or Declining then Straight Line, or simply Straight Line.

The Gross Value/Duration will be computed when you select the Straight line. It will be determined based on residual value in the case of declining. Finally, a minimal depreciation value equal to the straight line value will result from a decline followed by a straight line, but with a declining trend. The number of depreciations required to depreciate your asset can then be allocated in the Duration box based on Years or Months.

Depending on the value entered in the computation section, the depreciation calculation may be based on "No Prorata," "Constant Periods," or "Based on Days Per Period." No prorata indicates that the asset's acquisition date will not be taken into account, and that the depreciation period will begin at the beginning of the fiscal year.

When the computation is set to "Constant Periods," the depreciation board is determined starting from the purchase date or prorata date. Depreciation board each day for each period will be calculated using the third computing method, "Based on days per period." It will first calculate the daily depreciation taking into account the entire period. Based on the daily depreciation, a monthly or annual (duration frequency) depreciation board will be calculated.

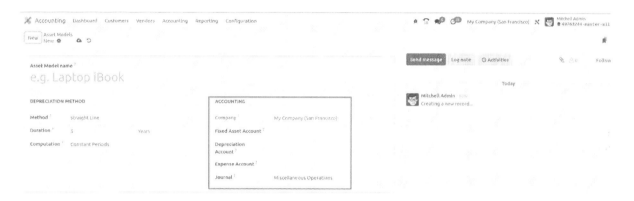

Similar to this, you may specify the Company associated operation in the Company field of the Accounting portion of the Asset models creation window. The system will automatically assign the field. The Fixed Asset Account area is where you can specify the account that was used to record the asset's initial purchase price.

The Depreciation Account, which is the account utilized in the depreciation entries to reduce the asset value, can then be selected. The Expense Account, which is the account used in periodic entries for recording a portion of the asset as an expense, can also be defined. In the Journal area, you can finally select a journal. Here, all of the accounts and journals that we have previously set up on the platform are shown in dropdown menus so that you can select the one you need.

The new Asset model will be saved into the system once you have provided all the necessary information. By selecting the Follow option located on the bottom left, you can now add followers to this specific Asset model. The system also offers the Attachment option and the Knowledge Article Search option, as seen in the image below.

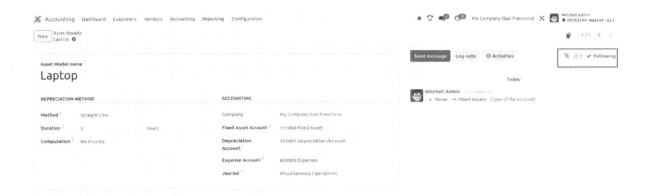

You may track the asset model's development using the Follow option, and you'll get alerts when anything changes. You can upload documents, pictures, and other types of materials that are relevant to the asset model using the Attachment option. The new feature included in the 17 version of Odoo allows users to browse the Odoo 17 Knowledge Base for pertinent articles that may be helpful during the building of an asset model. The Send Message, Log note, and Activities options are visible in the bottom left corner of the creation form, as illustrated in the image below.

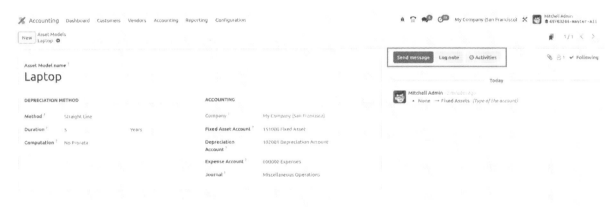

You can transmit information to the recipients of the asset model using the transmit messages option. In addition to having the ability to schedule an activity with the followers regarding the asset model using the Activities menu, the Log note option will feed all modifications made to the asset model. You can add, view, and keep track of activities associated with the asset model using this option.

We can learn about the Product Categories feature based on what we deduced about the Asset Management option that is already available in Odoo17 Accounting.

Product Categories

Large amounts of inventory can be organized and managed using Product Categories in business software. It makes it simpler to identify, order, and report on things while also assisting in the development of an effective system for tracking products. Making sure that clients are shown things that are relevant to them can also be accomplished by maintaining an organized list of products and commodities. Product categories can also assist firms in identifying patterns in consumer purchasing behaviors.

Product Categories are a feature of the Odoo 17 Accounting module that allows users to more effectively organize and manage the products in their inventory. You can categorize things using product categories, which makes it easy to find them in the inventory.

To make it simpler to set different prices for various product kinds, Product Categories also allows you to set various pricing criteria for each category. Additionally, reports that provide an overview of products and their sales performance can be produced using product categories. This function makes it simple to break down your financial information into several product categories. You may quickly classify your products into various categories and view the associated financial data. Additionally, you can use this capability to undertake budgeting and forecasting by product categories and assess how well they performed in comparison to industry standards.

Additionally, you may keep track of each product category's profitability and examine the effect that pricing tactics have on overall performance.
The Products Categories menu in the Management portion of the Odoo 17 Accounting module is located under the Configuration tab. You may quickly access the Product Categories window by using this option.

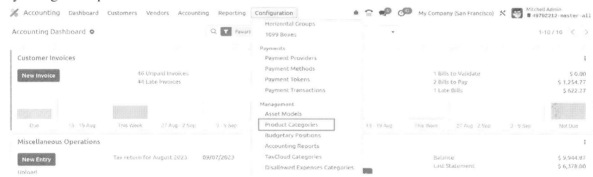

The window will keep a list of all the entries for previously defined categories, as seen in the illustration below.

You can quickly find and group the product category you need by using the Filters and Group By options. You can choose from any of the defined categories, view them in detail, and edit the records if necessary. Additionally, you can use the NEW button to add a new Product category.

You can enter the category name in the Category area of the Product Categories creation form at first. After that, you can assign the Ava tax category and the Parent Category. The next choice is TAX CLOUD, where a drop-down menu allows you to select the Tax Cloud Category. The TIC, or Taxability Information Code, is displayed in the TaxCloud Category field and is used by TaxCloud to determine the appropriate tax rates for each type of product. When the TIC is not set on the product, this value is utilized. If no value is entered, the invoicing settings' default value is applied.

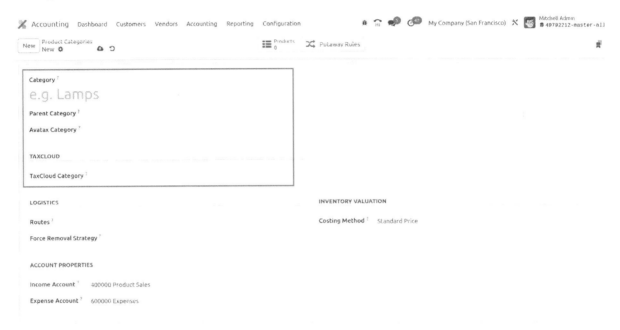

Similar to this, you can define fields relating to ACCOUNT PROPERTIES, such as the Income Account and the Expense Account, by selecting an option from a dropdown menu or by defining a new one. The revenue account will keep track of all the profits made from this product category, and the expense account will keep track of all the costs connected to it.

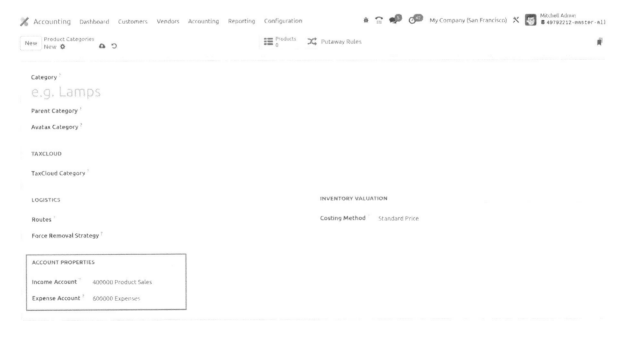

The 'Force Removal Strategy' the Routes and Reserve Packaging can be discussed in the LOGISTICS section. You can select a specific removal method using the dropdown menu in the Force Removal method column. In that case, regardless of the location of the source for this product category, the removal technique will be used. The many removal techniques proposed by Odoo17 include:

- **FIFO (First In First Out):** The First In First Out approach can be used when you want to sell the item that was stocked first. After that, the items or lots that were stocked initially will be removed. When products must be utilized or sold in the order in which they were purchased or created, this method is employed. When organizing product categories, this approach is frequently used because it guarantees that the oldest item gets used up first.

- **LIFO (Last In Last Out):** When it is necessary to transfer the item that was stocked last into first place, the LIFO approach might be used. When products bought or produced last are used first, this method—which is the opposite of FIFO—is applied. When prices are rising and taxes must be kept to a minimum, this tactic is most advantageous.

- **Closest Location:** The products must first be taken from the closest storage facility if you choose the closest location option. This is advantageous when things need to be transported to a client because it takes less time and effort to do so.

- **FEFO (First Expiry First Out):** The final method, FEFO, is utilized when products have an expiration date. It is crucial to make sure that the products with the earliest expiration date are used up first. This is crucial for products like food, medicines, and other goods with a short shelf life.

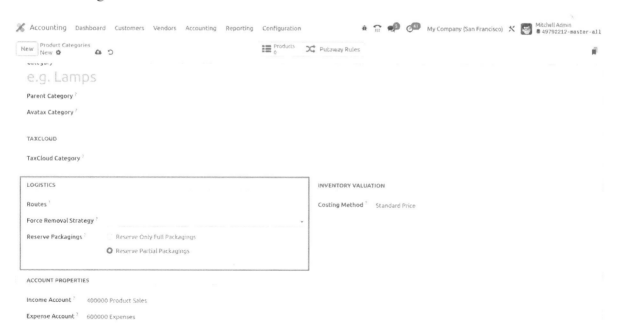

Reserve Packaging is related to product packaging. There are two options

- **Reserve Only Full Packagings:** This won't reserve partial packing. Only 10 units will be reserved if the buyer wants 2 packets of 10 units each and you only have 18 units in stock.
- **Reserve Partial Packagings:** This permits partial packaging in portions. The 18 units will be held for the customer if they order two packets of 10 units each and you only have 18 units available.

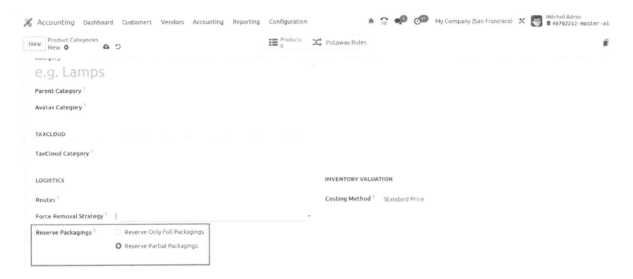

Additionally, under the INVENTORY VALUATION section, the configuration choices for inventory valuation, including Costing Method and Inventory Valuation, can be configured. Either Standard Price, First In First Out (FIFO), or Average Cost (AVCO) are definitions for the costing methodology. While FIFO and Average Cost are dynamic techniques depending on the product's purchase price and the quantity in stock, the Standard Price option enables you to establish a fixed cost per product. While FIFO uses the purchase price of the oldest stock on hand, average cost uses the purchase price of all stock on hand.

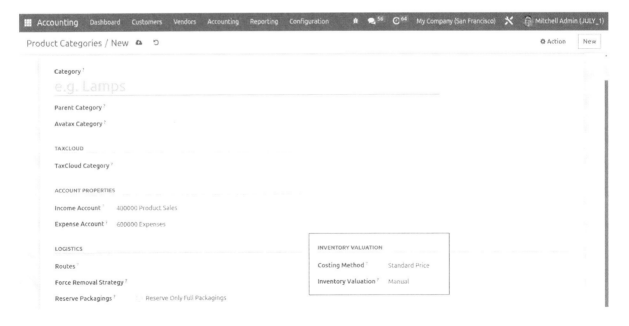

The Inventory Valuation is performed to confirm how stock journals should be defined for this specific category, and the platform provides you with the ability to carry out both manual and automatic activities. You must set up the necessary definitions of the stock accounting attributes under the ACCOUNT STOCK attributes section before starting Automated Inventory Valuation.

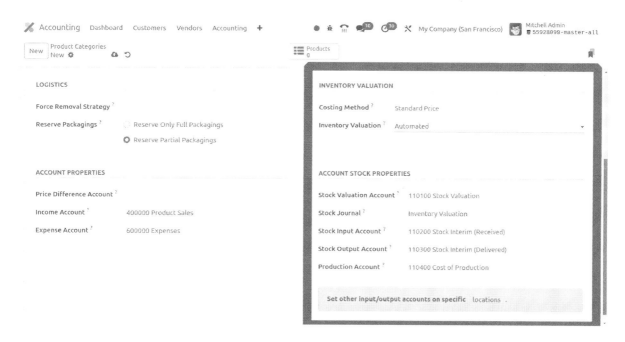

You can include the Stock Valuation Account in this section so that when automatic inventory valuation is enabled for a product, this account will contain the products' current value. The Stock Journal can then be brought up. When automating inventory valuation, this stock journal will be quite helpful. When stock moves are made, the entries will automatically be placed in this account journal. If there isn't a designated valuation account, you can define the Stock Input Account to publish equal journal items for all incoming stock moves. You'll close by mentioning the Stock Output Account, which is used to track all stock movement. This will be the default value for all products in this category if no unique valuation account is used at the destination location. Only after you choose the **Automatic Accounting** option in the **Settings** will the accounting tools become accessible here.

You have successfully set a Product Category once you have completed filling out all of these options. Along with all the options, the window will also reveal smart tabs in the upper right corner, as seen in the image below, where you can see the Products and Putaway Rules tabs.

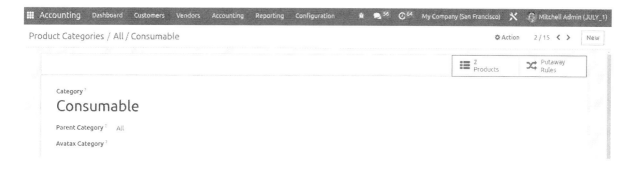

The smart tab "Products," which may be accessed by clicking the button, will show all the products that fall within this product category. As soon as you choose the smart tab, you'll be taken to the Products window, where you can see every item that fits into this category.

Based on the different stages and the construction of the specific category of the product that are stated, the product information in the product menu will be displayed. You can also view the entire products that are being stored if you remove the filters.

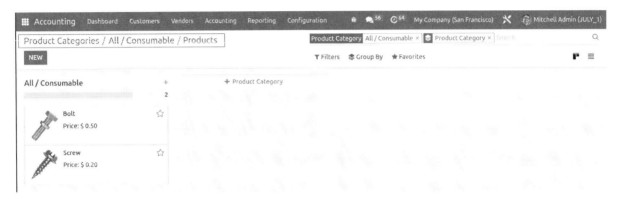

All configured putaway rules for the product falling under that specific category are displayed in the category form's smart tab Putaway rule. Define the routes and removal strategy under Logistics so that all items falling under this category will be taken out of the warehouse in accordance with the removal strategy specified.

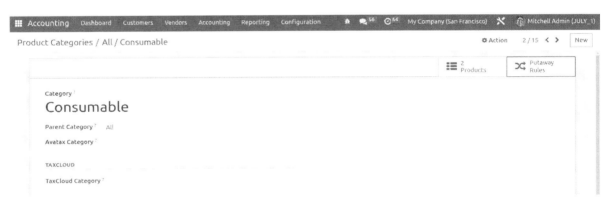

The created product category can be easily added to the product.

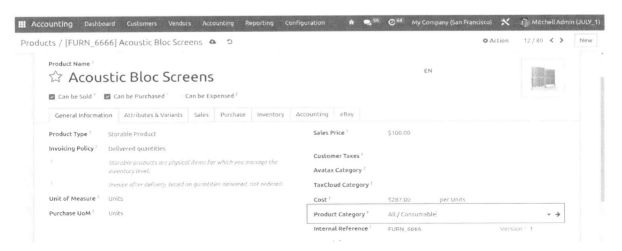

Let's move on to the following section, where the Cash Roundings setups are discussed, now that we are clear on the Product Categories configuration in the Odoo17 Accounting module.

Cash Roundings

You can quickly and precisely round off the total amount of a sale or purchase invoice using the Cash Rounding feature in the Odoo17 Accounting module. This can be used to quickly round up, down, or to the next whole number, depending on your preferences. This function guarantees that the whole invoice amount is rounded off correctly and accurately, making it particularly helpful for companies that accept cash payments. If necessary, this feature can be set up to selectively apply to particular invoices or to apply automatically to all invoices.

Avoiding using pennies or small bills as payment is beneficial. The quantity is automatically rounded to the next smaller denomination. Businesses that receive a lot of cash payments, like merchants, can benefit from this service. It assists in reducing both the time required to complete payments and the quantity of coins or tiny notes required for such payments. Businesses that frequently handle cash transactions must ensure that all currency amounts are rounded to the next denomination can use it.

In the Accounting Settings section of the Configuration page, this feature can be made active. Once enabled, users can choose between 0.05, 0.10, 0.25, or 1.00 as the rounding increment. The amounts will be rounded up or down to the designated increment when issuing an invoice or creating a receipt. In order to avoid the need for manual rounding off of cash payments, this tool is helpful for organizations that need to make sure that all cash transactions are rounded off to the nearest denomination. You can set up rounding rules in the Accounting module if this functionality is enabled. With the use of this tool, users can effortlessly round up or down any sum to the closest suitable denomination.

Users can set the system up to, for instance, round off all payment amounts to the nearest dollar. Businesses that accept cash payments and must round off consumer payments exactly can benefit from this functionality. Additionally, invoices and other financial documents can be automatically rounded off using cash rounding. This function aids in ensuring that all transactions are accurately recorded and that payment sums are correct.

The Configuration Settings of the Odoo Accounting module contain the Cash Rounding option. By turning on the Cash Rounding option, you can specify the smallest denomination of the currency that is used to make cash payments. You will be able to view the menu in the Accounting module once you have enabled the setting in settings.

You may view and define the Cash Roundings by selecting the Cash Roundings option from the Management section of the Odoo17 Accounting tab.

Here in the window, you can see a sneak peek of all the Cash Roundings records that have already been defined. The specifics are shown, including Name, Rounding Precision, and Rounding Method. These fields are all configurable and have detailed views available. Additionally, you may use the many pre-set and programmable filters and grouping options to quickly search for and locate the necessary data. You may access the Cash Rounding creation form with the help of the New button. The window is shown in the screenshot that follows.

You can assign the name of the cash roundings in the Name field of this form view. The smallest denomination with a non-zero value can then be represented in the Rounding Precision field. The Rounding Strategy section is where you may define how the invoice amount will be rounded to the desired rounding accuracy. Here, you have two options for using the rounding strategy: Add a rounded line or Modify tax amount.

When producing invoices in the Accounting module of Odoo17, you can use these parameters to specify how you want Odoo17 to handle rounding amounts. When you choose Add a Rounding Line, you add an additional line at the end of the invoice with the Rounding Amount, and when you choose Modify Tax Amount, you can change the invoice's tax amount to include the Rounding Amount. When the rounding amount is not substantial enough to merit its own line item, this can be utilized.

The Profit Account and Loss Account can be mentioned following the definition of the Rounding Strategy. Due to the rounding process, the total rounded value will eventually shift to a higher infinity, producing a profit that will be recorded in the profit account. A loss will be created and recorded in the Loss Account if the total round value shifts to the lower infinity. The Rounding Method can be specified as a final option. You have three options for defining it on the Odoo17 platform. UP, DOWN, HALF UP.

- **UP:** Value rounds to plus infinity when it is UP. By selecting this option, the value will be rounded to the nearest stated amount. For instance, if the specified amount is 20 cents and the amount is $15.20, the outcome is $15.40.
- **DOWN:** The value rounds to the negative infinity. In this instance, it will round the sum down to the closest given figure. For instance, if the specified amount is 20 cents and the amount is $15.20, the outcome is $15.00.
- **HALF-UP:** The decimal value will be rounded up if it is larger than 0.5 and down if it is less than 0.5. In other words, the sum will be rounded up to the

135

nearest given amount. When using an example, the outcome would be $15.20 if the amount was $15.20 and the required amount was 20 cents.

After you've specified Cash Rounding, you may save it, and it will then appear in the menu. To round the total amount, this rounding can be used on vendor or customer invoices. Rounding can be used on the invoice's additional info tab. Additionally, you have the option to change your defined Cash Rounding setup whenever you like.

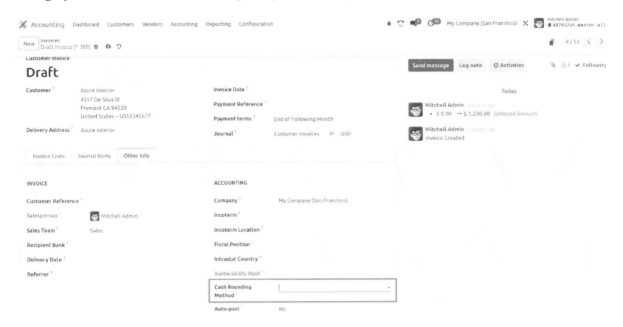

Let's go on to the next section, where the budgetary situations are discussed, now that we are clear on the configuration of Cash Rounding.

Budgetary Positions

An innovative tool to design and manage various budgeting positions, which offers a structure for tracking funds allocated to particular projects or departments, is available in the Odoo 17 Accounting module. Each budgetary position has a set of budget lines that users can designate. The money can then be spent in accordance with the established budget thanks to their real-time monitoring of budget expenses. Additionally, you may specify a budget cap for each position and get warnings if the cap is surpassed. Users can also create a variety of reports to monitor budget allocations and expenditures.

Tracking budget allocations, expenses, and associated data is made very simple by the advanced feature featured in the Odoo17 Accounting module. It makes sure that resources are being used effectively and aids in keeping your finances organized.

You must enable the Budget Management feature available in the Configuration Settings window of the Accounting module in order to make the Budgetary Positions menu accessible on the Configuration tab. As seen in the figure below, you can find the option in the Analytics area.

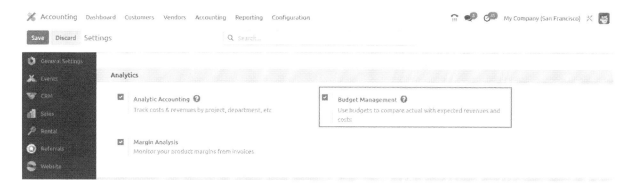

You may now access the Budgetary Positions menu from the Configuration tab's Management section.

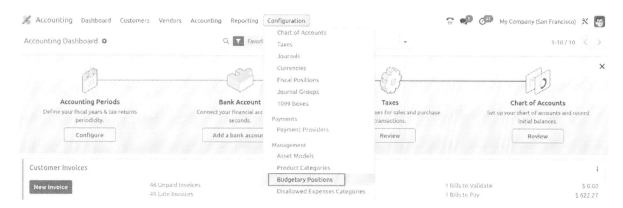

You may access the Budgetary Positions window, which is displayed in the screenshot below, with only one click on the Budgetary Positions menu.

The Odoo17 platform's Budgetary Positions window controls all of the previously stated Budgetary Positions and lets you define new Budgetary Positions. You can simplify your search using the filters, group by, and search options. The Save current search, Import records, Link menu in spreadsheet, and Insert list in spreadsheet choices are all found on the Favorites tab, as shown in the figure below.

To set up new Budgetary Positions, use the NEW button. The accompanying screenshot shows the clear window used to create budgetary positions. You can enter a name in the Name area of the creation window. Next, you have the Company filed, which can be updated and will be automatically allotted. The accounts for the Budgetary Positions can then be described in the Accounts tab.

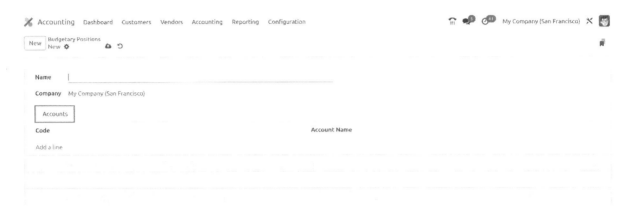

You can select the Add a Line option to add accounts. You will now draw the pop-up window where the system lists every account that has ever been set up. If it's a new account, you can choose it from the pop-up box or use the New option to create a new one.

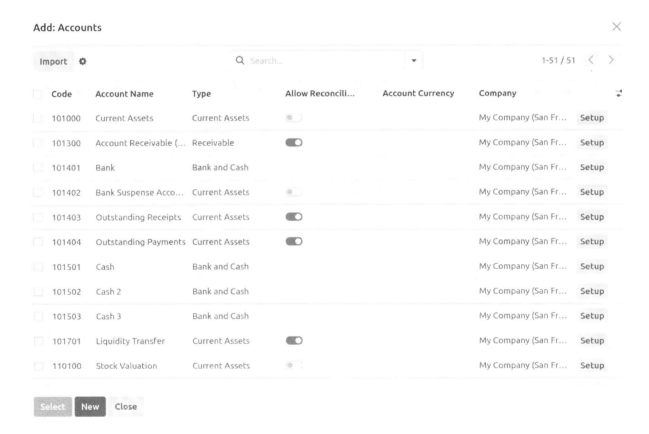

You can choose the New option to create a new budgetary position. This will display the creations box shown below, where you can first provide a Name.

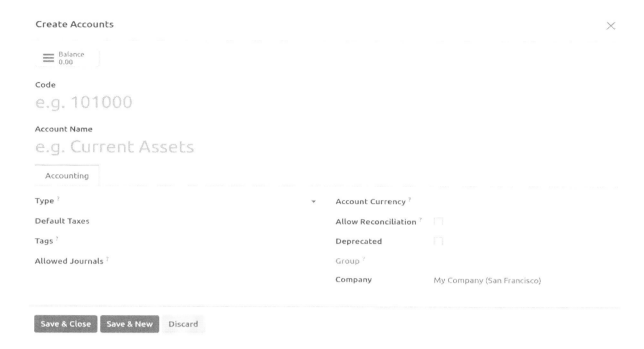

By choosing the Add a line option, you can also offer the Accounts of the Budgetary Positions, which have an impact on this.

You can also add the necessary accounts. We have been talking about the Odoo 17 Accounting module's Budgetary Positions Management option up to this point, which serves as the ideal remedy for budget management for organizations. Let's move on to the following section, where we'll talk about the Accounting reports portion of the configuration menu.

Accounting Reports

The Accounting reports in Odoo 17 are yet another improved feature. Financial reports from earlier versions can be viewed as an enhanced version of accounting reports. Accounting reports give customers the ability to somewhat customize the financial statements by setting rules and formulating new lines.

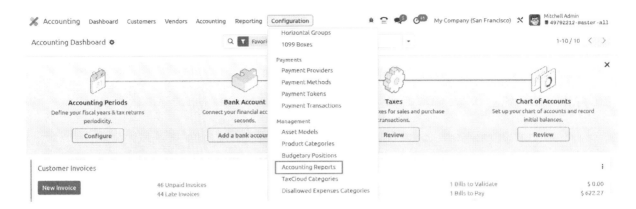

Odoo 17 allows users to customize practically all financial reports, in contrast to the previous version. Users of Odoo17 can add additional rows to each report and define domains, equations, and related values. These values will then be updated in the new line in accordance with the equation supplied.

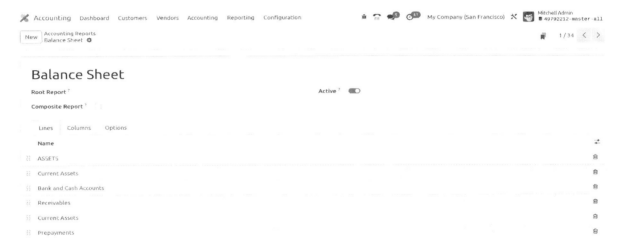

You can add new lines once the report has been opened by selecting the Lines tab.

You can add the parent line's code while drafting a new line so that it will appear below the parent line. Additional information may be included, such as the foldability of the line, whether or not the text that follows this line prints on a new page and the under-label calculation for the new line.

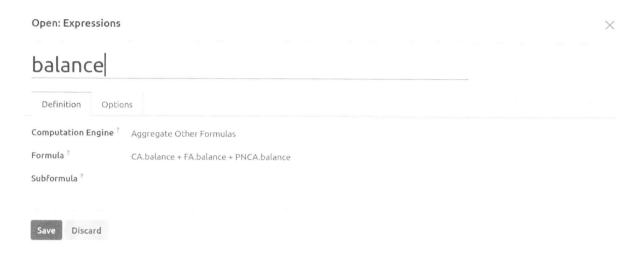

You can define the computing engine, the formula, and the sub-formula after adding the expression on the definition tab. We can compute the formula thanks to the computation engine. Various computing engines are available with Odoo17, as shown in the screenshot below.

The columns in the corresponding financial statements are defined on the columns tab of the accounting report.

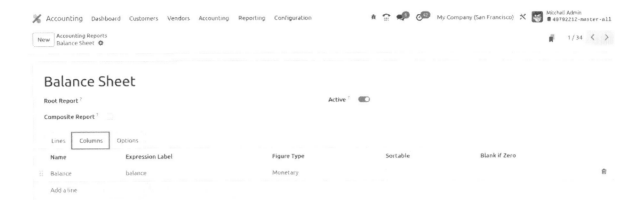

The financial statement filters for the accounting report can be chosen under the 'Options' tab.

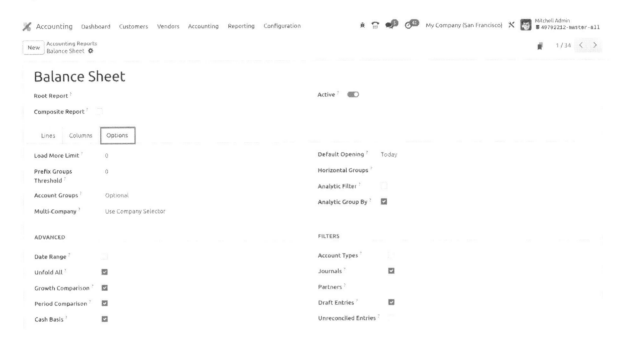

When it unfolds, the amount of rows that are visible is limited by the 'Load more Limit' parameter. The default filter data that will be based on this year, this month, today, etc. is defined by the default opening. Additionally, additional settings can be made for account groups, multi-company, default horizontal groups, analytic filter, and group by. We will also be able to check the necessary default filter for the financial report under advanced and filter by section.

Moving on to the following topic, Disallowed Expenses Categories, let's continue our discussion of Odoo 17 accounting reports.

Disallowed Expenses Categories

Disallowed expenses are those that cannot be reported as deductible expenses or items for tax purposes and are listed in the Accounting module of Odoo 17. These include costs for food, entertainment, travel, presents, and other non-work-related expenses for the individual, the household, and the family.

Disallowed expenses have a variety of advantages, including

Reduced taxable income: Unallowable expenses lower the amount of taxable income that applies to an individual or corporation. By reducing tax liabilities, this can increase cash flow and profitability.

Avoid penalties and interest: By failing to claim Disallowed expenses as deductions on tax returns, individuals and corporations can avoid the penalties and interest that may be imposed.

Better Accuracy: The Internal Revenue Service (IRS) may have issues if disallowed expenses are not properly reported. Organizations can improve the correctness of their filings by correctly classifying these expenses that aren't claimed on tax returns.

Streamlined Compliance: Making a distinction between costs that are authorized and those that don't help people and businesses comply with tax laws, lowering the likelihood of an audit.

Therefore, you can subtract the appropriate charges from the bookkeeping result without deducting them from the fiscal result with the use of Odoo17's Disallowed Charges function. As a result, by configuring prohibited spending categories and obtaining periodic updates, you will receive the financial results in real time. First, you must activate the Disallowed Expenses modules from the App Store in order to have access to this option's rights in your system. You can search for Disallowed Expenses in the search box after removing the Apps filter to install the module. The system will now display the outcome as seen in the below-displayed image.

The Disallowed Expenses Categories menu may be found in the Management part of the Configuration tab of the Odoo17 Accounting once the module has been activated.

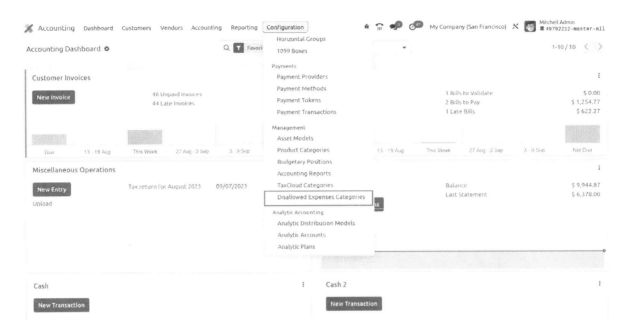

You can add new Disallowed Expenses Categories using the NEW button, and the system will assist you in keeping track of all the configured Disallowed Categories.

You can first enter the Code and the Name when creating a new category of disallowed expenses. then, utilizing the list of preconfigured accounts, you can select associated Accounts. Additionally, new accounts can be made right from this page. Additionally, you can assign the Current Rate by selecting the SET RATES option located on the far left. The window where you can specify the rate under the Rates tab will then be fully visible to you.

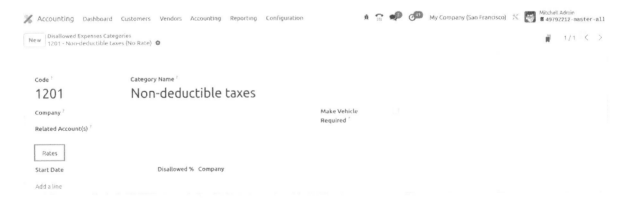

When you choose the Add a Line option, the Company field will be automatically assigned once you provide the Start date and the rate of the Disallowed Expenses. This field is helpful for managing multiple companies.

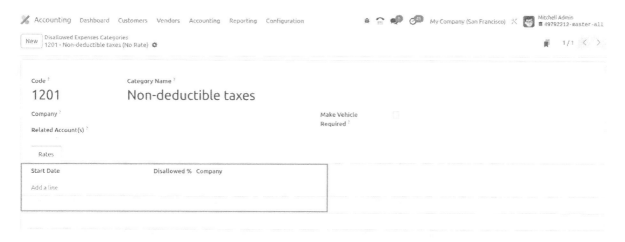

Additionally, when you set up a Chart of Accounts, the Disallowed Expenses Category is directly linked to the Expense Account. Go to the Chart of Account window where you can build up a Chart of Account with an expenses type in order to view it. You can now see the Disallowed Expenses Category selection option, and it will be closely related to the respective account.

Under the module's Reporting menu, you may access the new report titled Disallowed Expenses.

The platform's ability to create a variety of Disallowed Expenses Categories is one of its main advantages. Now that we are clear on these characteristics, we can look at the next features, which manage the analytical items.

Analytical Accounting

Analytical Accounting is a feature of the Odoo 17 Accounting module that enables users to track financial data more precisely. This is accomplished by adding new dimensions that can be used to classify and examine financial data, such as departments and projects. Users of analytical accounting can monitor the financial performance of particular projects or departments and base their business decisions on this data in order to make better-educated choices. Users can also create thorough financial reports that can be utilized for forecasting, budgeting, and other types of financial research. You can see where your money is going and where it is coming from since it gives you a more in-depth perspective of your spending and income.

To prepare financial reports, plan for upcoming expenses, and monitor spending trends over time, utilize this module. Other financial components including Accounts Receivable, Account Payable, and General Ledger can all be used in conjunction with the analytical accounting capability. To manage client invoices and vendor bills, it can also be utilized with the Sales and Purchase modules. Businesses can also monitor their inventory levels and make sure they have enough goods on hand to satisfy their customers' needs by employing analytical accounting.

Any industry can use this cutting-edge accounting system to manage its financial operations. Additionally, the feature includes the ability to filter or analyze specific accounts without publishing a journal article. This means that a new Analytic Account can be formed for a certain product or service if it is necessary to comprehend the expense specifics of a particular product or service in comparison to the expense of all products and services. The

146

analytical accounting aspect's well-defined tools and features will make even the most complicated accounting processes simple.

You must enable the 'Analytic Accounting' feature from the Configuration Settings of the Accounting module in order to examine and configure the analytic accounts in Odoo 17. where, as demonstrated below, you may find the menu in the Analytics area.

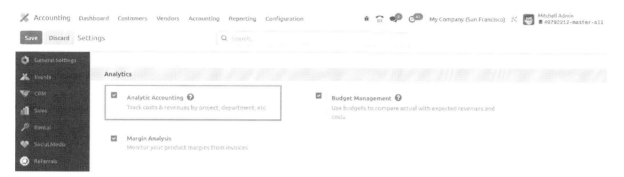

The Odoo17 Accounting module also has a unique section and cutting-edge features that support Analytical Accounting activities. The following part will provide a detailed examination of the main management tools and capabilities present in the Odoo17 Accounting module.

Analytic Plans

The Accounting module for Odoo 17 is arguably the greatest and most popular module available. Since its beginning, this module has consistently been among the most popular modules. It enables better account and financial management for the user. Analytic Plans, a feature, that helps you manage financial data in the most practical way possible. You may make and maintain your financial plans with this function. By doing so, you'll be able to monitor your financial condition and make wiser choices regarding your money.

You may examine the Analytic Plans menu in the Analytic Accounting portion of the Odoo17 Accounting module's Configuration tab, as illustrated in the figure below.

You may find a list of all necessary analytic account plans using the Analytic Accounts menu.

The Analytic Plans panel will methodically save and maintain all configured Analytic Plans, and it will show the key details for each plan, including Name, Default Applicability, Colour, and Company. You can choose any of these records to view it in more detail. You can manage a large number of analytical plans with this capability. You may rapidly select the necessary Analytic Plans information from the entire list using the many preset and custom Filters and Group By options.

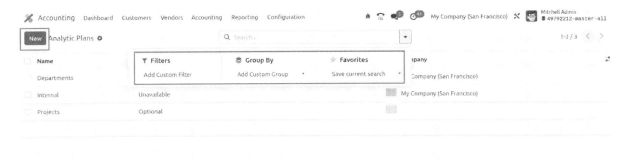

You must select the "New" option in order to set up a new financial plan. The NEW button will take you to the Analytic Plans creation window, as displayed in the screenshot below.

The Name, Parent, and default applicability of the plan can be entered in the Creation window and marked as Optional, Mandatory, or Unavailable.

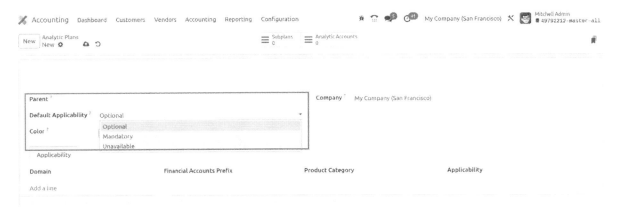

Comparing Odoo17 to earlier versions, some improvements have been made to the analytical plans. Under the applicability tab, it is possible to define the application of these plans across several domains. Plans can be used for costs, purchase orders, sale orders, vendor invoices, and other items. In addition, we will be able to specify whether these plans are Mandatory, Optional, or Unavailable for the specified analytic plan and whether they apply to a specific product category or financial accounts with a specific prefix.

Additionally, sub-plans can be set up for an analytical plan, which we can see in the smart tab displayed in analytical plans.

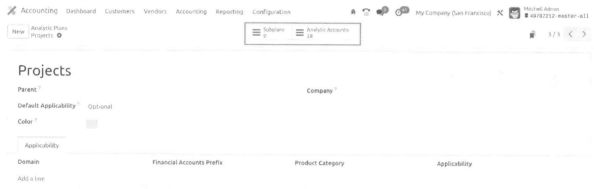

Analytical sub plans will immediately update where you view the parent once they are opened. There are two sub plans for the analytic plan "Project" in the aforementioned example: "Project Planning" and "Project R&D." If an item states that any expense from the project is generated, it will be recorded in the analytic account under the planned project later on when analytic accounts are assigned with these plans.

Let's go on to understand the following management choice, the Analytics Tags, in the following chapter of the book now that we are clear on the Analytic Plan tool in the Odoo 17 Accounting module.

Analytic Accounts

The main purpose of the Analytic Accounts function is to keep and monitor your company's financial data. It can also be used to analyze your financial data and gives you the option to examine your financial data graphically. The denotation of the analytical accounts will be the first step in the management of analytical accounting in Odoo17. You have the option to create, amend, and delete your own analytic accounts using this tool. Additionally, you may view your analytic accounts in graphical, tabular, and pivot representations with this function.

Under the Configuration tab in the Analytic Accounting section, you may quickly access the Analytic Accounts menu.

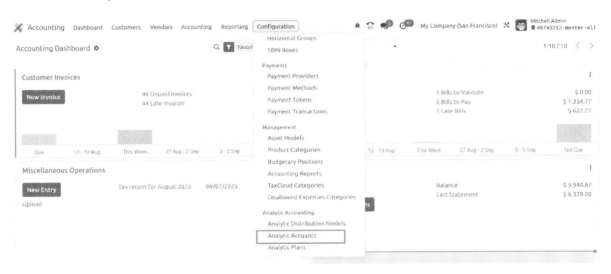

All of the accounts that are configured for the organization's Analytic Accounting processes will be managed through this Analytic Accounts pane. Additionally, this box has choices for Filters, Group By, Favorites, and Search.

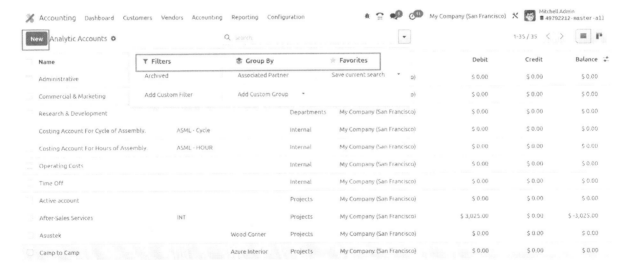

You can also view the window in Kanban format by selecting the Kanban view menu item. The names, references, customers, plans, companies, debits, credits, and balance amounts for each analytic account are recorded here. Clicking on any of these account details will give you the chance to update them.

Selecting the New button will bring you to the creation form shown in the image below, where you can mention a new one. You must enter a name for the analytic account in the Analytic Account field of the form view of the Analytic Accounts creation window. The Customer, Reference code, and Plan can then be mentioned in the designated fields. According to their operational bases, the Company and Currency fields will be automatically assigned.

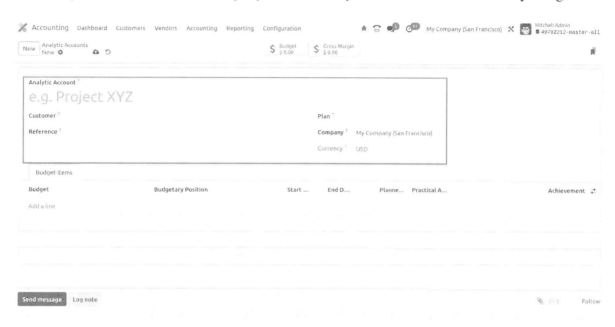

You can add the necessary budget items using the Add a Line option found under the Budget Items tab. The budget, the budgetary position, the start date, the end date, the planned amount, the practical amount, and the achievement can all be added here. You can add numerous budget elements to the analytical account using this option.

151

Additionally, the Action button at the top of the window will show the Duplicate, Archive, and Dashboard options for carrying out the appropriate activities.

Additionally, the available smart buttons at the top of the form, which are noted in the screenshot below, will allow users to check the Gross Margin and the overall Budget of the various Analytic Accounts.

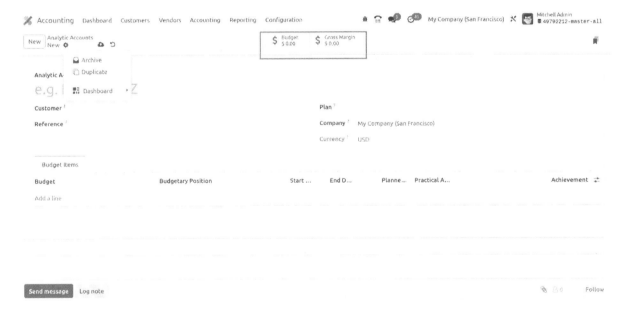

Analytic Distribution Models

We can use rules to automate the accounting entries using Odoo17's Analytics Distribution Models. A sales invoice, for instance, has several line items. We can design a rule that divides the invoice's total into fixed or percentage-based payments for each line item. We can avoid having to manually make journal entries for each line item in this fashion.

The flexibility of the Analytic Distribution feature allows for a wide range of application possibilities. It can be used, for instance, to allocate the cost of products sold to various expense accounts or the proceeds from a sales invoice to various income accounts. We must first develop a model before we can create an analytical distribution model. By heading to Accounting -> Configuration -> Analytic Distribution Models, we can accomplish this.

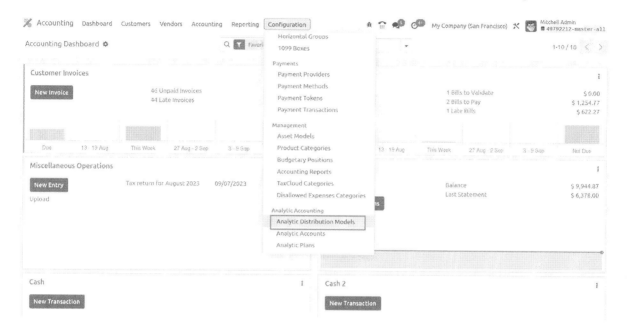

Using the creation form shown below, we must enter some conditions as well as the analytic distribution for the model.

Any transactions that fulfill the criteria outlined in the analytic distribution models will automatically be subject to the analytic distribution established there. The partner, partner category, product, product category, and accounts prefix can all be used to establish conditions.

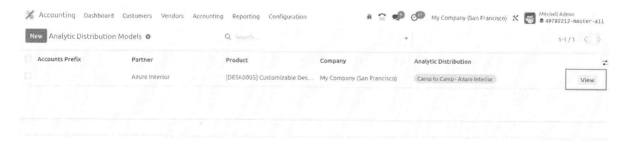

The analytic distribution will automatically apply when an invoice is issued for the product category as seen in the model's snapshot above.

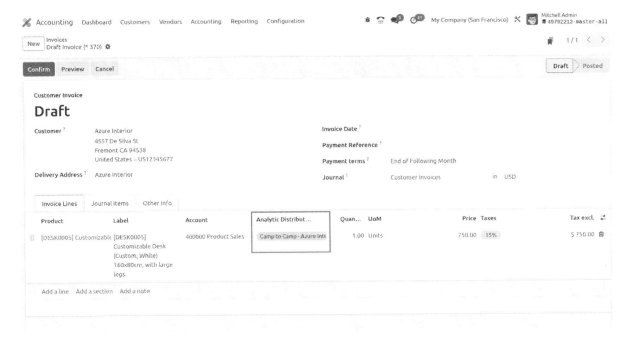

The distribution will be noted in the relevant analytic accounts as a result.

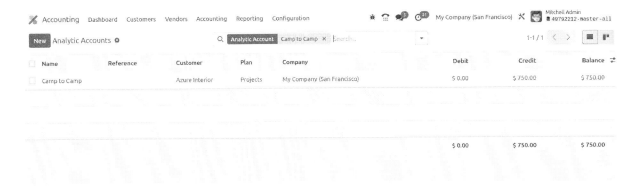

We have been talking about the management tools linked to the analytical accounting features of the Odoo17 Accounting module that are available under the Configuration tab. Now that we are clear on it, let's move on to the next chapter of the book where we will discuss how to configure the invoicing features for the accounting operations of the firm management.

Configuring Invoicing

A corporation should handle invoicing and invoice administration with the utmost attention and accuracy using respectable tools and solutions. Both the Accounting and the Financial departments of every organization are in charge of creating and managing invoices. With the aid of a supporting Invoicing module that is integrated with the Accounting module of the Odoo17 platform, the operations of invoicing and invoicing administration are supported by the Odoo17 Accounting module. When the Accounting module is installed, the Invoicing module also does so automatically.

Along with the Invoicing module, Odoo17's Accounting module offers a number of configurations to support operations. These configurations are accessible via the Accounting module's Configuration tab. Numerous menu options that support the components of invoicing are available in the Configuration tab. Let's continue by learning about each component of the invoicing configuration individually.

Payment Terms and Early Payment Discounts

You may manage your payment terms and conditions using the Odoo 17 Accounting module's Payment Terms feature. Businesses that need to monitor and manage their payment terms and conditions will find this tool helpful. With the help of this tool, you may view a list of all payment terms, add a new payment term, update an existing payment term, delete a payment term, and search for a particular payment term. Businesses will benefit greatly from defining the conditions under which they will collect payments from their clients. By detailing when they will receive payments and providing a transparent record of what payments have been made, this feature can help firms manage their cash flow more effectively.

The Accounting module's Configuration page has an Invoicing section where you can locate the Payment Terms menu.

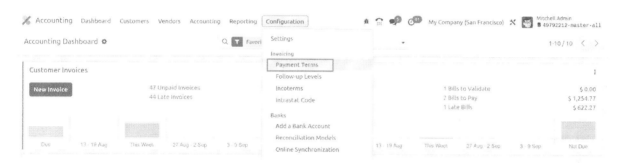

You may access the Payment Terms window using the menu, as seen in the screenshot below. Along with the pre-set and user-configurable choices, the Payment Terms window will contain all of the configuration-specific information.

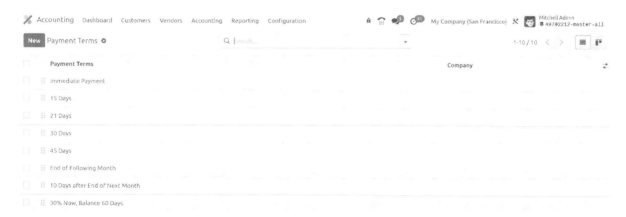

The necessary tools will be listed for each payment period. You can choose and learn more information about any of these listed payment terms. It is also possible to change it if you want to. You can drag and drop the payment terms in the window's sequencing feature to arrange them in the order you like.

Additionally, additional actions can be taken by checking the checkbox located on the extreme left of each payment terms record. When the box is checked, the Action button, which has menus like Export, Archive, Unarchive, and Delete, will be displayed, as shown in the screenshot.

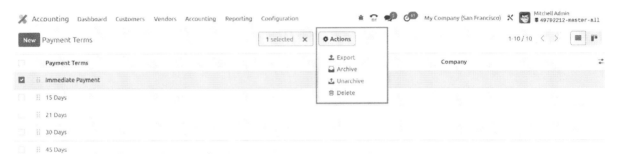

Additionally, the criteria option simplifies the search process and allows for better search results through the use of a variety of preset and customizable criteria. To simplify data processing, you can create a variety of groups of payment terms that are fully customized using the Group By option. Numerous additional options are included under the Favourites tab, including Save Current Search, Import Records, Link Menu in Spreadsheet, and Insert List in Spreadsheet.

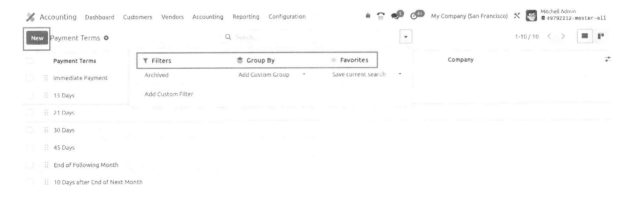

Additionally, using the Kanban menu icon in the top right corner, as seen in the screenshot below, you can access the window in Kanban format.

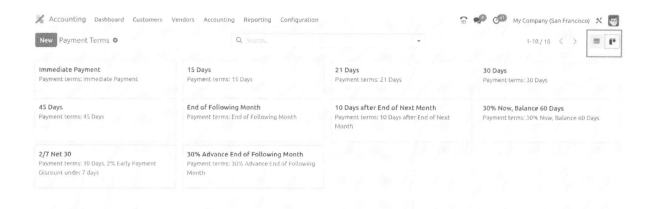

The payment terms can be thought of as the time frame that the business gives its clients to pay for the associated goods or services. The related payment will be marked as due if the customer doesn't make it in time for the payment deadline. Additionally, based on the sales payment term or the buy payment term according to the due date, the relevant payment will be shown in the aged reports, which means in the aged payable or aged receivable.

You can select the New button to open the creation form when you want to create new Payment Terms, as shown in the following screenshot.

In the Payment Terms area of the form view, you can first enter the name of the payment terms. Also, the user has the option to mention the Company name and early Discount and then we have a Due term section that includes the filed Due and the type such as Percentage, and Fixed Amount. Additionally, it is possible to define the Due Date Computation Details of the Terms by supplying the relevant fields on a date and the computation details.

With the addition of the feature of offering early discounts, Odoo 17 provided new field discounts and discount days in the due lines. You can include the discount and the number of days it is effective on field discount days.

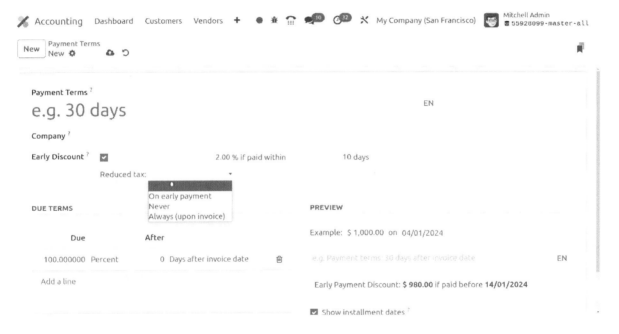

After being defined, these payment expressions can be used in bills and invoices.

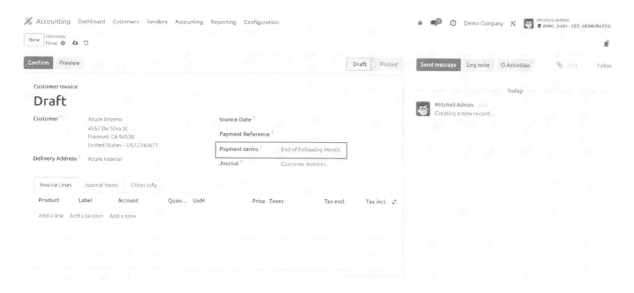

The Odoo17 platform gives you the option to select and update the necessary Payment Terms that you have set up.

Now that the payment terms configuration in Odoo17 has been clarified, the next part will address the Follow-Up Levels management function that is available under the Invoicing management area of the Configuration tab.

Follow-Up Levels

You may configure and manage the follow-up levels for client invoices using the Follow-Up Levels functionality in the Odoo17 Accounting module. The menu can be found in the Accounting module's Invoicing section's Configuration tab.

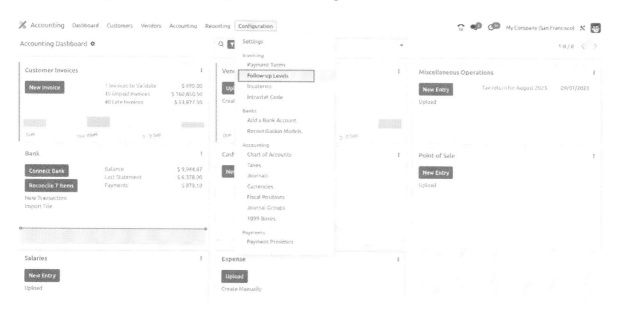

It is a great system for classifying and monitoring client invoicing. Customers who wish to see a breakdown of their invoices by follow-up levels and organizations who want to keep track of which invoices are past due may find this beneficial. Additionally, you can use this option to select the level for each customer and to view which customers are on which level. You may also set up automated follow-up emails and texts with its assistance.

The Accounting module's Configuration tab provides access to the Follow-up Levels menu, which lets you manage and set up the follow-up levels for your business. We can select the appropriate option to define the Accounting operation's Payment Follow-up. The Payment Follow-up window, as seen below, is what you will draw in the following situation.

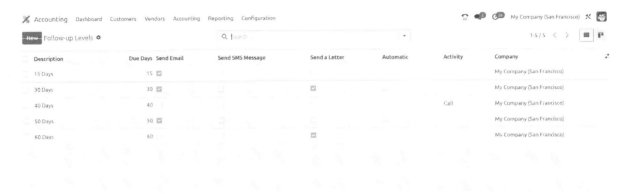

With the use of this function, you can make sure that you have the right resources to monitor any unpaid invoices for clients. The Follow-up Levels window will present a polished preview of each Follow-up Level that has already been established together with important details like Description, Due Days, Send Emails, Send SMS Messages, Send Letter, Automatic, Activity, and Company. Depending on the user's preferences, the follow-up actions on the Send Emails, Send SMS Message, Send a Letter, and Automatic can be activated or deleted. Here, you can also access the other standard Odoo window options like the Filters, Group By, Favorite, Search, Kanban view icon, and Export All icons.

The New button can be gently clicked to open the creation form for configuring new Follow up Levels. Below is a screenshot of the creation window.

Initially, you can set the name of the follow-up action in the Description field and the follow-up's due date in the available space. It is the number of days after the invoice's due date that must pass before a reminder is sent. If you want to send the reminder prior to the invoice due date, you can change this value to negative. You can enable the actions for each follow-

160

up, such as sending an email, an SMS message, a letter, etc. You can check "schedule activity" and add the sign activity to the designated individual under the "Activity" page, where manual action options are provided.

Additionally, based on the situation, the Options for Payment Follow-ups, including Automatic and Attach Invoices, can be enabled as well as disabled. The content template 'Payment Reminder' will display the message in response to the Payment Follow-ups being conducted. As invoices become due, a follow-up report is generated based on the following levels that have been defined.

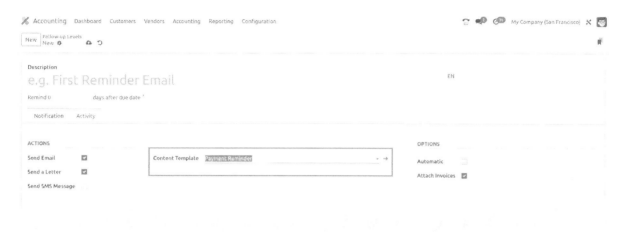

Since it is obvious that the Follow-up Levels function is sufficient for managing and customizing the follow-up levels for customer bills, you can track customer invoices with the help of this effective tool and make sure that they are paid on time.

The Schedule Activity boolean can be used to schedule activities inside of follow-up levels. Indicate who is in charge of the task in the Responsible field. Next, select the Activity Type and make reference to the Summary.

161

Now let's move on to the section that describes the Incoterms settings menu.

Incoterms

The international commercial terms known as Incoterms outline the obligations of buyers and sellers with regard to the delivery of products. They are used to identify when the title to the goods goes from the seller to the buyer as well as who is liable for paying the freight and other transportation costs.

Incoterms are used in Odoo 17 Accounting to automatically fill in shipping-related fields on the Sales Order and Purchase Order forms, such as the Incoterms and the shipping address. When products are sent, they are also used to create the proper accounting entries.

The most crucial thing to keep in mind about Incoterms is that they should only be utilized for shipments that are being sent internationally. Incoterms should not be utilized for domestic shipments because the terms and conditions are frequently different. You can navigate the Incoterms window as shown below by lightly pressing the Incoterms menu, which is located in the Configuration tab's Invoicing section.

All the aspects of Incoterms activities that were previously demonstrated in the platform will be shown in this window. The platform anticipates the requirement for sorting capabilities and includes all standard and resizable sorting as well as other functional menus like Filters, Group By, Favourites, Search, and Export All, as seen in the screenshot.

With the help of the New button, it is simple to construct new Incoterms. When you click the New button, a new creation line is shown in the same window where the new Incoterm can be set.

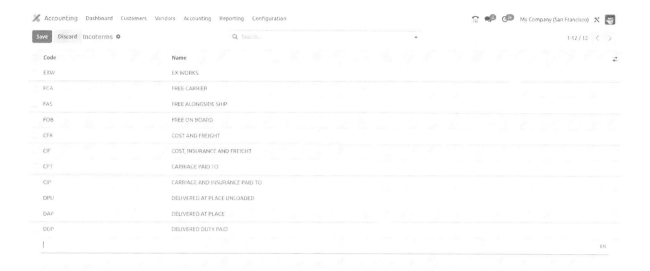

It is possible to apply incoterms to invoices and even establish default incoterms in the accounting configuration settings section devoted to customer invoices.

The invoice will also include the applicable Incoterm.

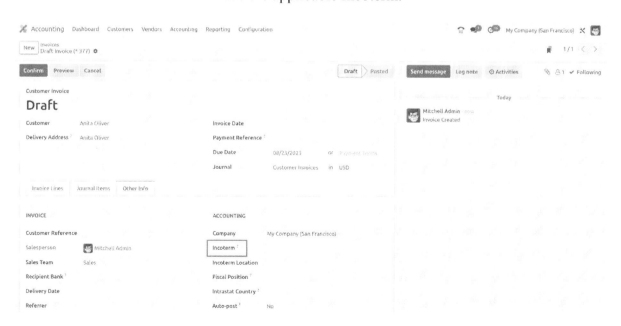

Let's move on to the platform's Intrastat Code setting now that we have covered the management of Incoterms in the Odoo17 Accounting module. To safeguard the buyer and seller, each incoterm calls for a defined location at the origin or destination. These requirements should be as explicit as feasible.

Intrastat Code

To identify items transferred between nations in the European Union, a code called the Intrastat Code is employed. This code is used to trace the flow of goods and figure out the appropriate tariffs and taxes that must be paid on them. The value of international trade in goods is also determined using the Intrastat code. It serves as the identification code for monitoring the flow of products between several nations. Customs officials use this code to keep track of the value of imported and exported items.

In Odoo17 the Intrastat Code must be enabled from the Configuration Settings. Default invoice transaction code and Default refund transaction code can be added from there also.

The European Commission assigns a product an eight-digit code called the Intrastat Code. For statistical purposes, the product is identified by the code. The Configuration tab's Invoicing section is where you'll find the Intrastat Code menu. The Intrastat Code window, which has the appearance seen in the screenshot below, will appear as soon as you click on this menu.

164

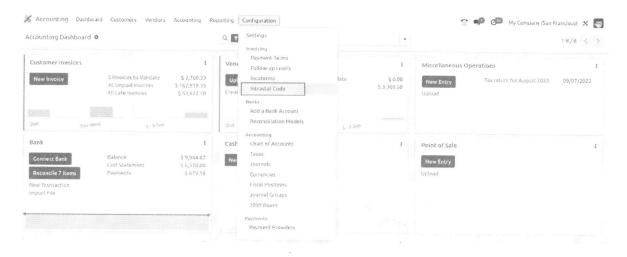

The Intrastat Code menu will show all of the platform-defined characteristics of the Intrastat Code. You can read a general description of each code defined in the preview itself.

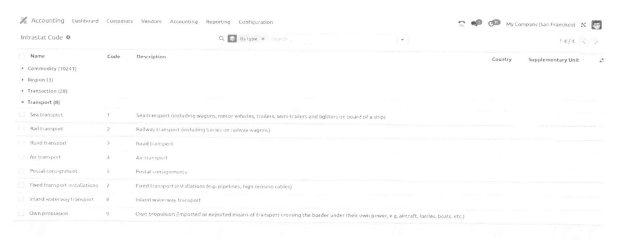

As seen in the screenshot above, you may view the Name, Code, Description, Count, and Supplementary Unit. Under the Filters menu, you may select from a variety of preset and personalized filters. You can use it to rapidly get the Intrastat code you need. Active, Commodity, Transport, Transaction, and Region are the accessible default filters here. The 'By Type', and 'By country', are included in the Group By tab by default. The Save current search, Link menu in spreadsheet, and Insert list in spreadsheet options are additionally available on the gear wheel icon.

Select one of these defined Intrastat Codes to explore it in more detail.

The Name, Code, Type, Supplementary Unit, Usage start date, Expiry Date, and Description may be seen here in the extension form, as shown in the screenshot above.

We have been looking at the setting options available in the Odoo17 Accounting module's Invoicing section up to this point. Let's move on to the Configuration of Bank Payments, the platform's final management tool for Odoo17 Accounting.

Configuration of Bank Payments

For effective and seamless finance management operations, it is necessary to integrate bank activities at the appropriate moment with corporate accounting. The platform provides outstanding support and guidance to it, and the Odoo17 Accounting explores a fantastic route for it. You are urged by Odoo17 to create the bank accounts and the business payments linked to those accounts. Configuring bank payments in business accounting software has a number of advantages, such as,

1. By decreasing the need for manual data entry and processing, automating bank payments can help your accounting and finance staff work more efficiently.
2. By removing mistakes that can happen when processing payments manually, automating bank payments can assist in increasing the accuracy of your accounting records.
3. You can gain more insight into your company's financial operations by configuring bank payments in your accounting software. This can aid in the detection and prevention of fraud.
4. Automating bank transfers can assist in cutting back on processing fees like postage and office supplies.
5. Additionally, the platform's reconciliation feature will validate that there is a strong correlation between the organization's operational ledgers and bank account operations.

Add a Bank Account

The Odoo 17 Accounting module contains the 'Add a Bank Account' option. With the help of this functionality, the user can expand the Odoo17 database with new bank accounts. The account type, bank name, and number can all be entered by the user. The user may additionally provide the account's currency, owner's name, and owner's address. It is helpful for businesses that need to keep track of their transactions and balances across various bank accounts. The easiest and fastest way to add bank accounts is with this method. By enabling you to automatically reconcile your bank statements, this can be seen as a good way to keep track of your finances and can also save you time and money. The Configuration tab's Banks section contains the Add a Bank Account menu as its first menu, as shown below.

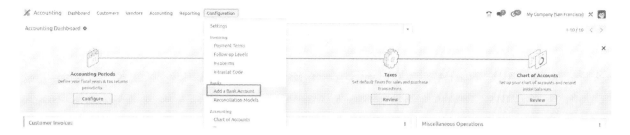

You can set up different bank accounts using this Add a Bank Account menu in accordance with your company's needs. As soon as you select a menu item, a pop-up window for adding a bank account will appear, allowing you to see the default bank's details. You can select your bank from this pop-up and confirm that it will be configured for use with the Odoo17 platform operations.

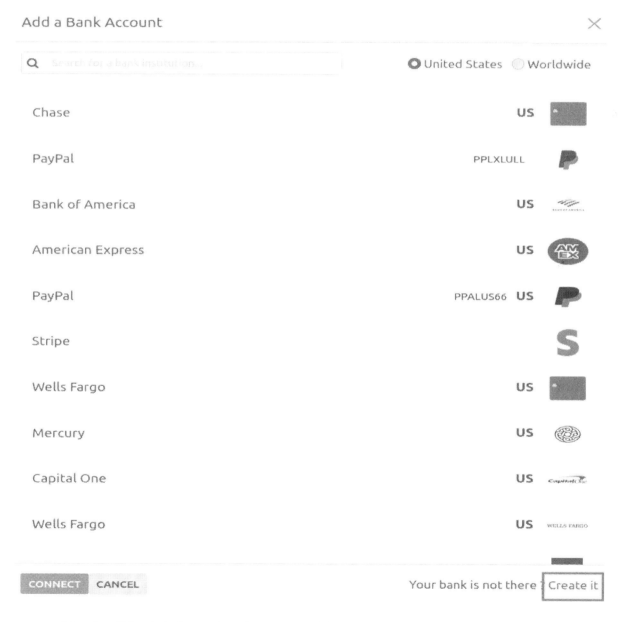

Nearly all bank information from around the world will by default be presented in this window. You can select the "Create it" option from the menu in the bottom right corner if your bank isn't listed in the window. As a result, a new pop-up window for configuring a bank account will appear as shown in the illustration.

The Account Number, Bank, Bank Identifier Code, and Journals can all be entered in the appropriate fields here. You have the option to choose an existing journal to link with the bank account, or you can leave the Journal form blank to create a new diary for this bank account. After providing all the information, activate your bank account in the Odoo17 system by clicking the CREATE button in the pop-up's lower left corner.

We can now move on to the Reconciliation tool found in the Configuration tab of the Odoo17 Accounting module since it is clear how to Add a Bank Account to the Odoo17 platform at this point.

Reconciliation Models

A Reconciliation Models tool is very helpful for reconciling account transfers in the Odoo17 Accounting module. You can pick and reconcile numerous move lines with this tool at once. To make sure that the books of accounts are in sync with the actual transactions, this tool is important in Odoo17 Accounting. This is accomplished by making the necessary adjustments to the entries after comparing the transactions reported in the books of account with the actual transactions. This procedure guards against financial irregularities and maintains the correctness of the financial accounts.

The Configuration Bank section includes a reference to the system's Reconciliation menu. As shown in the screenshot below, one mouse button is sufficient to reach out to the window.

For efficient operations in Odoo17, the Reconciliation Model window that you can see in the screenshot will maintain all the records of previously described Reconciliation Models. To provide you with a general overview without opening and carefully reviewing each record, the preview includes the Name of each Reconciliation, Type, and Auto-validate field. Additionally, it is quite straightforward to filter out and group necessary reconciliation models because of the default and custom Filters and Group By capabilities. As seen in the screenshot below, the Favourites tab is where you'll find the Save Current Search, Import Records, Link menu in Spreadsheet, and Insert list in Spreadsheet menus.

The Odoo17 platform gives you the option to specify Reconciliation models in one of three categories by default. Those are

- Button to generate counterpart entry
- Rule to suggest counterpart entry
- Rule to match invoices/bills

Button to Generate Counterpart Entry

The button reconciliation model, in which you create a button on one or more journal items to generate a counterpart entry. This button makes the reconciliation automatically when you click it and offers a counterpart based on the selected journal article. In contrast, you can set up a set of rules for "Rules to suggest counterpart entry." When you click the suggest button, these rules are used to recommend a counterpart based on the selected journal item and automatically produce the reconciliation. It will confirm that only the immediately adjacent counterpart values need to be verified. Additionally, this model will ensure that the automation takes place in accordance with the Reconciliation model's set of rules.

'Rule to match invoices/bills' The ability of the reconciliation model to automatically post the accurate customer invoices and vendor bills that correspond to the payment amount. The reconciliation activities are completed automatically if the entries are confirmed. Additionally, each and every reconciliation is carried out in accordance with the guidelines established in this mode during configuration.

In Odoo17 Accounting, establishing a new Reconciliation Model is simple. Simply review the New button that is there in the Reconciliation Models window. You will enter the creation window shown in the frame below as soon as you select the New button.

In the Name field, you can first give the Reconciliation model a name. The next step is to define the Type by selecting one of the previously covered options for creating a counterpart entry. The three types include Button for counterpart entry generation, Rule for counterpart entry suggestion, and Rule for matching invoices and bills. The additional fields that are accessible will be presented based on the type. This implies that if you select the "Button to generate counterpart entry," a field titled "To Check" will appear, which you can activate or deactivate depending on your needs.

When this option is enabled, the matching rule is used when the user is unsure of all the counterpart's information. Additionally, you may use the dropdown menu to provide details about the Journals Availability under the Bank Transactions Conditions tab. The Add a Line menu can then be used to allocate the COUNTERPART ENTRIES. When you select Add a Line, a new line will appear with a drop-down menu where you may select the Account to see a list of all the available procedures.

Next, choose the Amount Type, where you'll also discover a drop-down menu with options for Fixed, Percentage of Balance, Percentage of Statement Line, and From label types.

You also have the option to make it display extra fields in the counterpart entries, along with the Amount, Analytic, and Journal Item Label. Click the icon that is present on the right end to do that, as seen in the screenshot below.

It will be added to the line if you turn on the Journal, Taxes, and Tax Included in Price fields. The equivalent entries can also be removed by selecting the Delete option that is present at the right end of each line. The reconciliation model will be usable once the Button's setting to create a counterpart entry is complete.

Rule to Suggest Counterpart Entry

Applying the 'Rule to suggest counterpart entry' as the Reconciliation model type will result in the addition of extra fields and tabs, as seen in the screenshot below. This type offers more customizations, as shown in the screenshot above.

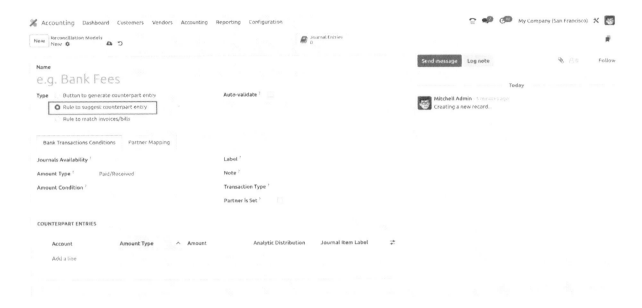

You can choose whether or not to auto-validate the statement line first. The Bank Transaction Conditions can then be set up under the relevant tab. You can specify the reconciliation model under the Journals Availability option to make it accessible in a certain journal. The amount type can then be allocated in the designated field.

You can select it from the dropdown menu to be Received, Paid, or Paid/Received. So that the chosen transaction type will be the only one to which the reconciliation model is applied. Only when receiving an amount does the option "Received" apply. You can only apply using the Paid option after making a payment. In both situations, the third one, "Paid/Received," will be used. The Amount Condition can be examined next.

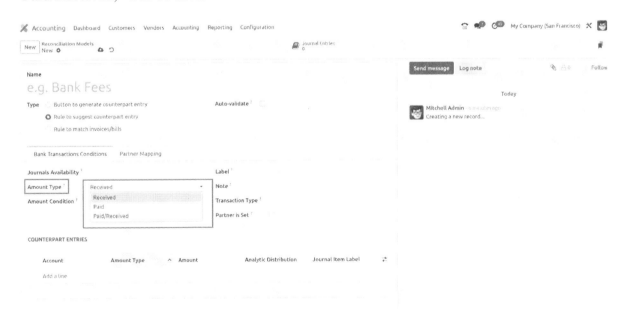

It will also show a dropdown menu with alternatives like Is Lower Than, Is Greater Than, and Is Between.

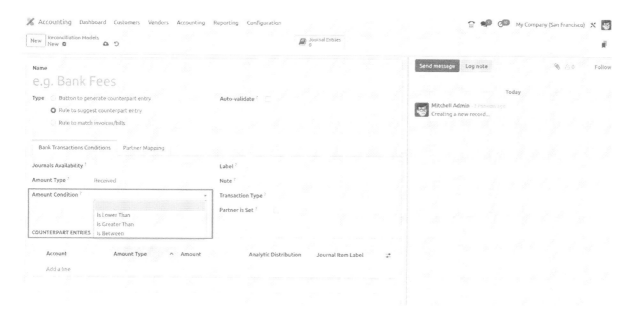

You can now complete the fields label, note, transaction type, and partner is set on the right side of the tab. The dropdown menu, which has options such as, is located in the Label field.

- **Contains:** When this option is selected, the reconciliation model will only be used if the preposition label contains the specified string.
- **Not Contains:** The opposite of "Contains" is "Not Contains."
- **Match Regex:** Create a regular expression on your own.

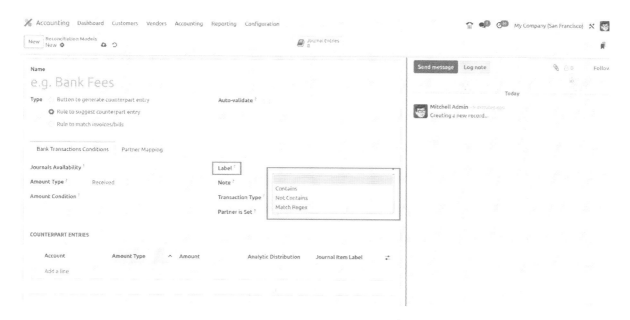

The reconciliation model will only be used when the note satisfies the requirement, so you can assign the note in a similar manner. The Player Should be set option, which will provide you with more possibilities to choose the partners as shown below, can also be used to configure the partners. You can choose the Transaction Type as well. You can also enable or disable the Partner Set field. The chosen reconciliation model will only be used if a customer or vendor is set if the field is activated. By turning on this option, other fields like "Matching partners" and "Matching categories" will become available. as seen in the following screenshot.

By turning on this function, a dropdown menu will appear with a selection of predefined partners and categories, from which you can select the partners and categories that match. You can add the entries in the COUNTERPART ENTRIES column.

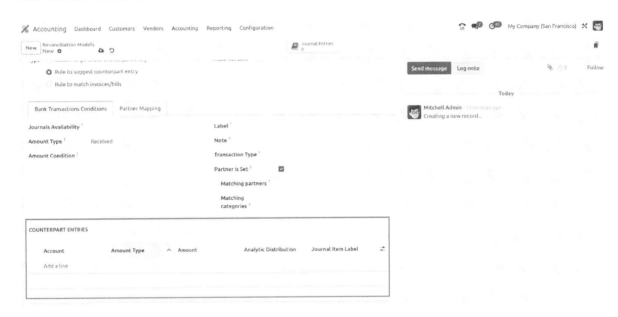

The setting can then be started by assigning the Find Text in Label and Find Text in Note fields, as well as by selecting the appropriate partner using the dropdown menu available under Partner, under the next tab, which is called "Partner Mapping."

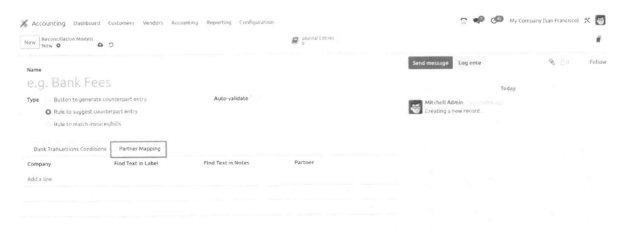

The newly built Reconciliation model will be instantly saved into the system after all the necessary information has been provided. If not, you can save the record manually using the icon that is provided at the top, as seen in the screenshot above.

Rule to Match Invoices/Bills

'Rule to match invoices/bills' is the last reconciliation type. You must complete the extra fields that we will cover below in order to configure the reconciliation applying this (Rule to match invoices/bills).

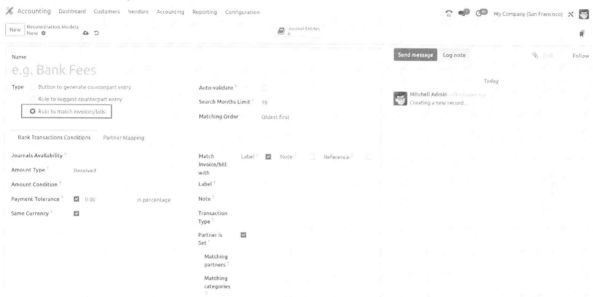

The 'Search Months Limit' field, where you can define the number of months to be utilised for the reconciliation process, must be filled in after you have mentioned the Name, Type, and Auto validate. This can be used to restrict the reconciliation process's application, for as by limiting it to transactions from the last three months or something similar. Additionally, the dropdown option allows you to fill up the Matching Order box using either the Oldest First or Newest First order. You can arrange the reconciliations in order of importance using this field.

Later, under the Bank Transactions Conditions tab, the condition on the bank statement can be specified. Here, you must first determine the Journal Availability in order for the reconciliation model to only be accessible from the designated journals. Then, as we said before, the Amount Type can be set to Received, Paid, or Paid/Received. Then, by selecting the appropriate option from the dropdown, you can define the Amount Condition. Additionally, if any underpayment happens, the Payment Tolerance feature can be activated to accept the payment difference. It may be configured percentage-wise. Similarly, whether or not the reconciliation procedure should utilize the same currency for all sums included in the reconciliation is indicated by the boolean field Same Currency being activated.

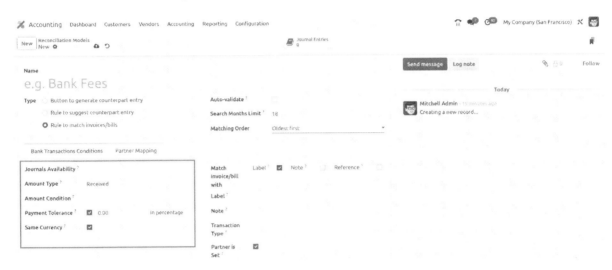

Additionally, the 'Match Invoice/bills with' option can be set to Label, Note, or Reference on the right side of the tab. Then, using the appropriate options from the dropdown, you can describe the Label, Note, and Transaction Type fields. The bank statements can be filtered with the use of these options. In order to mention the Matching Partners and the Matching Categories, you can activate the Partner is Set field.

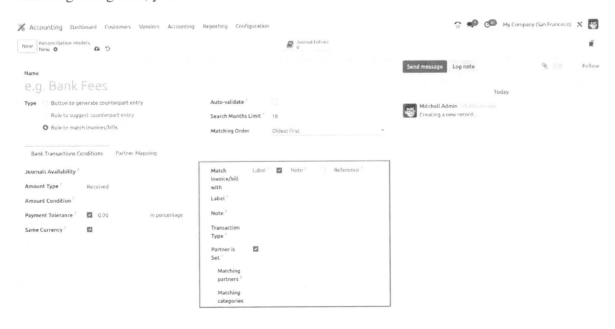

176

In order to complete the Partner Mapping tab, use the Add a Line button to provide information about Partner, Field Test in Label, and Find Text in Notes. You can automatically associate accounting entries with various partners using this tab. It enables you to instantly spot any anomalies or irregularities in the accounting and reconcile transactions with ease. When it comes to minimizing data entry errors and improving decision-making, the Partner Mapping tab is extremely helpful.

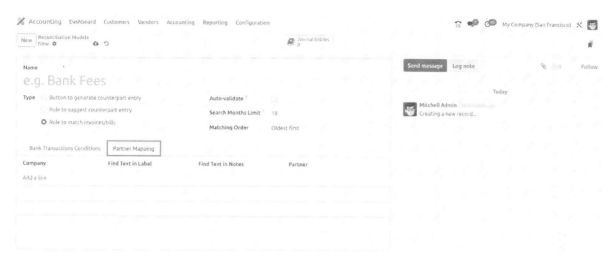

The configuration procedures for various Reconciliation model kinds are as follows. The Reconciliation Model Creation Form also shows a smart button named Journal Entries, which is highlighted in the screenshot below. By clicking this button, you can access all the Journal Entries connected to the Reconciliation Model that has already been defined.

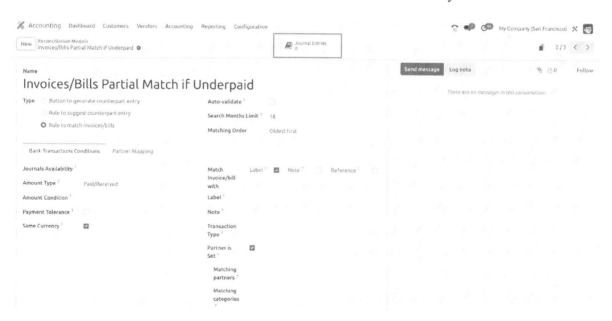

The form view in Odoo17 has changed, and the 'NEW' button now allows for the creation of bank statements.

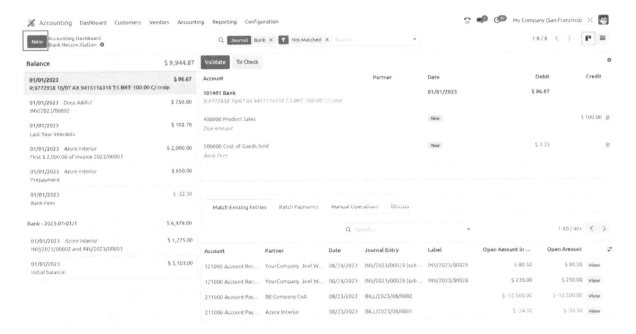

To reconcile the corresponding invoices or bills, select the line that corresponds to the statement. Or, entries are reconciled automatically in accordance with the rules and reconciliation model established.

You may automatically match bank and other financial transactions to the relevant accounts in their Odoo17 Accounting system by using the Reconciliation model, which is an essential component of the accounting process. As transactions are automatically matched to their appropriate accounts, this assures accurate and timely accounting while reducing the need for manual data entry. Additionally, since transactions are automatically reconciled, it aids in removing errors and discrepancies. This makes it easier to make sure that the financial data entered into the system is accurate and current.

Therefore, we covered every aspect of the unique Configuration tools and menus available in the Odoo17 Accounting module in this chapter. The many tabs of activities in the Odoo17 Accounting module, which support efficient financial administration, will be the subject of the following chapter.

Chapter 4
Odoo 17 Accounting:
Navigating Financial Management with
Customers and Vendors

Odoo 17 Accounting: Navigating Financial Management with Customers and Vendors

The Accounting module of the Odoo platform enables efficient processing of payments and other financial transactions related to customer and supplier activities for the company. Both customer and vendor payments can be efficiently managed using the special menus and tools included in Odoo's accounting module. In the previous chapter, the main topic of discussion was the functions related to setting up the accounting module. Each setting menu and option had a detailed explanation.

This chapter focuses on how your company manages financial relationships with customers and suppliers.

This chapter covers the following topics:
- Accounting module Dashboard
- Customer Finance management with Odoo Accounting module
- Vendor management

This chapter contains a detailed definition of all sub-functions related to the defined topics with relevant descriptions and illustrations.

Accounting Module Dashboard

Odoo, which works in a modular way, includes a special Accounting module where you can perform all the functions of the financial management of the company with considerable menus and options. We will continue to understand the dashboard of the Odoo accounting module, where users will be directed when entering the accounting module because the configuration parts were discussed in the previous chapter. With the well-defined dashboard of the Odoo accounting module, you can get detailed information about the many functional features of the various functions.

A Descriptive Overview of Accounting Module Dashboard

You can get an overview of the financial processes carried out in the organization using Odoo accounting from the Dashboard of the Accounting module. In addition, by using the different tabs, you can get an idea of how operations are performed and what happens to the financial components of each tab. When you use the dashboard for the first time, you will see filtered data based on the configuration defined during platform development. In addition, you can remove the filter if necessary. Also, you can customize the panel with a selection of custom filters, some of which are preconfigured.

The information displayed in the menu can be changed according to your functional needs using the Group By option in the Dashboard. You will also see a table that illustrates the layout of the accounting module and subsequent business financial operations. From there, you can get information about how all functions related to financial management should be organized. The Dashboard of the accounting module with the configuration description window is shown in the following image.

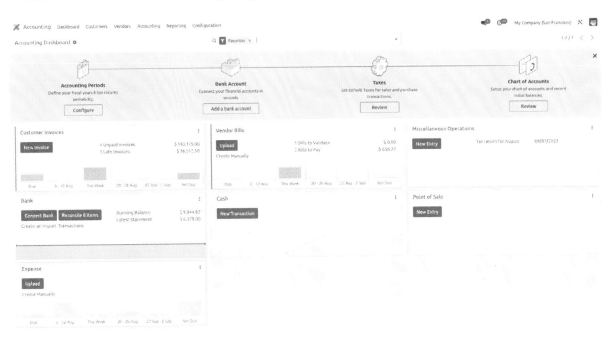

You can set up the first bill for vendors directly from the overview by clicking on it. The Let's Get Started option takes you to a window where you can instantly generate vendor bills based on functional requirements. By selecting Add Bank, which takes you to the same interface where a bank account was created for the company, you can also set up a bank account for company operations. Then you can change the accounting period and the Tax Return Periodicity for various periods, such as quarterly, annually, and on-demand, by selecting the settings button under Accounting periods.

Additionally, the Review button for the chart of accounts displays all currently installed locations with corresponding Charts of Accounts. Additional accounts can also be created or imported if needed. Users can add a starting balance by clicking the Review button below the Chart of Accounts. The credit/debit amount of each account can also be added to make the platform work, and the changes can be saved. For Opening Balance in Journal Entries, the associated Journal Entry will be created. Odoo automatically adds any debit/credit differences to "999999 Undistributed Profit/Loss" for automatic balancing, if any.

You can close the indicated window as needed to see the Dashboard, which is shown in the following image. A number of tabs, such as Customer Invoices, Vendor Bills, Miscellaneous Operations, Bank data, Cash information, and many more, will be presented based on the Dashboard's Favorites as they are set up and used. Furthermore, the Dashboard will include all of the generated Journals and operations. The ones you use frequently can also be added to the Favourites list based on your demands. This will be beneficial for journal filtering, depending on necessity. The following picture shows a useful flowchart of the processes related to how each tab operates. The distinct information on each chart will be displayed to you when your mouse pointer is hovered over it, according to the definition on the chart.

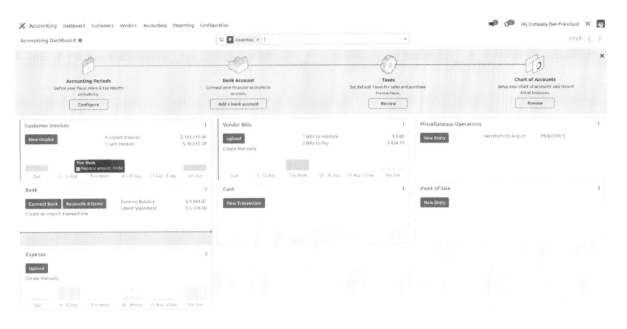

There are also shortcuts to the respective menus of each of the defined tabs. Additionally, unique configuration options have been developed under each of the tabs based on each tab's functioning aspect. The color configuration choices enable you to generate diverse color coordination for each tab, allowing you to categorize them clearly if many tabs are present.

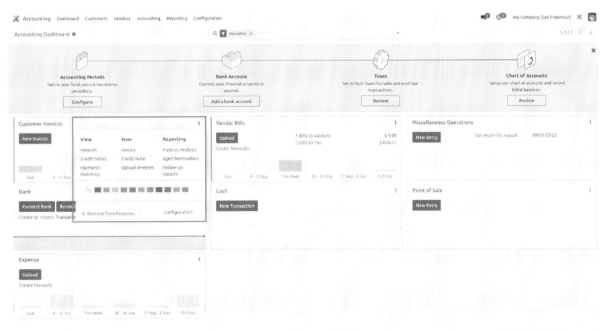

If you want to remove the corresponding tab from the accounting module Dashboard, you can remove it from favorites. In addition, you can see relevant documents for each journal, such as invoices, bills, and credit or debit items, from the overview, as well as create new documents and get reports for documents in each journal. In addition, there is a settings option that will take you to the settings menu in this tab. Each tab has a separate configuration setting, and you usually need to configure the journals for the tab you are configuring. For example, the Customer Invoices tab is currently selected, and the attached screenshot shows its Settings menu. You can learn more about each journal, including its types, by visiting this page. In addition, journal entry setup information, including currency information, short code, Dedicated Credit Note Sequence, and Default Income Account. By selecting the Edit option in the settings panel, you have the option to change all the journal information you need.

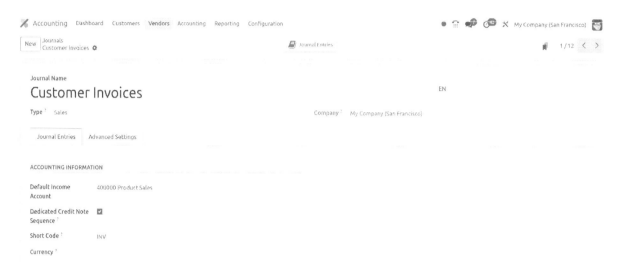

Additionally, the specified Journal's Advanced Settings may be configured, allowing you to adjust menu items such as Control Access information such as Allowed Account Types and Allowed Accounts, as well as activate or disable the Lock Posted Entries with the Hash function. Mentioning allowed accounts allows you to record journal entries to those particular accounts only. Also, by enabling the feature Lock Posted Entries, Odoo restricts editing of the posted entries. You may also add the Email Servers from which Accounting emails are sent by utilizing the Configure Email Servers option. Electronic Data Interchange and Electronic Invoicing through Factor-X(IN) can be enabled or deactivated for each Journal.

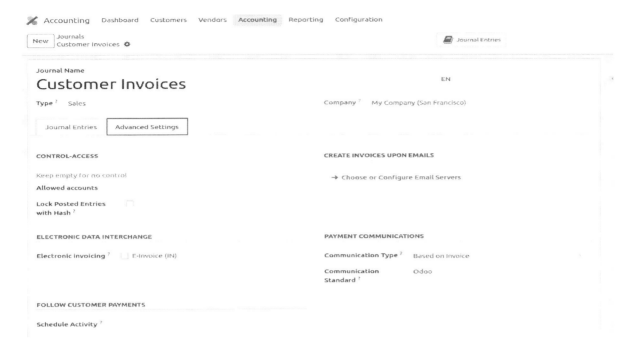

Furthermore, Payment Communication settings, such as Communication Type and Communication Standard, can be changed. The communication type depicts which is the valid communication to make payment for the invoice. It can be the customer or invoice number itself. The Scheduled activity may be set in order to Follow Customer Payment depending on the follow-up activity and adjusted as necessary.

How is the Opening Balance added?

The Opening Balance for the Business Operations should be introduced in order to display the amount of cash that is readily available in each account of operations. The components of the opening balance will provide you with information about the finances that are accessible when the firm is just getting started. Let's go on to understand how to define the starting balance of the firm in Odoo.

Step 1: The accounting module's onboarding panel will provide us the opportunity to examine and add starting debits and credits for your chart of accounts.

When you click the Review option, you will be sent to a screen where you may add initial balances.

Step 2: Opening balance can be added by mentioning the debit or credit amount in respective ledgers.

Save the details after adding the balance of each account.

Step 3: A new Journal Entry with the reference "Opening Journal Entry" is created automatically upon saving in the Accounting menu > Journal Entries.

Step 4: If an account opening debit of credit fails to add, it can be added by modifying a journal entry that has already been written.

Step 5: Once a draft journal entry has been opened, we can view all the entries we entered into each ledger, with a reference to the 'Opening Journal Entry.' The difference between the Credit and Debit values is immediately sent to the '999999 Undistributed Profits/Losses Account,' which Odoo provides for automated balancing.

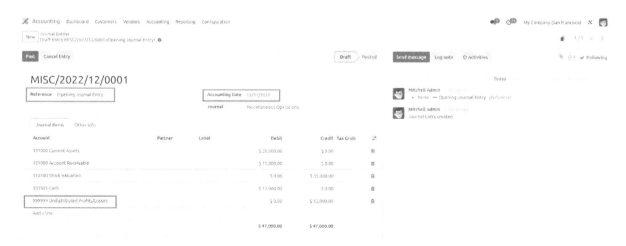

Step 6: Additionally, alter the accounting date for when the account ledgers are affected by the Opening Balance added. Now, post the journal entry.

Step 7: The data is added to the balance sheet once it is posted.

Step 8: If we need to update account ledgers with a specific Credit or Debit sum that was missed while entering the Opening Journal, they can be added by manually entering them in a journal entry with a reference 'opening journal entry'. It is critical to remember that when posting, you must supply the right accounting date, which must agree with the date the entry was entered in the balance sheet.

With the release of Odoo 17, we will be able to evaluate and import data from the accounting module's configuration settings.

With the 'Review Manually' option, the user may check the balance in the chart of accounts, and the 'Import' function allows the importing of contacts, charts of accounts, and journal entries.

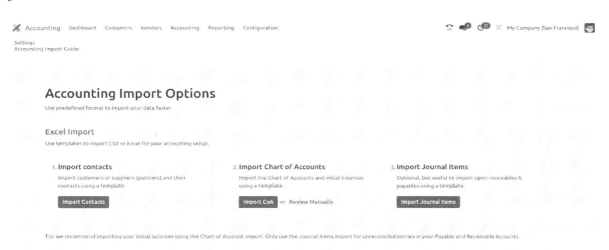

The sophisticated Odoo Accounting module Dashboard provides a comprehensive picture of the actions that were taking place regarding the accounting administration of the firm. Now that you understand it completely, let's move on to the section where the Odoo Accounting module's customer financial management component is discussed.

Customer Finance Management with Odoo 17 Accounting Module

Customer management is critical to the efficient operation of a business since, without it, you risk losing control over processes such as payment collection, product transportation, and many others. The financial parts of client operations are vital, as you will want specialized operational tools to handle them. Using a specific tab of menus, you may control client financial management processes in Odoo. The Customer tabs on the Accounting module's dashboard give you various options, such as Invoices, Credit Notes, Receipts, Payments, Batch Payments, Follow-ups, Direct debit Mandates, Products, and Customers. The financial management factors related to client activities towards the firm will be added up using each of these choices. Now that we have thoroughly discussed each configuration choice, let's move on to the section that covers client finance management.

Creating your Customer Invoices

Customer invoices must be processed quickly, carefully, and very carefully. You should have special programs for this. Customers can access the invoice management menu in the Odoo accounting module by going to the Customers menu in the accounting module. The Invoices menu in the Accounting module displays all business invoices owed to customers, as shown in the screenshot below. It shows invoice number, customer details, invoice date, due date, future activity, tax information, invoice amount, invoice status, and payment status. The Due date and status correspond to the colors as shown in the following screenshots. With this complex feature of Odoo, you can identify and categorize many activities. If the deadline is today, a yellow color appears, and if it is red, it means that the date has passed or become due. The invoice status says whether it is posted or not and the Payment status defines whether the invoice is paid or not.

If required, you may amend the current invoice data, providing you the freedom to modify it as needed, but only by authorized persons to avoid interruption of security. You may also create new invoices by selecting the Create option from the Invoices menu. As seen in the picture below, the customer invoice number will also be displayed in the invoice production menu along with the short code INV, which is connected to journal activities and is changeable.

INV is used as the invoice prefix. Additionally, you may select the Customer, Payment Reference, Invoice Date, Due Date, and Journal where the entries should be defined.

The Sales Product may be specified under the Invoice Lines tab. When adding items or additional sections to the invoice lines, you may do so here using the Add a Line or Add a Section choices. By selecting the 'Add a note' option, you can also include a note to the client right on the invoice. The following fields can be added: the Product, Label, Account, Analytical Account, Analytical Tag, Intrastat, Quantity, Price, Taxes, and Subtotal of the products being defined. You can also include the Terms and Conditions in connection with the particular Invoice. The Untaxed Amount will be described together with the Tax, its percentage, and the Total Amount.

The Journal Items for the appropriate Invoice will be specified by the menu based on the items and other data provided in the invoice. As soon as the products are added to the invoice, the pertinent ledgers will be added to the journal entries.

It consists of the Receivable Account, Tax Account, and Income Accounts listed under the Product/Product category. The Account information, Label, Analytical Tags, Debit, Credit, and Tax Grids will all be defined. You will also be able to observe the Cut-Off of the relevant Account, as seen in the image below.

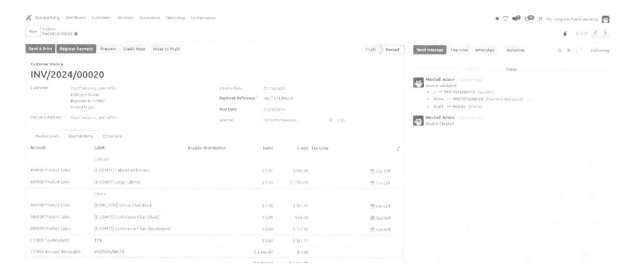

Odoo uses Continental and Anglo-Saxon accounting in its general ledger entry procedures, allowing both to be fully understood. In Continental Accounting, when an invoice is produced, the Account Receivable is debited, and the Income Account is credited. The Account Receivable is debited when the Assets' value increases because, by definition, the Account receivable is an "Asset." Similarly, the Income Account gets credited when income rises because it is of nature "Income." Since the tax account is a "Liability" by definition and is credited when liabilities increase.

On the Other Info tab, which also gives you more details, you may customize a number of the created invoice's components. In the Other Info tab of the invoice menu, you can include customer references, salespeople, sales team, receipt bank, etc. Fiscal Position, Incoterms, Intrastat Country, and Cost Rounding Method are further concepts included in the definitions of accounting other information tab. 'Auto Post' is another option that may be enabled or disabled to determine whether this item will be posted on the specified accounting date and any related recurring bills. Invoice auto-posting options include "No," "At Date," monthly, quarterly, and yearly. 'No' invoices are those that are not automatically posted but can be manually uploaded; 'At Date' invoices are those that are posted on the specified date, and Monthly, Quarterly, and Yearly defined invoices are posted every month, quarterly or yearly.

Additionally, based on the Accounting Date set, the journal entries are automatically posted when the Post Automatically option is activated. In case you or another user of the Odoo platform is unclear of how they operate, the To Check options can also be selected to indicate that the pertinent document needs to be checked.

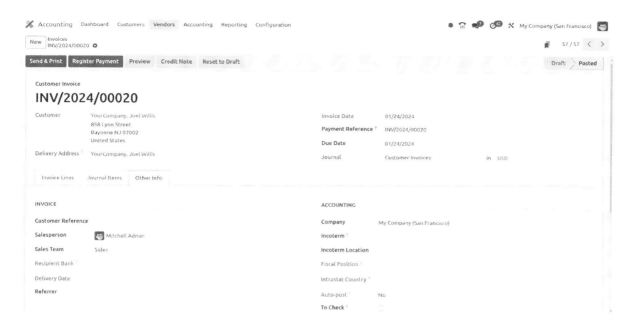

Once the customer's invoice setting is complete, you can select the Send & Print option to send the invoice to them and print a copy for yourself if a printer is connected to the system. The printed version may be used to handle the invoice with the customer or to mail it together with a personalized letter to them. If you want to preview how the invoice that will be sent to the client will look before you send it, you may utilize the Preview option.

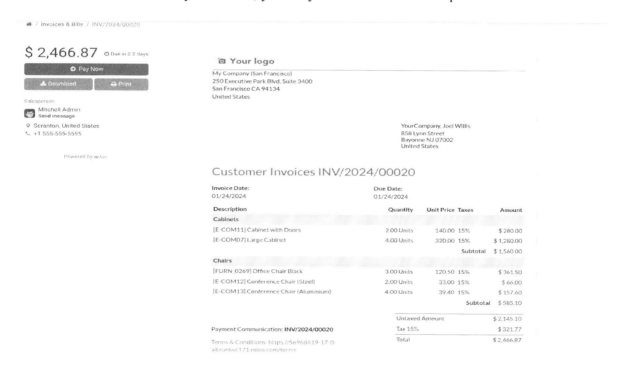

This screenshot depicts how the invoice would seem to the client; all information defined during invoice preparation will be displayed here, except for information based on the internal business operations of the company. Additionally, specifics like the Journal and Chart of Accounts won't be shown.

You have the option of sending invoices to the customer after they have been sent and modifying them as needed. Depending on the conditions, the buyer will get the invoice through mail or post. You may keep track of the money owing to you by using the Register Payments option in the appropriate invoice box as soon as the client makes a payment in connection to the issued invoice. After deciding to register the payments, you will see the following pop-up window, where you may choose the Journal Payment Method from Manual, Branch Deposit, or SEPA Direct Debit. You can provide the specifications of the Receipt Bank Account in addition to the Amount and Currency. The memo and the Payment Date can both be defined. Finally, to register the payment in the Odoo platform, choose the Create Payment option.

It will be feasible to manage how the company's accounting activities are handled by knowing how the payment revival methods of Continental Accounting and Anglo-Saxon Accounting vary. Let's look at the operational features of them. When a payment is received, the Continental accounting system credits the Account Receivable and debits the Outstanding Receipts Account. After bank statement reconciliation, the Bank Account is debited, and only the Outstanding Receipts Account is credited. An Outstanding Receipt Account will be utilized to store all incoming payment entries brought on by invoices and refunds. During reconciliation, they are compared to the pertinent transaction rather than Account Receivable and shown in blue in the widget. On the invoice, the ribbon PAID will take the place of IN PAYMENT. The Expense Account in Anglo-Saxon accounting also modifies upon the posting of the invoice. The Anglo-Saxon accounting expenses are affected after the Sales process has been validated. As a result, the stock output account is credited, and the expense account is debited.

As seen in the example below, the associated invoice menu will show an In Payment label after the payment has been received. If the payment has been made in full, the status of the related invoice will be shown as Paid.

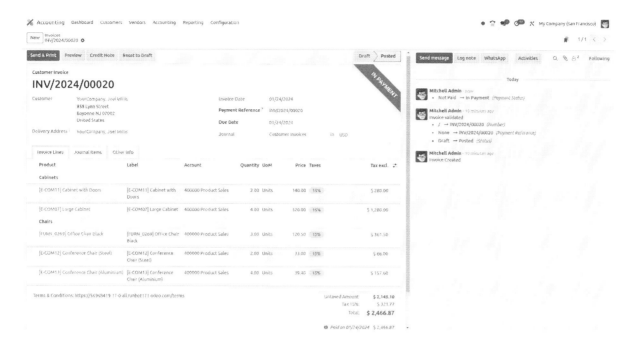

Once the payments have been received and you need to repay part or all of the money for internal reasons, you may attach a credit note to the relevant invoice by selecting the credit note smart invoice option. The following menu will display, where you may define the credit note's parameters, such as the credit method, the cause for the refund, and the reverse date (which can be a journal entry date or a particular day). Additionally, you may customize the Refund Date and Use Specific Journal details to suit your needs. Select Reverse if you want to change the amount that will be returned to the customer; otherwise, select Cancel.

With all the functional menus and windows related to managing invoices in the Odoo accounting module, you can create customer invoices and perform various related functions. From now on, with the help of the Odoo accounting module, the aspects of managing invoices are clear. Now we go to the next menu related to customer management, the Credit Note, in regards to customer management.

Credit Note Management on the Customer Invoices

The characteristics of credit note activities that will allow you to refund the invoice amounts in the section prior may be clear to you. Credit note operations will probably need to be specified in a real-time business context; hence, Odoo offers a particular menu to make managing all credit note activities easier. In the Credit Notes menu, which is available from the Customer page, all Credit Notes will be described with the Number, Customer information, Invoice Date, Due Date, Next Scheduled activity, Tax Excluded, Total, Status, and Payment Status. To get the required Credit Notes, you can provide custom and default Filter and Group by settings.

By hitting Create, you will also have the opportunity to create Credit Notes and create new ones. You can see that the Credit Note number starts with the RINV label, which stands for the reverse invoice when it is defined in the Creation menu. The invoice number, however, will begin with the letter RINV. The Customer Details and the Payment Reference Details may be defined. The Invoice Date, Due Date, Journal, and Electronic invoice for the Credit Note will also be displayed.

The invoice lines can also be set using the Add a line option. Additionally, by selecting the Add a section option, you may add a section to the invoice, and you may add a remark by choosing the Add an available note option.

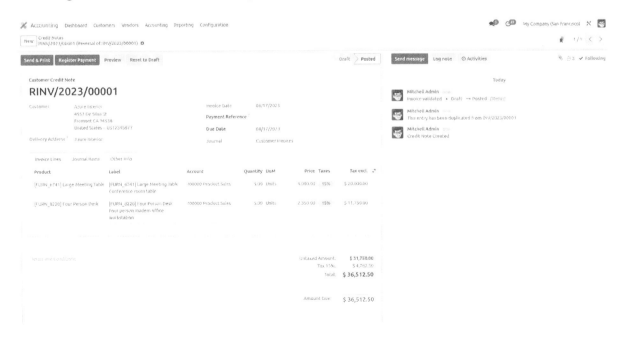

194

The Journal Items will populate the Account data, Label, Analytic, Debit, Credit, and Tax Grid information. Once the product has been included on the reverse invoice itself, the impacted accounts will show up on the Journals items page. The Account Receivable is credited during this process, while the Income Account and Tax Account are debited. This shows that when an invoice is reversed, income decreases and is debited, but account receivable, an asset by nature, decreases and is credited.

Both the Invoice and Accounting data may be specified under the Other Info tab. Invoice data such as the customer reference, salesperson information, recipient bank, and payment QR code can be defined. The Incoterms, Fiscal Position, Intrastat Country, Cash rounding Method, Post Automatically, and To Check can be added depending on the business requirement.

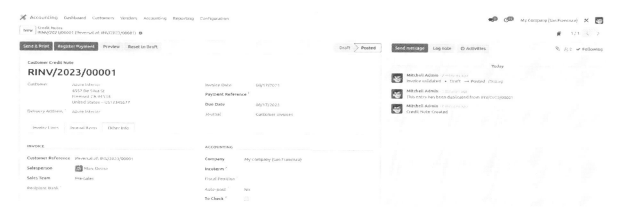

You may get a preview of the reverse invoice for a Credit Note by selecting the Preview option from the applicable Credit Note menu. A reverse invoice must be sent back to the customer. The screenshots that follow show the reverse invoice that will be sent to the customer. All of the information will be explained here in the exact same terms as they were in the credit note you sent us.

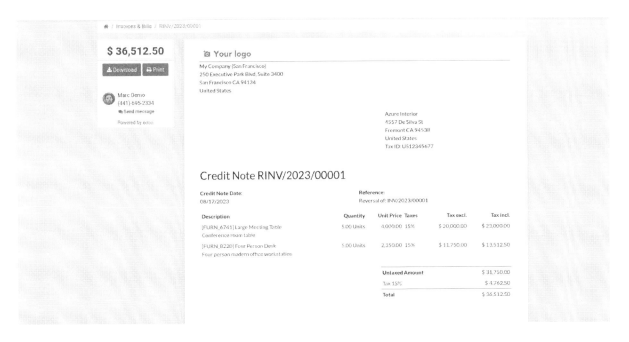

If the Credit Notes' descriptions are correct, they can be delivered or emailed to the customer. Reverse payments, as well as Credit Notes, may be made to the consumer. After making the payment, you must record it in the necessary client payment journals of the financial operations on the platform. When you select the Register Payment option, a pop-up window where you may enter the payment register's details will display. Journals, manual or check-based payment mechanisms, and other components. You can also mention the recipient's bank account details.

It is also possible to specify the Amount, the currency in which the payment must be made, the Payment Date, and the Memo. Once the information has been entered, you may select the Create Payment option.

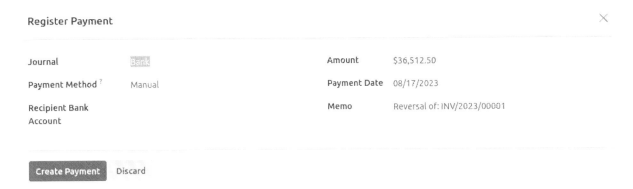

If a payment is made but not yet authorized or completed, the credit note for that payment will indicate that it has been received by marking it as In Payment. If the transaction goes through successfully to the bank or cash account after reconciliation, the label will read "Paid."

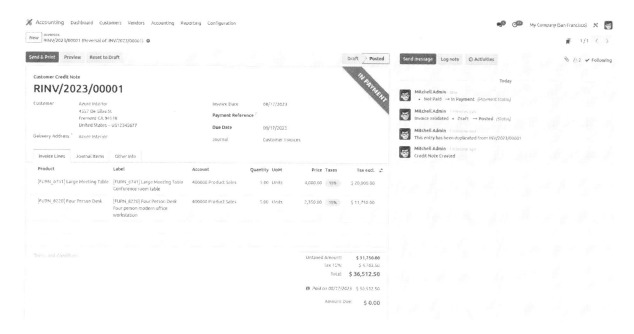

You will be familiar with the Credit Notes operations, how they function, and the management elements of them as of now. In the section that follows, we'll go into more depth about how the Odoo Accounting module manages client receipts.

Customer Receipts Management

Receipts are an important aspect of ensuring that payments to the invoices record are made. In many businesses' real-world situations, the operations for producing receipts are carried out both before and after payments are received. Only corporate activities are responsible for this. The company's operations for client sales receipts will be supported by a particular tool for handling receipts that is offered by the Odoo platform. The Receipts menu may be accessed from the Customers tabs of the Odoo Accounting module. The menu will define all operation receipts. Number, Customer, Invoice Date, Due Date, Next Activity, Tax Excluded, Total, Status, and Payment Status will all be shown. The activities will have a foundation, and the understanding of it will be obvious thanks to the color-coordinated representation of the Status section of the menu.

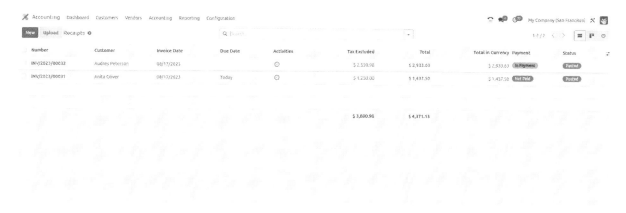

Receipts defined in the menu may be changed, and there is also the opportunity to produce new ones using the accessible Create option. The choice for producing receipts will provide the Customer name, Reference, Payment Reference, Invoice Date, Due Date, and the Journals description, along with the Currency used. Under the invoice, lines are also listed Product data, Label, Account details, Analytical Accounting details, Analytics Tags, Intrastat, Quantity, Price, Taxes, and Subtotal.

By choosing to include a line, it may be defined. You may also add a new section to the invoice by selecting the Add a section option. You may add remarks to the customers by choosing the Add a note option. It is possible to delete or alter the sections, product lines, and remarks that are being provided.

The amount of the invoice, as well as the tax information, will be shown in the relevant invoice window at the bottom of the page.

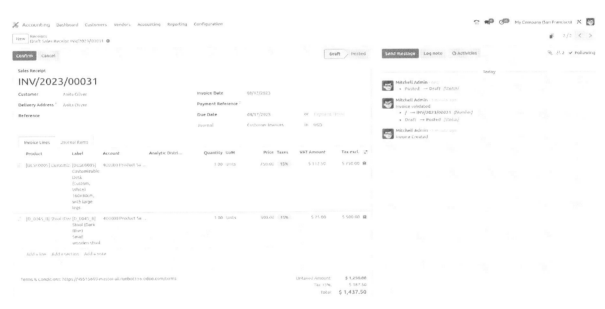

The Journal Entries option will additionally provide every journal entry detail for the pertinent invoice. Detailed information will be provided for the Account, Label, Analytical Tags, Debit, Credit, and Tax Grids.

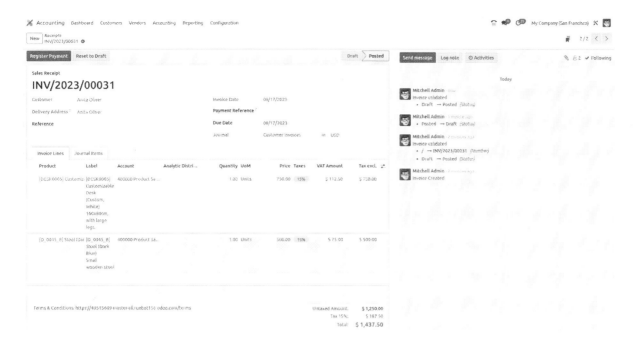

Once the reverse invoices are configured, you may proceed to register the payment by selecting the relevant option. At that time, a pop-up window similar to the one in the picture below will display. Here, you must select whether to use manual, batch, or SEPA direct debit as your payment option. Next, you must provide the recipient's bank account, payment sum, payment date, and payment note.

Finally, you must select the Create Payment option.

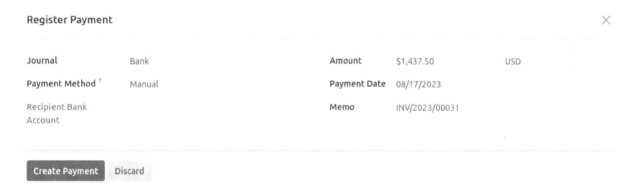

Once the payment has been entered again in the relevant Receipts menu, a label indicating that the pertinent Invoice is In Payment will display. Otherwise, the label will display as Paid if the payment is successful.

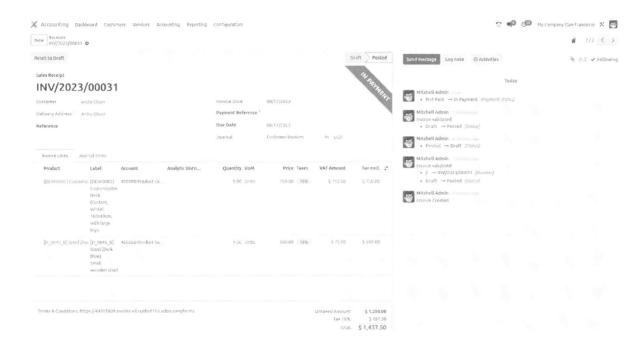

Additionally, you have the choice to modify the platform-defined receipts as needed, but only authorized users of the Odoo platform—those who may be identified during platform setup—are allowed to do so. Now that you know the basics, let's talk about how the Odoo Accounting module manages client receipts. In the next part, we'll learn more about the elements of client payment administration that are described in the Odoo Accounting module.

Customer Amounts to Settle

Here, we record the bills to settle for the customers by the company due to any reason. Odoo 17 added a new function called Customer Amount to settle since there is a possibility that the company would occasionally need to settle a customer's condition. Thus, by employing this, users may quickly determine how much to give consumers.

Within the **Customers** menu is the **Customer Amount to Settle** option.

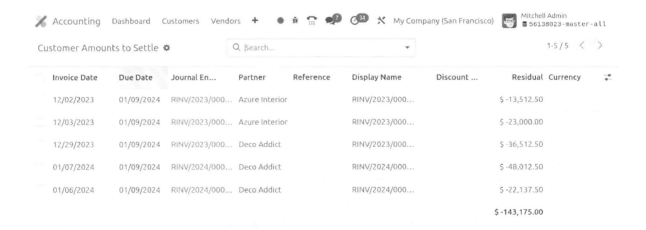

Within the list view are the following details: invoice date, due date, journal entry, partner, reference, display name, discount amount, residual, and currency.

Customer Payments

The Odoo platform's specific Payments management menu, which is accessible in the Odoo Accounting module, enables the effective administration of client payments for invoices that have been issued for them for specified purchases. The Payments menu will reveal each of the Payments activities that have been defined for the operation of the business, as seen in the following screenshot. Together with the Payment, Date, Number, Journal, Payment Method, Customer, and, if appropriate, a description of a Batch Payment, the Amount, Status, SDD Scheme, and Currency will be defined. The state will be decided based on the color indicator that will display the operating state of the pertinent Customer Payments.

You may add new Customer Payments by selecting the Create option, and you can modify the data related to the particular Customer Payments that have been defined.

Choosing to generate new customer payments will trigger the window seen in the following screenshot. Here, you may select the payment method of either sending or receiving money. Additional details, such as the Partner Type and customer or vendor information, could also be given together with the destination account. The receiver of the Send Money is the Partner Type Vendor, whereas the recipient of the Receive Money is the Partner Type Customer. Additionally, the destination Account of the Customer will automatically be displayed with the Account Receivable after choosing Customer as the Partner Type and Receive Money as the Payment Type. Additionally, this function will be useful for keeping track of client accounts and obtaining payment for billed sums. If the payment is made to the organization or one of its partner firms, you can enable the Is Internal Transfer option.

Along with the Journal and Payment Method (Manual, Batch Deposit, or SEPA Direct Debit), you may also enter the Amount, Currency, Date, and Memo. The Recipient Bank Account can also be specified for the relevant Customer Payments.

201

When a customer's payment is received, any outstanding bills for that customer are added to the payment list. The payment can be added to the invoice using the payment matching option if the customer "Azure Interior" has a $1000 invoice and has made a payment of, say, $3000.

Then, open invoices for that client that need to be matched with the payment are shown when we click on payment matching; the pertinent invoice with the same amount that the customer needs to pay can then be picked with the payment and reconciled. Payment Matching is a function available on the Odoo platform.

Once the payments have been matched with the payment matching, the Account Receivable and the Outstanding Receipt Account are also deducted. After the account has been tallied up with the bank statement, the bank account must be debited and the unpaid receipts must be credited.

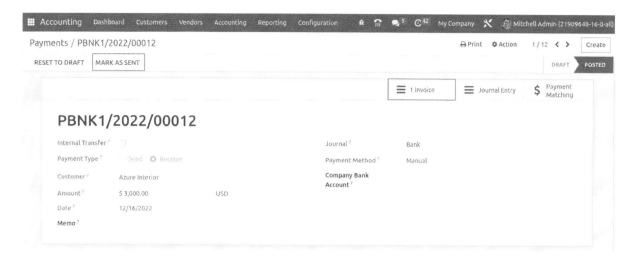

Once the Customer Payments setting is complete and the money has been delivered, you may register the payment, at which time the appropriate Payments menu will display a Sent label, as seen in the picture below.

Additionally, you may choose to Mark As Sent and Reset To Draft in order to modify the Payment's configuration. These settings will only be exposed to authorized Odoo platform users to guarantee that configuration operations are safely kept to the relevant managers and executives of the organization. All payments may also be sorted by a number of other criteria, including Draft, Posted, Sent, Reconciled, and Un-reconciled. Now that you know how the Odoo Accounting module manages customer payments, you can use it effectively. In the next section, we'll talk more about how to set up batch payments in Odoo Accounting.

Batch Payment Configuration

Your company will have many regular clients who are trustworthy and who you know in person, giving you the confidence to trust each other in business and in personal matters. These types of interactions may be found in small and medium-sized firms as well as huge and global corporations. One such example of a trust-related feature is the payment, where the client will pay for the invoices both in advance and in full at the conclusion of a term.

The Odoo platform has batch payment features that will let the company post payments in groups and help with efficient operation. The Customers page of the Odoo Accounting module is where you can adjust the Batch payment setup. When you select a menu item, all of the configured Batch payments will be displayed to you. Like with every other menu in Odoo, there are also obvious choices for Filtering and Grouping.

When you wish to generate a new batch payment, you can select the Generate option to see the window shown in the following picture.

You must first establish the Batch Type, Bank information, Payment Method, Date, and Reference of the relevant Batch payment before you may build new Batch payment configuration aspects.

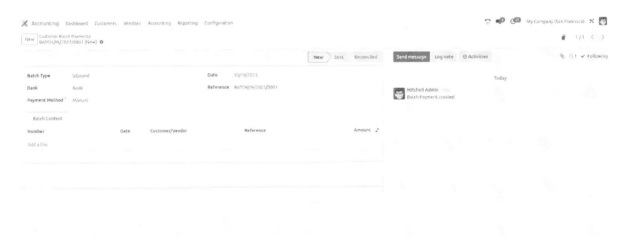

By selecting the Add a Line option from a different menu that is also used to specify the batch content, you may add the invoices for the batch payment. When you select the Add a Line option, a pop-up box, as seen in the picture below, will emerge, displaying every payment that has to be made. The Payment will be displayed based on the batch type that has been configured for the batch payment. All of the payments that the client is anticipated to make to the company will be displayed if it is an inbound transaction. If the transaction is an outbound one, all of the payments that the company must make to the vendor will be displayed. Additionally, the Filters and Group By options under the Add: Payments menu may be utilized to exclude particular payments from the Batch payment that has to be configured. For Odoo's Vendor operations, there is also a Batch payment setup option that will be discussed in more detail in the following chapter.

Once each payment has been selected to be a part of the batch payment, you may confirm the decision, and the batch payment will include each payment. Additionally, upon the confirmation of the Batch Payments, all of the Payments in the Batch have been marked as Sent.

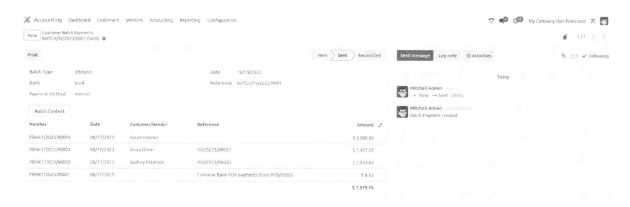

The stage will be changed to "Reconciled" after this batch has been reconciled. The firm will be able to provide the client with full payment of the invoices at the conclusion of a term or based on the customer's financial situation, thanks to the batch payment operations. Now that we have clarity on the component of the Batch payment setting, let's move on to the portion that establishes the Follow-Up Reports of the Odoo Accounting operations.

Follow Up Reports

In the real-time operations of the companies, it is possible that, for a number of reasons, the client will create a payment towards the firm for the sales given to them. Therefore, it is the owners' job to keep an eye on both the payment of those activities and the sales operations. Odoo's Follow-Up feature was created with these considerations in mind, and it allows the business owner to follow up with clients for payments using a range of activities that may be scheduled either internally or externally.

The Follow-Up Reports option is accessible from the Customers menu in the Odoo Accounting module. The Follow-Up Reports option will display the Name, Total Due, Total Overdue, Follow-Up Status, and Follow-Up Level of each Follow-Up Report. By utilizing the available Filter and Group By options, you may get the relevant Follow-Up Report from the menu. Additionally, these Follow-Up Reports are generated using the Follow-Up Levels that have been configured on the platform. Additionally, the Follow-Up Levels may be configured in the Odoo platform's Accounting module's Configuration tab > Follow-Up Levels, each Follow-Up activity's action, such as writing an email, printing a letter, or sending a letter, sending a text message, taking a manual action, or doing any other Follow-Up activity., is specified by the Follow-Up Level.

To see additional details about a Follow-Up Report, you can choose it. When you do, a window such as the one in the screenshot below will emerge. Here, details about the consumer and the contest will be displayed. The Next Reminder Date, which is customizable, will also be displayed. If the initial reminder is sent through email, a description of its contents will be sent.

Additionally, all the information related to the invoices defined in the pertinent Follow Up Report will be provided, as seen in the table in the picture that follows. There are several details displayed here, including the invoice number, date of the invoice, payment due date, source document, communication, reminder date, and the total amount owed. The Exclude option, which is offered, can be activated.

By choosing the Print Letter option from the Follow-Up Report menu, you may print the report and see a sample of the letter along with the other configuration options that are offered. There are four different types of layouts: background, boxed, light, and clean.

Additionally, the company logo can be specified and modified with the use of colors, a specific font, the company tagline, a footer description, and a paper format. The configuration varies depending on the operations option you select, and the Preview of the Letter may be found on the right side of the window. Last but not least, you can choose the Preserve option to save the Letter's setup and print the Letter.

Selecting the Send By Post option will take you to the window shown in the following screenshot, where you can send the Follow up by mail to the customer. You will see a warning message about the cost of the stamp(s) to send the letter here.

For the Postal Services integrated with Odoo, Stamps can be purchased through the Odoo website. If you are okay with the Stamps being used and have enough remaining Stamps to complete the transaction, you can choose the Send By Post option.

Send and Print   ✕

ACTIONS

☑ Print

☑ Email

☐ Sms

☐ By post

Email Recipients   Deco Addict <info@agrolait.com>✖

Email Subject   My Company (San Francisco) Payment Reminder - Deco Addict

Letter/Email Content

Dear Deco Addict,
It has come to our attention that you have an outstanding balance of $ 36,512.50

We kindly request that you take necessary action to settle this amount within the next 8 days.

If you have already made the payment after receiving this message, please disregard it. Our accounting department is available if you require any assistance or have any questions.

Thank you for your cooperation.

Sincerely,
--
System

Attach Invoices ☑   Content Template   Payment Reminder

✎ Attachment

[Send & Print]   Cancel

The integration of the Snailmail postal service for the letters, invoices, reports, and other components of the business operation to be sent to the clients is done to demonstrate how the operations function here. If you want the Follow-Up Report or the Follow-up letter to be mailed to the client, choose the Confirm option. Just be sure to include the customer's address and zip code.

By choosing the Send By Email option found in the appropriate Follow-Up Report, you can also choose to send the Follow-Up Report by email. In this case, the default email with the current template will be shown to you. Additionally, you have the option to change the email's details or select a different mailing template that has been defined.

Follow-Up Reports through text messages: To send text messages based on the Follow-Up Reports, choose the Send By SMS option found in each of the aforementioned Follow-Up Reports. You will be presented with the following window where you can customize the message after choosing to send a text message. The recipient and the responsible party's mobile number will be automatically defined, and a predefined message template will be produced that may be customized to meet your needs. However, you must check that the text message is no longer than 65 characters. If it is, the message will be split into two SMSs, and you may then choose the Send SMS option.

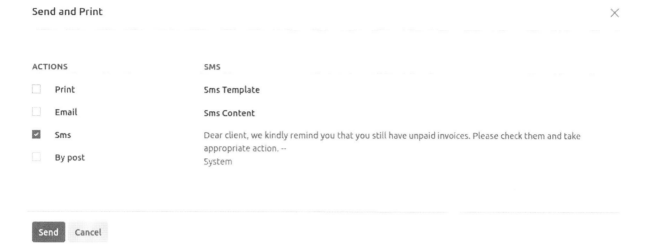

Send and Print   ✕

ACTIONS	SMS
☐ Print	**Sms Template**
☐ Email	**Sms Content**
☑ Sms	Dear client, we kindly remind you that you still have unpaid invoices. Please check them and take appropriate action. --
☐ By post	System

Send   Cancel

The next step is to select the Done options and then select to reconcile it in order to match the invoices with the bank payments that have been detailed after all setups and sending activities pertaining to the follow-up reports have been completed.

Once the Follow Up Report setting aspect is complete, the next step, as previously noted, is to reconcile. To do this, pick the distinct Reconcile option inside the Follow Up Report menu, which will display the reconciling menu as seen in the accompanying screenshot. Here, the name of the customer, the amount, and account information, such as whether the account is payable or receivable, will be described. Furthermore, the Miscellaneous Matching details of the respective Reconciliation will also be described.

Additionally, the Manual Operations for each of the Reconciliation operations' components can be set up with unique operational capabilities. For the operations to be going forward for the accounting management, the specifics such as Account, Taxes, Analytical Accounting, and Analytical Tags should be defined.

In order to manage the follow-up of payment operations, the Odoo platform's Follow-Up Reports management will be a helpful tool. It will also be one of the most helpful tools to assist you when operating in real-time. Let's move on to the section that follows, where we'll talk about the direct debit requirements for customer management in Odoo Accounting.

Direct Debit Mandates

Direct Debit Mandates are one of the most complex instruments and terms of operation used in corporate operations. By using the Direct Debit Mandates, you may be sure that the customer has authorized your firm to collect payment for any future business activities. The direct debit mandates are formed whenever the consumer and the business have agreed to a contract or a trust that has been established between them on the elements of the administration of the business operation.

The Odoo platform employs an appropriate menu that is present on the Customers tab of the Odoo Accounting module to facilitate the handling of Direct Debit Mandates. You may use the menu to establish new Direct Debit Mandates for operations on the Odoo platform. The customer's name, IBAN (international bank account number), journal, SDD Scheme details, Identifier, Start date, and End date can all be entered in the creation window. Based on the Start Date and the End Date, the operational period for each of the eligible Direct Debit Mandates is determined.

Product Management

Product management plays a significant role in the business operations of a firm focused on products. With the characteristics of a specialised management tool, you will have complete control over the items being described. Using Odoo product management, you can specify every product and service your company provides. The Accounting module's items menu, which can be accessed through the Customer menu, displays all of the items defined in your business's operations.

Under the Products menu, you'll discover filtering and grouping options to assist you find the product from the list of ones described there. The Products menu may be seen in List, Kanban, and Activity views, with the last one being very helpful due to the image and a list of activities.

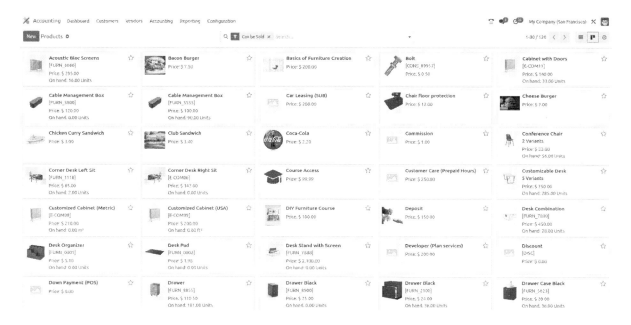

You will be able to change the product details provided under each product and add new ones by selecting the Create option from the menu. When you select to create a new product, a window will open asking you for details such as the product's name and whether it can be sold or purchased. You may also describe the product's look by selecting the image icon and a photo from your computer. Now that the essential characteristics of the product have been stated let's move on to the next stage of product configurations, where we will discuss the parts of how it may be specified in operation.

First, need to set up the general information sections. Here, you may specify whether the product category is a consumable, a service, or a storable good whose inventory should be managed by the platform's in-house inventory management module. Consumables are products that may be consumed or are perishable in a short period of time, typically food and other perishables with a limited shelf life.

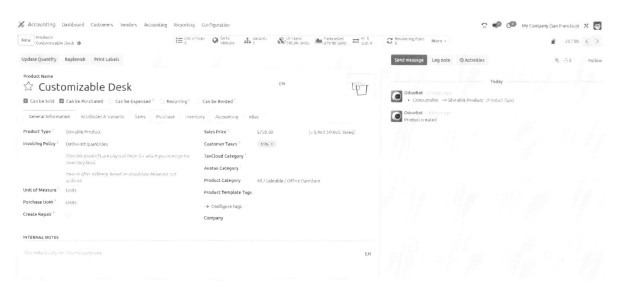

Products that can be stored have a longer expiration date and are less likely to be damaged. All non-consumable products are also included in this category. Service-based items are those that may be provided to the client as a service based on their requirements but are not physically present. If the product is only consumable, it will be possible to specify inventory. The product category can also be specified and selected from a drop-down menu. After we've established the sales price for the goods, you may specify the extra prices. Additionally, you may specify the Customer Taxes and the TaxCloud Category by selecting them from the dropdown menu. You can also provide any Internal Notes that must be specified for the particular product.

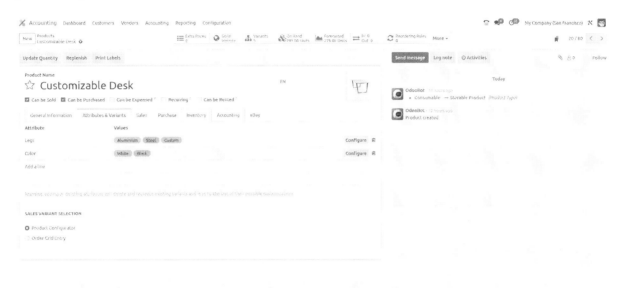

Additionally, under the variants page, all product variants used in business operations may be described. The "Add a line" option allows you to provide both the variant's values and characteristics. The number of alternatives will be shown on a smart button, as seen in the screenshot that goes with this sentence. You are able to add as many variations for a single product as you want, and they will all be shown under the same product description.

Purchase information elements, such as vendor bill management aspects, can be changed under the Purchase tab of the product description menu. Here, the vendor taxes that are connected to the product and that the vendor has indicated are defined. This section can be used to specify different taxes for operations at a certain time.

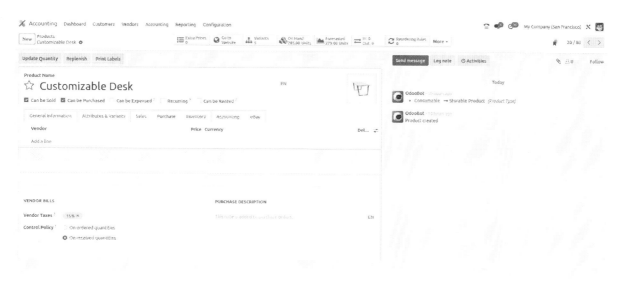

The Accounting tab of the product description window allows you to define the product's Accounting details. The drop-down box allows you to select one of the receivable components, such as the Income Account in this example. The Expense Account may be defined in the same way as the Payable elements. The income account keeps the earned revenue while selling an item to the customer and the expense account keeps the expense generated during the purchase of that item from any vendor.

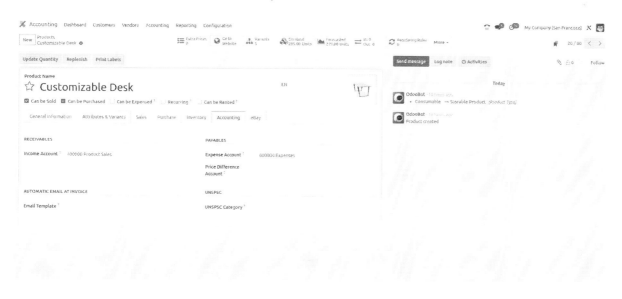

The Email Template may be specified under the section automatic email upon invoicing, which will send the customer a product-specific email after the invoice has been confirmed. After selecting one of the Variants choices in the Product creation description box, you will be directed to the Product Variants menu, as seen in the picture below. Name, attribute values, sales price, and cost are all defined here, as well as internal reference information. The Filtering and Group by options are also useful for excluding the essential Product Variants.

Additionally, as already stated, the Products tab allows you to define products that are also services. For example, hotel accommodation is one of the services provided by the hotel and is classified as a product. If your hotel offers different rooms and packages for each product catalog, you can define each product as a different product or a variation of it. In order for it to function as a service-based product, the product type is additionally defined as a service. The other characteristics of a service-based product are the same as those of a consumable-based one.

The product's financial management components will serve as the foundation for the Odoo Accounting module's product management characteristics. With the aid of the specialized Product management menu, you will be able to control the operation based on the needs of your organization. Moving on, the customer management aspects of Odoo's accounting operations will be covered in the part that follows.

Customer Management

The management of customers will be the main objective of running a range of businesses, but the majority of them will fall short in terms of having specialized management, which will make it simpler to run tasks. The well-defined Odoo ERP solution enables effective business administration throughout the whole organization. Furthermore, specialized business management capabilities covering all aspects of corporate operations, including customer management, are available.

In the Accounting component of Odoo-based company operations, a dedicated customer management section menu is provided for all operations connected to customer management activities in the Accounting components. As seen in the following picture, you may view a depiction of all of your company's clients, including both businesses and private people, by selecting the Customers option from the Customers page of the Accounting module dashboard. Users will be given access to all of the data through the Customers menu, which can be seen in List and Kanban views, as shown in the picture below. Additionally, you may filter data by utilizing the Group by and Filter options that are offered.

You may edit the customer's data at any time by selecting it from the list, and you can add a new client by clicking the Create button.

Before entering the Name, you must first select whether the client is an individual or a business in the client creation box. You must also include the company's address, functioning location, and zip code. The Tax ID must also be provided for the operational financial components.

Additionally, contact details like a phone number, a mobile number, an email address, and a website link should be included. Additionally, the platform's specified Customer Tags may be assigned, which will be defined in the Odoo platform's Customer administration element. Additionally, you will have the option to directly create new Tags from this menu.

Then, utilizing the available ADD option in the distinct tab 'Contacts & Addresses', we must define the required Customer's Contacts & Addresses. It is possible to specify many addresses for the activities of a certain business or individual.

If you select Add contacts and addresses, the following pop-up window will appear where you can specify the contact. First, it is necessary to determine what address is assigned in this case. Billing address, shipping address, other addresses, private address, and tracking address are just a few examples of contact information type options. The tracking address is the address where tracking reports are sent.

Contact information must now be specified after specifying the address type. It is necessary to specify the name, address, postal code, and country of the contact person. In addition to the email address, phone number, and mobile phone, you can also specify all the comments about the respective address. You can add different contact details for a specific customer. You can do this by choosing Save and New, or you can use Save and Close instead.

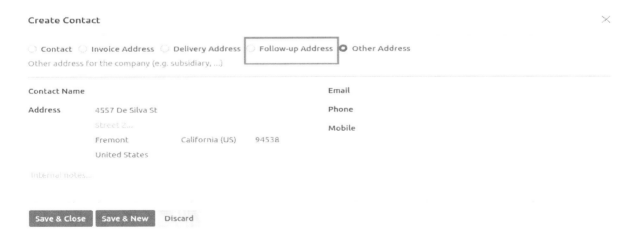

The Contacts & Addresses page for a specified customer displays all addresses specified for that customer. Then the customer's sales and purchase settings must be filled. The seller's details, payment terms, and price list must be specified on the Sales tab. In the Purchase tab, you can also set the payment terms and payment method. The Financial Information tab contains a definition of the Fiscal Position. Other factors were also taken into account, such as the customer reference received and the industry or sector.

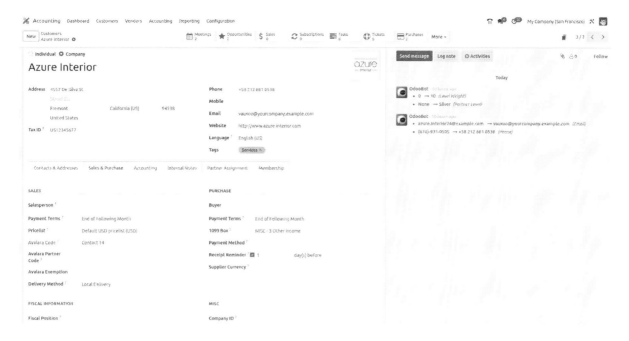

Additionally, the given Accounting tab may be utilized to specify the Customer's Accounting element. Account Receivable and Account Payable accounting entry components should be established using the available drop-down menu options.

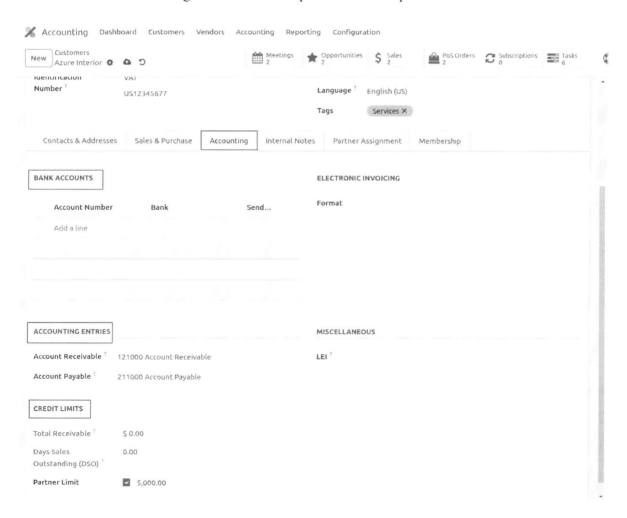

You can add company bank account details using the Add Line option, which is available if you need to create multiple accounts. You can use the "Accounting" tab to view a description of your account information. The menu shown in the following screenshot appears when you select the Add Row option. Here you can describe the account number and bank details.

To keep the accounting entries accounts receivable and payable can be added to the respective fields. In the credit limit section, you can set the credit limit of the partner, and the total amount that the customer owes you, which we see as the total claim.

All internal functions of the system can be explained in the Internal Notes tab. In this case, the data can be provided together with the invoice warning, which can also be a notice depending on the situation. Depending on the characteristics of the action, alerts and notifications can be configured separately.

On the smart tabs of the partner form, you can see the partner's scheduled meetings, completed sales and purchases, partner invoices and totals, supplier invoices, and the partner book, which lists the partner's debts and claims.

218

By selecting the available Smart Tab for "Due" which will take you to the Follow-up report menu as shown in the following screenshot, you can further select the specified due amount. Information about the invoice and Transmission amount is defined here. For a clear understanding of the operations, you can refer to the Follow-Up part described earlier in this book.

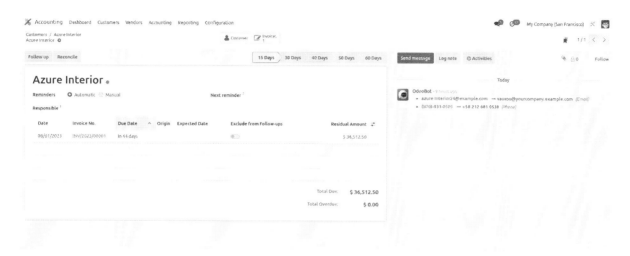

As shown in the following image, you can also select the Invoice tab to view all invoices associated with the relevant customer, providing comprehensive information. Invoice number, customer details, payment period, follow-up information, tax exemption amount, total amount, status, and payment status.

Furthermore, if the client is also a business partner, a Partner Ledger will be generated and may be accessed by selecting one of the choices under "Partner Ledger" in the customer creation menu. The Partner Ledger will include a description of each invoice as well as information on the invoice, including the number, journal information, account information, references, due date, matching number, beginning balance, debit amount, and credit amount.

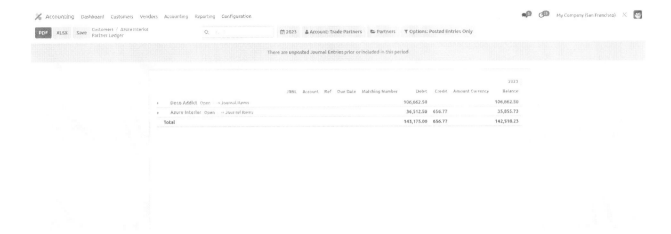

Once each component of the customer has been established, the client may be stored for future operations. You can also modify the customer data whenever you want by choosing the Customer from the list and then choosing the modify option that is shown.

Now that we've covered the many customer management capabilities available in the Odoo Accounting module, let's move on to the next portion of the chapter, where we'll look at the vendor management features and the several Odoo alternatives.

Vendor Management

Just as customer management is essential for business, supplier management must be effective for the business to run smoothly. You can choose from multiple vendors for each product in your enterprise, and likely have multiple vendors for the same product. The best provider for your business depends on various operating factors, including price, product or service quality, and other important factors.

Enterprise operations require a management solution that can efficiently meet the challenges of managing multiple vendors. Effectiveness in managing the accounting component is very important, and this can only be achieved with the help of dedicated accounting applications. The management of single and multiple suppliers in business operations is supported by the Odoo Accounting module. Additionally, the Odoo platform includes a supplier management tab specifically designed to improve your efficiency with exclusive and powerful tools and menus.

The Vendor management page has options for handling vendor bills, refunds, vendor receipts, bill payments, batch payments on vendor bills, items based on vendor descriptions, and a separate vendor management menu. Let's go on to analysing each of these menus and choices under the Vendors tab of the Accounting module in the section that follows.

Vendor Bill Management

Managing invoices for purchases made is an important part of the operation. Suppliers prepare invoices according to the agreed terms regarding the price of the products and the quantities to be supplied or delivered. The Vendor tab of the Odoo accounting module gives access to the Dedicated Vendor Bill management menu. All vendor bills created and sent to the company are displayed here. The bill number, vendor, bill date, due date, reference, next action, details of unapplied taxes, total amount due, and status are provided. By selecting the appropriate invoice and using the edit option, you have the opportunity to change the information on the specified invoice.

The Create option will present you with the Bill creation window, seen in the accompanying screenshot, if you want to create a new bill. The vendor bill number will be automatically displayed, but you'll need to specify the vendor's information, including the bill reference, payment reference, receipt bank, and auto-complete information. Bill Date, the date the bill is created, Accounting Date, the date the entries are to be recorded in the ledger, Due Date, Journal Details, and the Currency in which the transactions are carried out are all examples of dates that should be noted. Furthermore, by choosing the Add a Line option, the Invoicing lines for the relevant Vendor Bill can be specified. Here, the product information, label, account information, analytical accounting information, Quantity, Price, Tax information as well as the Subtotal will be defined. By choosing the Add a Section option, new sections can be created, and the Add a Note option can be used to add notes to the invoices.

Additionally, the bill of purchase orders can be quickly generated using the Autocomplete fields. We can select Purchase Order from the Autocomplete form rather than entering the Products, Quantities, Price, and other details one at a time in the Order Line. As a result, the Bill form will automatically receive updates to all the Purchase Order data. A single bill against several purchase orders for the specific vendor can be generated if we include multiple purchase orders as well. The Vendor Bill Number is generated automatically after we save all of this data, and the source document for the generated bill, which is the Purchase Order numbers separated with a comma, is shown in the list view of the bill.

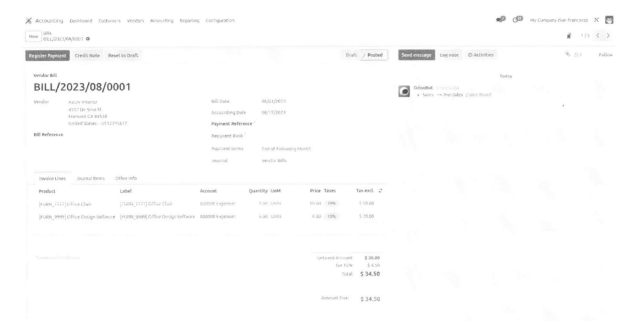

Once the products have been added to the Order line, the Journal Items page will automatically display the Accounts that are affected and the amounts that are credited or debited. The Ledgers involved during the Bill production can be seen here. Furthermore, the Account Payable, Expense Account, and Tax Account are impacted in Continental accounting throughout the Bill preparation process. Because the Account Payable is an asset by nature and the asset is losing value, the Account Payable gets credited. Additionally, the expense account is by its very nature an expense, and as the expense rises, the expense account is debited together with the tax account.

While in Anglo-Saxon Accounting, the Ledgers are affected when a bill is created. Here, the stock input account and tax account will be debited while the Account Payable will be credited. because after the sales have been confirmed, the Anglo-Saxon Accounting Expense Accounts will be impacted.

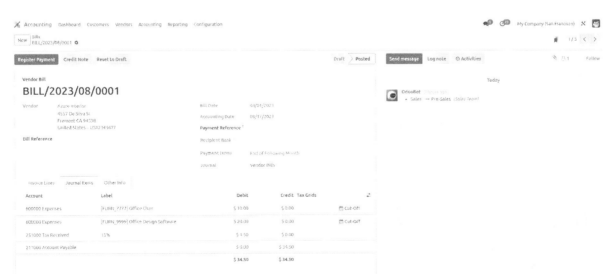

Once the vendor bill has been generated, you can choose to confirm the payment by selecting the option to register the payment. The Register Payment menu will appear for you, as shown in the accompanying screenshot. In this case, the payment mechanism can be either manual, SEPA credit transfer, or checks. It is possible to define the Receipt Bank Account information as well as the Amount, Payment Date, and Memo information. You should choose from the various Create Payment choices once all the aspects have been defined.

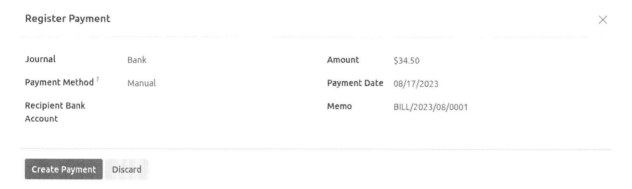

The Account Payable will be debited once the payment has been made, and the Outstanding Payments Account will be credited. This Outstanding Payments Account will be included in the setup of the Bank or Cash Journal for which the entries are transferred to the Outstanding Payment Account, and only after a bank statement reconciliation will the amount be transferred to the bank. This means that the outstanding Payment Account will be used for reconciliation rather than the Account Payable.

Thus, after reconciliation, the Bank Account is credited, and the Outstanding Payments Account is debited. The relevant Vendor bill will be provided with a label as In Payment once the payment has been registered and completed, as illustrated in the screenshot below. The label will show as Paid if the payment has been completed.

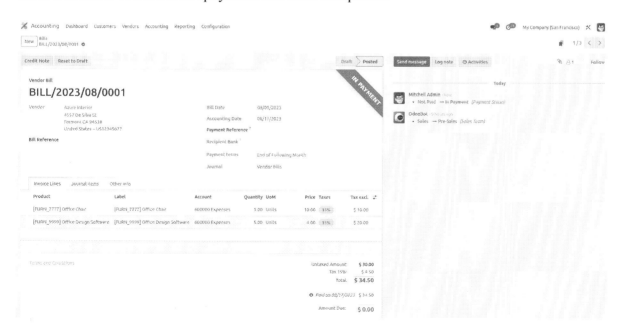

By choosing one of the Debit Note options from the menu, it is also possible to define the Debit Note for the specific vendor bill. You will be led to the pop-up window seen in the following screenshot after choosing to create a debit note. Here, the Use Precise Journal section allows you to specify the specific journal to be used, the Debit Note Date, and the Reason for the Refund. Additionally, the Copy Lines option can be enabled, which is helpful for copying the Credit lines when necessary for adjustments.

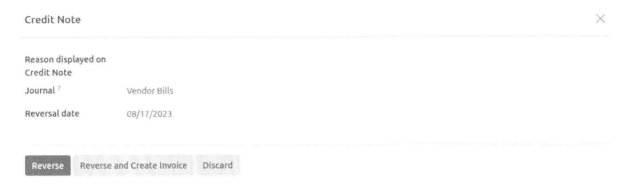

Once the description of the debit note is complete, you can choose one of the alternatives to reverse the produced vendor bill payment and send the credit note to the appropriate vendor. For the accounting operations management of the specific vendor operation, the Credit Note function, which is available in the Customer's configuration here as well as in the Vendor menu, is a beneficial tool. Let's proceed to the Refunds option in the following section, which is the next highlighted menu under Vendor management.

Manage Your Refunds

Similar to giving refunds to vendors based on business operations, receiving refunds from vendors likewise happens as part of a business' operations. The Vendor Management tabs in Odoo's Accounting module include a unique menu that supports the Refunds on Vendors sections. Here, all completed refund operations as well as those that have already been started will be defined. The Refund will be described along with the Bill Number, Vendor Name, Bill Date, Reference Information, Next Activity Scheduled for the Refund Operations, Tax Excluded Amount Along With The Total Amount, and the Status of the Operations.

You will be able to edit the defined Refund procedures that have already been carried out by using the Edit option present in the relevant menu where each of the Refunds is being defined. You can choose the Create option from the Refund menu to open the window depicted in the following screenshot in order to create a new refund operation.

Along with the vendor's name, the bill reference, payment reference, and recipient bank can all be added in this field. Additionally, the Bill Date, Accounting Date, Due Date, Journal Details, and Currency can all be defined. The Product Details, Label, Account Details, and Analytical Accounting Details can all be defined under the Invoicing Lines. The Subtotal, Quantity, Price, and Tax information will all be defined. The Add a line option now allows you to define products, and the Add a section option allows you to expand the Product Lines with new sections. A determined custom note may also be included in the Refund description. The Total of the refund bill both taxed and Untaxed Amounts along with the Tax details will be defined.

The details of the Journal Account, Label, Analytical Tags, Debits, and Credits, as well as the Tax Grid, will be defined under the Journal Items of the relevant Refund. Additionally, the Account Payable will be Credited and the Expense Account will be Debited throughout the Reverse Billing procedure. By choosing the accessible Add a Line option, you can add new Journal details.

Additionally, you can adjust the Accounting specifics, such as the Incoterms, Fiscal Position, Intrastat Country, Intrastat Transport method, and the Cash Routing Method, in the Other Info tab of the relevant Refunds menu. Additionally, the options to specify and put into action in the specific Refund procedure include Post Automatically and To check.

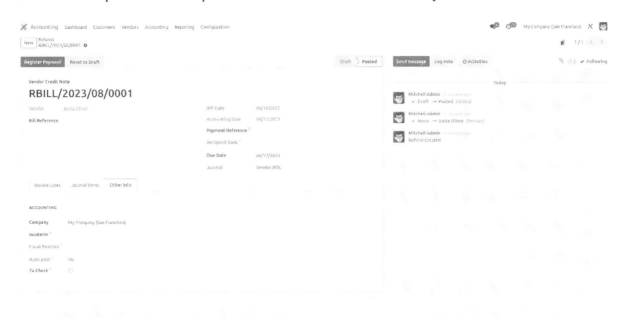

The Register Payment option will bring you to the Register Payment box, as shown in the accompanying screenshot, once all the Configurations components of the Refund have been established. You may then choose to save the description. The Journal and the Payment Method can both be set to Manual, SEPA Direct Debit, or Batch Deposit in this case. Along with the Payment Date and the Memo on each return, it is also possible to define the Amount, Currency, and other details of the refund. You can choose the Create Payment option once the configuration details for the Register Payment have been finished.

When the payment is registered, the Account Payable will be debited and the Outstanding Payments will be credited. Once the payment is in processing, you will be debited with the In Payment the appropriate Refund menu. You have the option to Reset To Draft on the specific refund that has been mentioned if the payment has been made; otherwise, the label will show as Paid.

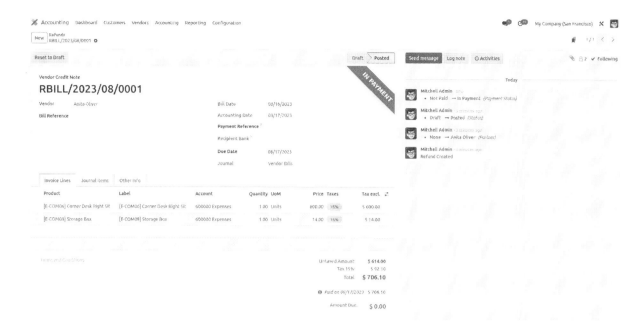

The defined menu can be used to manage refunds for vendor operations in an efficient manner. Let's move on to the following section, where the management of vendor receipts will be covered, now that we are clear on the aspects of refund management.

Vendor Receipt Management

You must give the vendors an acknowledgment of the received products as soon as the products are received in accordance with the purchase orders that have been received. The Vendors tabs of the Odoo Accounting module make it easy to create and maintain receipts as well as their financial components. All receipts created in conjunction with business activities are listed under the Vendor Management tab of the Receipt Management menu of the Accounting module. To retrieve the necessary Receipt from the menu, you may Filter and Group by the list.

Additionally, you may edit the data included in any specified receipt by selecting that receipt from the menu and then choosing the Edit option. To access the box where new receipts may be made, select the Create option. Below is a screenshot of this window. Here, the purchase receipt number will be shown automatically, and you may define the vendor, bill reference, payment reference, receipt bank, bill date, accounting date, due date, journal, and currency of operation by typing them in manually or selecting them from the drop-down box.

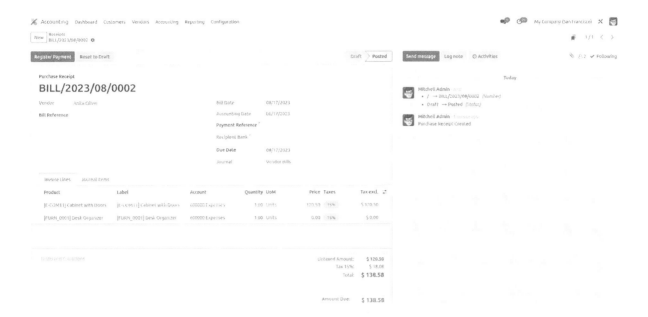

The Products can be specified in the Product Lines by choosing the Add an Available Line option. By selecting the Add an available section option, new sections can be added to the invoice. Additionally, much like in the Refunds management section that was described earlier in this chapter, the Journal Entries may be defined in the relevant menu along with the Other Information for the Receipts. You may register payment after making the necessary adjustments for the relevant receipt by selecting the corresponding option from the menu, which will take you to the pop-up window shown in the picture below.

Here, you can define the Journal and the Payment Method as SEPA Credit Transfer, Manual, or Checks to specify many parts of the Register Payment procedure. In addition, you may create a new recipient bank account or select an existing one from the drop-down menu to set the recipient bank account data.

It is also possible to specify the amount and kind of currency to be used for payment. Additionally, the Payment Date and the Memo details of the relevant Payment can be defined.

As seen in the following screenshot of the Receipts, a label indicating that the Receipts is In Payments will appear once the Payments have been registered in the appropriate Receipts. In this situation, the label will show as Paid if the payment is successful.

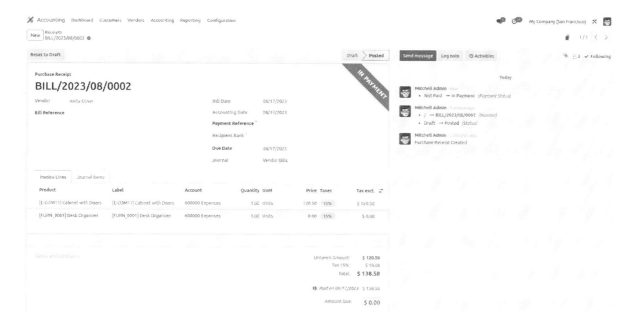

Receipts and their administration will be a valuable resource in the management of the accounting components of product delivery that must be described concisely and precisely. Using this feature of the Odoo Accounting module, you may improve the financial management skills of your business. Moving on, let's discuss managing vendor bill payments in the part that follows.

Vendor Amounts to Settle

Comparable to the Vendor amount to settle, the opportunity to view all of the vendor repayments that the business must make is included in the Vendor amount to settle.

Within the **Vendor** menu is the **Vendor Amount to Settle** option.

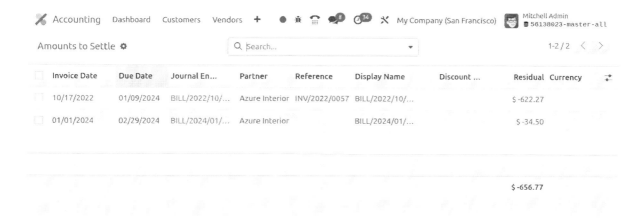

Within the list view are the following details: invoice date, due date, journal entry, partner, reference, display name, discount amount, residual, and currency.

Manage Vendor Bill Payments

To effectively manage vendor invoices and related payments, use the special management menu in Odoo's accounting module. A company's product supplier operations are dominated by vendor invoice payment management, which requires a dedicated operating system. You can define the elements of supplier invoice payment management in a coordinated and methodical way as part of business operations using Odoo's accounting module.

The screenshots below illustrate the vendor invoice management menu in Odoo's accounting module. All payments made with vendor invoices are displayed here. You will see the details of the payment, including the date and invoice number. In addition, information about journals, payment methods, suppliers, batch payments, embedded amounts and payment currencies, payment statuses, and the SDD scheme will be covered. You can sort the required payment information using the standard Filter and group by settings. Additionally, you can like unique filter and group settings for later use according to your filter requirements.

By selecting Create, you can make new payments. This will show you the creation menu shown below. Here, either money sent or money received must be initially set as the payment type. After that, you can set the partner type, customer/supplier details, destination account details, allocated amount and currency details, payment date, and note. You can also set the Payment as an internal transfer by selecting the Whether Internal Transfer option. The payment method can be either Manual or Cheque, and the journal can be selected from the drop-down menu. Depending on the situation, the account number of the Recipient can also be specified.

As soon as the payment setup is complete, the next step is to confirm the defined payments. This can be done by selecting Confirm and these vendor payments can then be added to vendor bills. As shown in the screenshot below, the text "Send" will appear when the payments are confirmed.

Now if you are paying by 'checks', you need to select the check payment method as shown in the screenshot below.

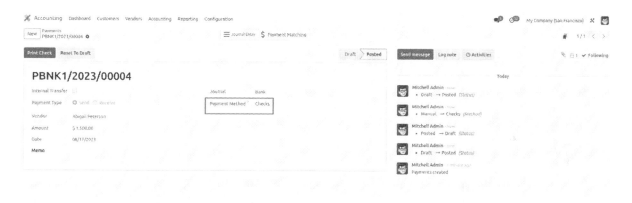

If the payment aspects are configured to use checks, you can select Confirm to see the pre-numbered checks that will be printed and set up the next check. The Print option can be selected when the Print Pre numbered Checks option is set.

Print Pre-numbered Checks   ✕

Please enter the number of the first pre-printed check that you are about to print on.

This will allow to save on payments the number of the corresponding check.

Next Check Number   1|

Print   Cancel

If Check Layout is not set, the following warning message will appear as shown in the following image. The Go to Settings Panel option is available.

Odoo Warning   ✕

You have to choose a check layout. For this, go in Invoicing/Accounting Settings, search for 'Checks layout' and set one.

Go to the configuration panel   Cancel

This will take you to the Settings menu in the Accounting module where you can configure Checks items under Vendor Payments. Control Layout can be enabled here and one of the three available options is Print Check (TOP), Print Check (MIDDLE), or Print Check (BOTTOM).

It allows you to make new payments to suppliers or payments created by them to the company. Odoo Payment Management is the best tool to manage the accounting functions related to the financial part of these payments. Let's move on to the next section where the components of the vendor bill batch payments are defined.

Batch Payments on Vendor Bills

In the real-time operations of the business, you will make numerous purchases from a vendor at various times while the firm is open for business. According to a formal agreement or an arrangement that both parties have reached, you won't be making payments for each individual vendor bill when it comes to the purchases you bought; rather, you'll be paying them all at once. Sometimes the agreement is based on the quantity of bills or invoices rather than their total cash amount.

In order to support the features of the Batch payments on vendor bills, the Odoo platform provides a special menu of operations where all Batch payments relevant to vendor bills are configured. Here, you can find definitions for the Reference number, Bank information, Batch Payment Date, Amount, and Status. To sort out all the declared Batch payments from the extensive list, utilize the Filtering and Group by options that are always available in any menu on the Odoo platform.

To make a new Batch payment on vendor invoices, select the make option, which will lead you to the Batch payments creation window as seen in the accompanying picture. Enter new values for the Bank Type, Bank, Payment Method, Date, and Reference in this situation, or select the relevant options from the drop-down box. Additionally, the Batch Content information where the Payments may be batched can be set by utilizing the available Add a Line option.

When you select to add the payment to the batch, a pop-up window with a list of all the payments that need to be made to the suppliers will display. You can choose from a variety of payments by utilizing the provided Tick Box. The relevant payment will be described here, including the date of the invoice, the bill number, the journal information, the payment method, the customer information, the amount, the payment status, the SDD scheme information, and the currency specifications. Using the also available Filtering and Group by options, you may order the defined Payments.

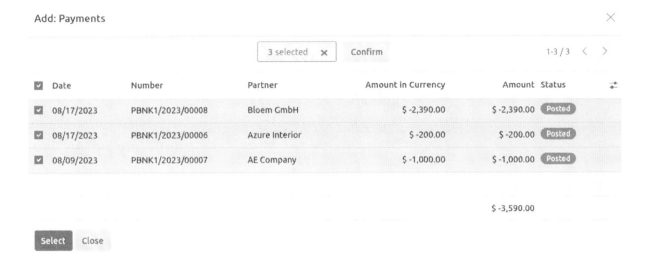

Once the payments have been added to the correct batch, you may approve the transaction and select the Register Payment option to have the batch payments show on vendor invoices.

Now that we've covered how to manage batch payments on vendor bills, let's move on to the next part, which will cover the Products menu based on vendor description.

Products Menu Based on Vendor Description

Vendor operations should be taken into account while determining the product of operation in business operations. The product descriptions should agree with how the vendors describe it for the business to operate properly. There is a unique Products option in the Vendor tab of the Odoo Accounting module where you may specify the Products depending on the Vendors. Similar to how it supports customer operation, this menu will support the product administration component.

The Vendor tab on the Accounting module dashboard allows access to the Products menu depending on the vendor description. The menu will specify each operation's product depending on the vendor, and it may be seen in List, Kaban, or Activity view. In addition to using the already available Filter and Group by options, you may additionally sort the necessary item out of the lengthy list. The snapshot that follows shows the Products menu as it has been set up in the Kanban view.

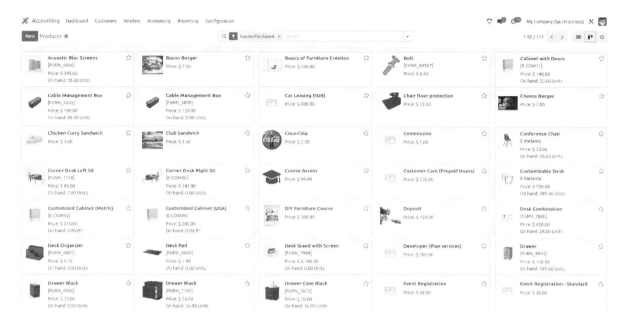

By choosing the Create Available option, you may add new items to the menu and be sent to the Creation window seen in the picture below.

Here, it is possible to define the Product Name as well as its features, such as whether it may be sold or purchased. Under the General Information tab, you may also set the Product Type, Product Category, Internal Reference, Barcode description, Sales Price, Customer Taxes, TaxCloud Category data, and Cost information. The criteria may also be used to define the Internal Notes. The other tabs in the Product creation window are similar to the one covered in this chapter's Customer management section's Product management section.

235

The product management component of vendor operations is managed similarly to how customer operations are managed. The section after this one covers the specific Vendor management menu.

Dedicated Vendor Management Menu

The management of the suppliers is equally important to a business as the management of the consumers since you will be cooperating with several vendors of operations in real-time. The numerous suppliers of operations for a particular commodity or service that are chosen based on internal business reasons should also be monitored. In Odoo, there is a distinct and well-designed Vendor administration menu located under the Vendor's tabs of the Accounting module. Along with the business partners who also act as vendors in the operations, all vendor information will be outlined here, exactly like in the customer menu.

All of the vendors for the defined operations will be presented in the menu, along with some basic information about them. The menu is also available in list style, which includes a list of each vendor. Filtering and grouping options are available by default, and you may create your own to assist you sort and filter out the essential suppliers from the extensive list.

If you wish to create a new vendor, select the Create option to bring up the Vendor creation menu, as seen in the picture below. The Vendor should be identified as either an Individual or a Company, and then their Name, Company Address, Operating Country, and ZIP Code should be provided. Additionally, the Tax ID, and contact information, such as the firm's phone number and cellphone number, email address, and website address, should be mentioned. On the relevant Vendor, you may define the tags for internal usage.

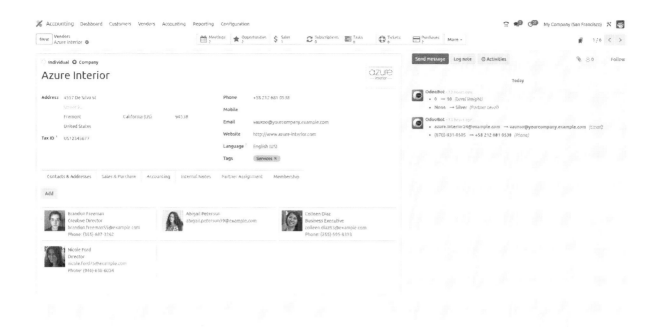

Under the Contacts & Addresses page, you may enter all the names and operational addresses of people associated with the Vendor as well as the names of people your company interacts with in regard to the purchase activity. Select the Add option in the succeeding pop-up box to specify the Contact and their address. First, it must be decided which kind of address is appropriate in this situation. Among the possibilities for Contact type are Invoice Address, Delivery Address, Other Addresses, Private Address, and Follow-up Address. After specifying the Address type, you must now elaborate on the Contact Information. You must include the Contact's Name, Address, Zip Code, and Country. Any Notes about the relevant address can be supplied in addition to the Email address, Phone number, and Mobile number. You can choose between Save & New and Save & Close from the available selections when entering new Contact information for a chosen Vendor.

The Sales & Purchases page must be established next, where you may configure every aspect of the Purchase operations with the vendor. In the event that sales are being conducted and the pertinent Vendor is also a business partner, you must set the elements of the sales activities. Under the Sales tab, specifics regarding the Salesperson, Payment Terms, and Pricelist should be defined. You may also set the Payment Terms and the Payment Method under the Purchase tab. The Fiscal Position is defined under the Fiscal Information Tab. Other nonspecific variables, such as references obtained from the vendor, may also be defined, along with the business or industries in which they operate.

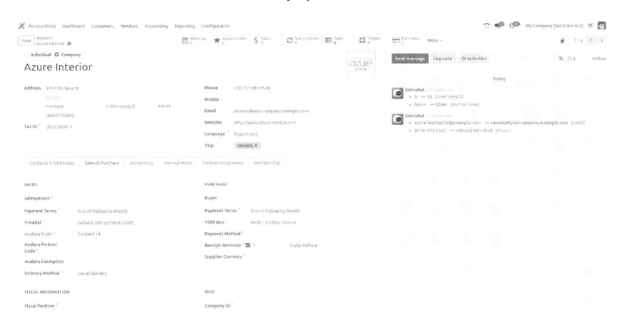

You may establish the bank account details for the company operations under the Accounting tab for the vendor by utilizing the Add a Line option. Additionally, if necessary, several accounts may be defined. To get a description of the Accounts' details, utilize the "Accounting" tab. A menu displaying the account number and bank details will appear when you select the "Add a line" option. We will be able to record various bank accounts for partners. Accounting Entities like Accounts Receivable and Accounts Payable can be selected for the specified Accounts of Company Activities.

Additionally, partner credit restrictions may be defined for partner receivables. The Total Receivable field will be able to display the total receivables from the partner. As a result, when an invoice for a partner is added, a warning notice stating that the partner has used all of their available sales credit will show.

Along with a warning on the invoice that may or may not be a message, the Primary Vendor information may also be seen under the Internal Notes tab. By customizing the warning and message definitions, you may always decide not to get any alerts or notifications about the vendor.

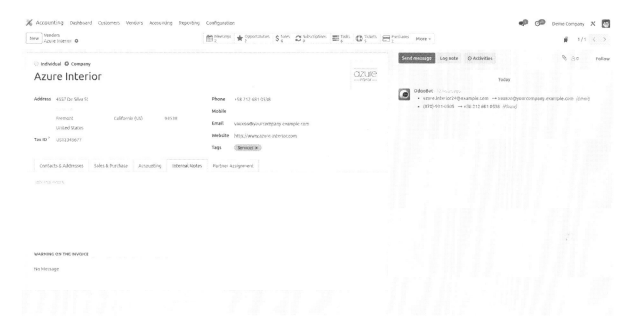

The effectiveness of the vendor operations inside the company will be aided by all of the stated vendor management tools, which may be managed and controlled by these distinct tools and features.

In conclusion, this chapter focused entirely on discussing the aspects of vendor and customer financial management that use the specialized Odoo Accounting module. In-depth coverage is given to all of the various tools and menus, as well as all of the functional tools for managing customers and vendors. The Accounting management functions of the Odoo Accounting module will be covered in detail in the next chapter, along with many of its numerous components.

Chapter 5
Mastering Odoo 17 Accounting Management Tools

Mastering Odoo 17 Accounting Management Tools

The Odoo Accounting module will assist with the company's overall financial management and will guarantee that the accounting operations operate smoothly and successfully. Furthermore, due to the specialized tools and functional possibilities that are supplied in connection to all aspects of the company's financial operations, the Odoo Accounting module may be regarded as one of the most advanced finance management systems on the market right now.

In the previous chapter, we focused on financial management, vendor, and customer factors using the Odoo Accounting module. We considered all of the menus available for managing customers and vendors, as well as the specialized choices available to assist operational performance.

In this chapter, we'll focus on the Odoo Accounting module's accounting management features, which will contribute to the efficiency of corporate operations and absolute control over its financial management. In this chapter, we will discuss the following Odoo Accounting module features:

Each of these features will be discussed in detail using examples and illustrated sample hosts from the Odoo platform to ensure a full grasp.

- The dedicated Accounting management tools
- Well-defined Accounting Management Action
- Useful Accounting Ledgers
- Journal Management aspects and
- Other miscellaneous tools and functions have been used.

Journal Entries

Effective record-keeping starts with journal entries. The act of recording any transaction, whether financial or stock, is known as a journal entry. A journal entry records the transaction of a business in debit and credit accounts.

From the Accounting menu, you can see every journal entry that has been made by the company. Odoo has five different kinds of journals. The several sorts of journals are sales, buy, bank, cash, and miscellaneous.

Inside the Journal Entries are all of the entries that belong to each journal. From there, you may see the entry's posted date, sequence number, partner name, reference, journal, firm name, total amount, and status.

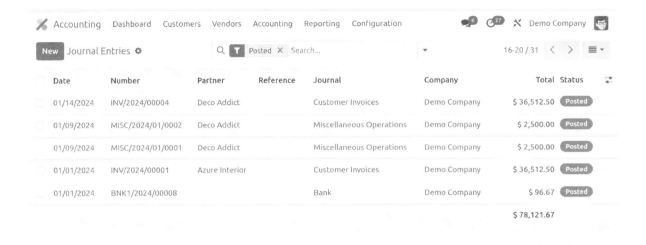

You can also manually add journal entries in Odoo, which is feasible if the New button is used. First, enter the Reference, Accounting Date, and Journal in the creation form. Users can designate the Journal items inside the Journal Items tab.

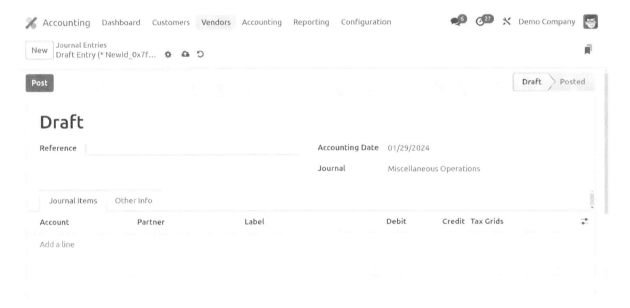

Once the required journal entries have been added, select the **Post** button at the top of the screen. The post will then be made.

Journal Items

From the Journal items menu under the Accounting menu, each journal item can be examined independently. From there, you may view the date, journal entry, partner, label, and credit and debit accounts. The entries can be reconciled using the Matching.

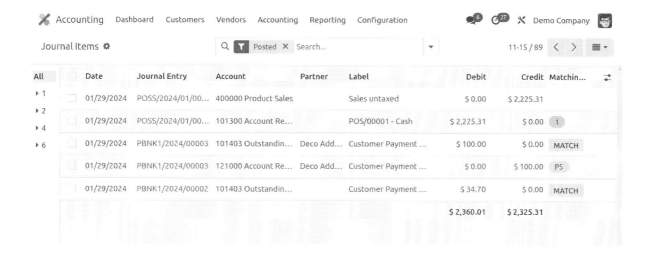

Accounting Management Tools

The Odoo Accounting Management module's primary function is to handle accounting and financial management. The preceding chapter examined the Configurations parts, the Accounting module interface, and the financial management capabilities for a company's customers and vendors. Thanks to Odoo's particular financial management features accessible under the Accounting tab of the module, you will have unique capabilities that assist total finance administration from a single platform. The Automatic Transfer, Analytic Items, Budgets, Assets, Reconcile, and Lock dates, for example, are well-defined functional menus that will assist the company's financial management activities.

Any Odoo user who has gained the necessary accounting management authorization will have access to these menus and capabilities. Furthermore, owing to the configurable tools and essential options in these menus, the Odoo Accounting component may be precisely specified. Let us proceed by completely understanding the various Accounting management menus and their components.

Automatic Transfer

Running an automated transfer operation in the accounting system of the organization may be advantageous for normal business operations. The primary purpose of using Odoo is to streamline daily chores, and Odoo Accounting assists with this by streamlining daily tasks. Using the Automatic Transfer feature menu, which is accessible in the Accounting menu of the module, you can configure the Transfer operations that will automate the function of sending funds from one account to another at particular intervals. The Automatic Transfers option, for example, can be utilized if you need to send money from one account to another within a certain time range and then repeat the procedure after each time frame. We can use this methodology if, for example, we use a given percentage of an amount for any type of business project and the required amounts should be transferred within a specific interval of time such as monthly, quarterly, or yearly, continuously until there is a manual stoppage of the process.

All newly generated automated transfers are defined in the menu, along with their names, start dates, stop dates, and frequency of operations. You can sort the desired Transfer data by utilizing the Filter and Group by options.

By selecting the Create option, you may create new automated transfer operations, which will take you to the Transfer Creations window, as seen in the picture below. Enter the Name of the Automatic Transfer first, followed by the Operation Period from the Start Date to the End Date.

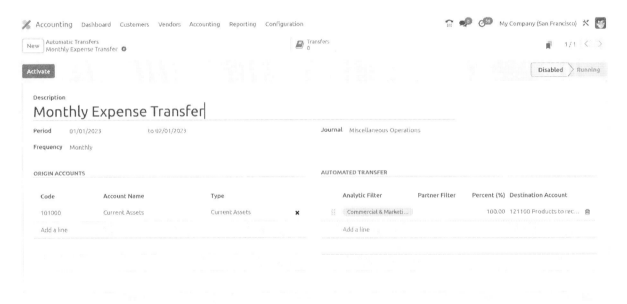

Furthermore, the Journal of Operations specification allows for the construction of a new Journal or the selection of the right Journal for the Automatic Transfer from a drop-down menu.

By selecting the Add a Line option, you may also set the Partner Filter, Account Percentage, Analytical Filter, and Destination Account, in addition to the Automatic Transfer information. A Transfer operation that you are about to create and implement in operations might have many Automatic Transfers added to it.

Additionally, the Origin Accounts for the appropriate Automatic Transfer may be set by selecting the Add an available line option on the relevant tab. When you opt to add an Origin Account, you will get a pop-up window similar to the one seen in the picture below. The account of operations for all of the company's accounting activities will be defined here. The accounts will have the following information defined: Code, Account Name, Type, Account Currency, and a setup option. You may also pick the Allow Reconciliation option, which will automatically reconcile the account using a slider.

Add: Origin Accounts

Import ⚙   🔍 Search... ▾   1-50 / 50 ‹ ›

	Code	Account Name	Type	Allow Reconciliation	Account Currency	Company	
☐	101300	Account Receivable (PoS)	Receivable	⬤◯		My Company (San Franci...	
☐	101401	Bank	Bank and Cash			My Company (San Franci...	
☐	101402	Bank Suspense Account	Current Assets	◯		My Company (San Franci...	
☐	101403	Outstanding Receipts	Current Assets	⬤◯		My Company (San Franci...	
☐	101404	Outstanding Payments	Current Assets	⬤◯		My Company (San Franci...	
☐	101501	Cash	Bank and Cash			My Company (San Franci...	
☐	101502	Cash 2	Bank and Cash			My Company (San Franci...	
☐	101503	Cash 3	Bank and Cash			My Company (San Franci...	
☐	101701	Liquidity Transfer	Current Assets	⬤◯		My Company (San Franci...	
☐	110100	Stock Valuation	Current Assets	◯		My Company (San Franci...	
☐	110200	Stock Interim (Received)	Current Assets	⬤◯		My Company (San Franci...	

Select   New   Close

Once you have done configuring the Automatic Transfer by identifying the Origin Accounts and other configuration criteria, you must save the applicable Automatic Transfer window. After adding the Origin Account, you must add the Destination Account to the Automated Transfer. You can optionally specify a percentage of the entire transfer to the target account. As a result, the relevant proportion of the amount from the Origin Account will be automatically transferred to the Destination Account at each interval (monthly or annually) that is set. At that time, the Automatic Transfer must simply be triggered and verified. Following that, you will find Activate choices that may be selected to activate and operate the related Automatic Transfer.

The Compute Transfer operations option will supply you with all the data about the Transfer that has been triggered to be in operation as soon as the relevant Automatic Transfer is enabled and operating and you need to compute the Transfer details in the long run. The smart tab Transfers in Draft Entry, which may be submitted manually or automatically, has a list of all the produced transfers. If the Post Automatically option is selected, the required journal entries will be automatically posted on the accounting date. Transfer operations will continue from the given accounts until the set period of operations is reached, at which point they will be automatically discontinued. There is also a Disable option that may be used to cease the applicable Automatic Transfer procedures.

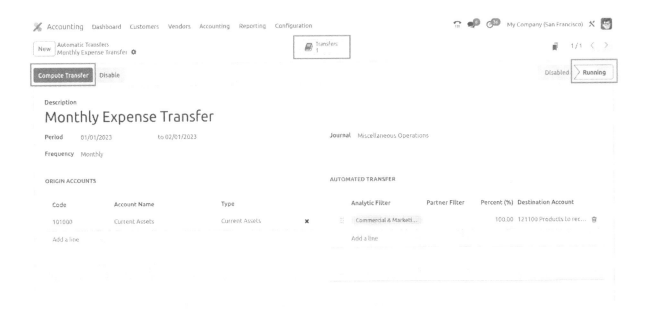

The Odoo Accounting module has an extra options menu called the Automatic Transfer Management tool, which allows planned transfer activities to be carried out automatically for a certain period. Let's move on to the part that discusses the Budget management option in the Odoo Accounting module.

Budgets

When it comes to how a firm does business, the budget and spending management are two critical components. Almost all organizations, large or small, will create a budget to plan for the following fiscal year. The Odoo platform supports budget planning with unique menu choices in the Accounting module. The Budget option, accessible from the Accounting menu on the Accounting module dashboard, displays all of the specifics of the Budgets that are presently being established. We will establish the Budget Name, Start Date, End Date, Responsible Person, and Status in this section. Users may filter the essential Budget from the extensive list by utilizing the Filtering and Group by option.

You can choose the Create option to bring up the creation window, as shown in the following image, to create new budgets. Here, the Budget Name, the Responsible Person, and the Operation Period, which specify the Start and End Dates, should all be stated at the outset. By choosing the Add an available line option, the Budget Lines for the specific Budget can also be defined. For the previously set budgets, you must indicate the budgetary position, analytical accounts, start date, end date, and planned amount. Additionally, while the relevant Budget is in effect, the Practical Amount, Theoretical Amount, and Achievement percentage will all be automatically described.

Furthermore, the budgetary position that we present in each budget specifies all of the accounts that are engaged in budget management.

The "Planned Amount," as mentioned, is the amount we have allocated for the specific item. The theoretical amount is the maximum amount that is expected to be made or spent from the beginning of the period to the conclusion of the budgeting period. For example, the Planned Amount for Budgetary Position in the picture below indicates income of $50,000, a period of 31 days from October 1 to October 31, and the maximum amount that may be spent or earned for each day is $50,000/31 = $1612.90. As a result, they must earn or spend $1612.90 every day. We are now on the 17th day of the budget, which is today, October 17, 2023. The Theoretical Amount for the day will be 17x$1612.90 = $27419.35. The Practical Amount is the total amount of money earned and spent up to this moment.

The success or failure of this budget is determined by the achievement. Divide the theoretical amount by the practical amount to get it. Furthermore, based on this achievement, the company may decide whether to maintain this budget or discard it.

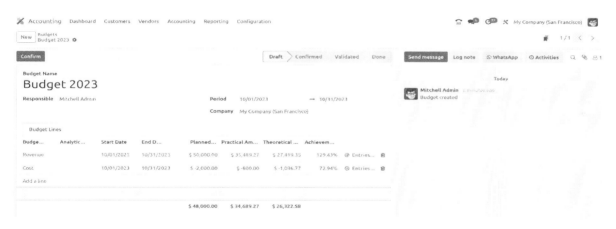

Once the various components of the budget have been set, you may save the menu and confirm the budget. After the budget is finalized, you will have the choice to accept or cancel it, as seen in the picture below. These will be given to approved executives and management, who will evaluate the budget's components and determine whether or not to approve or cancel it.

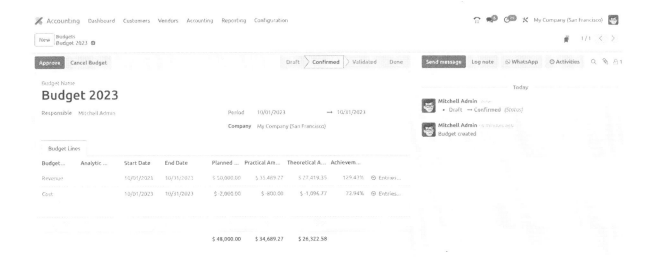

Once the budget is approved, the platform will be operational and capable of handling the financial components. Now that we've established the budget management aspects let's move on to the next part, where the asset management aspects will be completely covered.

Assets

Asset management is a key aspect of financial management operations. When an organization's financial and non-financial assets grow, the managerial components of the organization may become out of control. As a result, a particular Assets management system or tools are required. The Accounting module of the Odoo platform, which has a specific Assets management menu, may be used to specify all of the company's assets. To access the option, select Assets from the Accounting menu in the module, which will display the window seen in the picture below. The names, beginning depreciation dates, book values, depreciation value currencies, and asset statuses of all identified assets are displayed here. You may also utilize the filtering and grouping tools to find the right Assets from the menu.

You will be able to change the specified Assets by selecting them from the menu, and you will be able to create new Assets by selecting the Create option. After selecting Create New Assets, you will see the form presented in the following window. Before entering the Assets Values, such as the Original Value and the Acquisition Date, you must first input the Assets Name. In addition, you may create the Asset by selecting it from any associated transaction or by simply entering the Asset Value. As a result, the acquisition price will be added to the asset value. The next stage is to determine the current values, which might include currency, non-depreciative value, depreciative value, and book value. Only cash and non-depreciable values are updated in current values. The amount you will receive when you sell the thing and it will not lose any additional value is known as the non-depreciable value. As an example, if an asset has a value of 1000 and a non-depreciable value of 200, the depreciable value is 800, and it is this residual value that is utilized to calculate how much depreciation will be applied.

Aspects of the depreciation approach can alternatively be defined as a straight line, declining, or straight line then declining. When an asset is depreciated using the straight-line approach, the value of the asset does not vary during the period of the asset's usage by the business or for the specified Duration. Declining depreciation is a type of asset depreciation in which the asset's value decreases under the specified depreciation factor. A falling then straight-line depreciation is one in which the asset value depreciates first based on the preset depreciation factor and then changes to a straight-line model after a predetermined time.

Along with the Declining Factor, the duration of the Decline can also be specified in years or months. If asset depreciation is computed using "No Prorata," "Constant Periods," or "Based on days per Period," this is mentioned in the Computation column. The current worth of each asset can be characterized in terms of currency, not depreciable value, depreciable value, and book value.

Additionally, an Asset can be assigned to be operational with a Value at Import by providing the Depreciation Amount. When importing assets from new software, the value at import configuration ensures that their value is kept.

The accounting components of the fixed asset, where we will set the Fixed Asset Account, Depreciation Account, Expense Account, Journal, Analytical Account, and Analytical Tags, may be specified by selecting them from the drop-down menu of the relevant choice that is available.

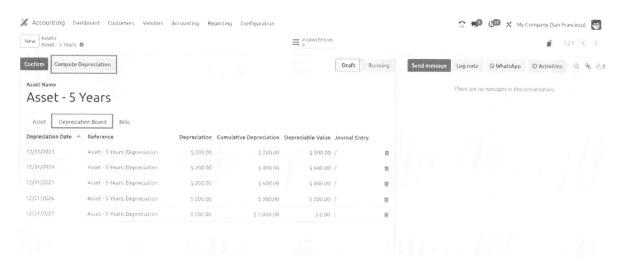

Once the asset's settings and data have been specified, you may save the item in the window and view choices for calculating depreciation. After selecting the Compute Depreciation option, the asset's depreciation will be calculated and shown on the depreciation board, as seen in the image below. The computation and depreciation aspects will be defined here. The Depreciation Reference, Depreciation Date, Depreciation Amount, Cumulative

Depreciation, Depreciation Value, and specifications of the Depreciation Journal Entry will be covered.

Once the asset has been defined, you may save the menu and confirm the procedures, which will display the 'Modify Depreciation' window. This will allow you to perform further actions such as dispose, sell, re-evaluate, and pause.

When assets are sold, a Loss account should be added in the specified field, and a depreciation entry will be posted on and after the provided date. The loss account will be updated with a disposal entry.

You can sell the assets using the Sell option. When selecting Sell, some information is required, such as the customer invoice to which the asset was sold. As a result, the invoice line will be auto-filled. The gain account in which the money from the sale of the item will be recorded, as well as a note, can be supplied.

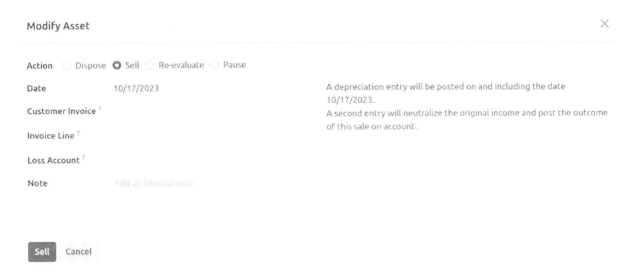

Re-Evaluate allows you to re-evaluate/modify the depreciation values of your assets.

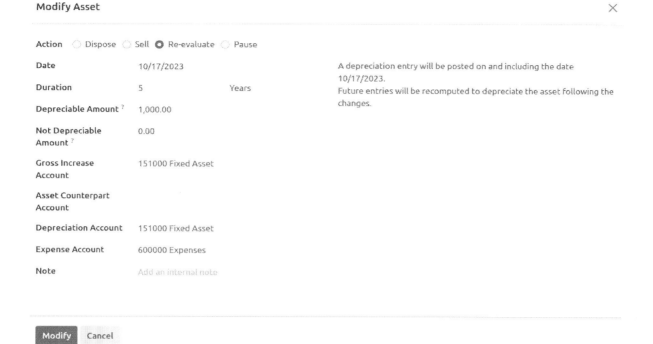

When assets are re-evaluated, the new depreciation amount is entered in the Depreciable Amount field, from which the new depreciation is computed. Other elements include the Cross Increase Account, Asset counterpart Account, Depreciation Account, Expense Account, and Notes. Once the information is entered, alter the asset and the asset will be produced for the asset's value rise. As a result, subsequent entries will be recalculated to depreciate the asset in light of the modifications.

Let's move on to the following section, where the components of Accounting Management Actions in the Odoo Accounting module will be discussed now that we are clear on Asset Management and the other Accounting Management tools in the Odoo Accounting Module.

Accounting Management Actions

The Odoo platform helps with financial management and accounting with capabilities that are detailed in this chapter. In addition to its unique tools and features that will aid with the effectiveness of the company's financial administration, the Odoo Accounting module provides a number of notable Action management capabilities. With the help of various activities, you may build the reconciliation operation and set the dates for the financial operations. Let's have a look at the two Accounting Action tools that Odoo provides.

Reconciliation

Reconciliation is a feature that allows you to synchronize your company's accounting and financial management procedures with those of a bank account operation, as well as the ledgers and the specified chart of accounts. The Reconciliation option will clearly aid you in all Finance Management actions relating to sales, purchases, and other business processes. You may access the Reconciliation option from the Accounting tab of the Accounting module's Actions tab, and once selected, the Reconciliation window will open, as seen in the picture below.

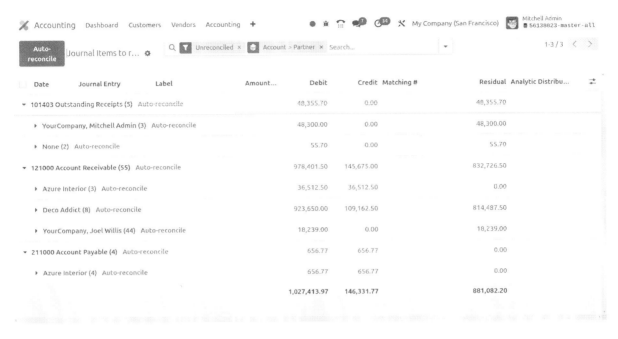

The company's whole payment-related aspects, as well as its operating Chart of Accounts, will be presented here. Each Chart of Accounts invoice will be offered for selection, along with the amount involved.

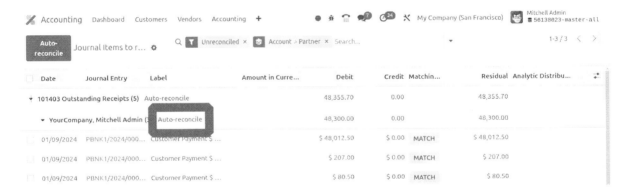

Every account has an Auto Reconcile option; select it to launch a new window with the entries that need to be automatically reconciled. Select the search mode from within the Reconcile field after the window displaying the dates from and to appears. After that, the Partners and Accounts can be selected. In order to reconcile the entries, click the Launch button.

In addition, as seen in the picture below, there is an Auto-reconcile button in the upper left corner of the screen. The users can quickly reconcile the entries by using that.

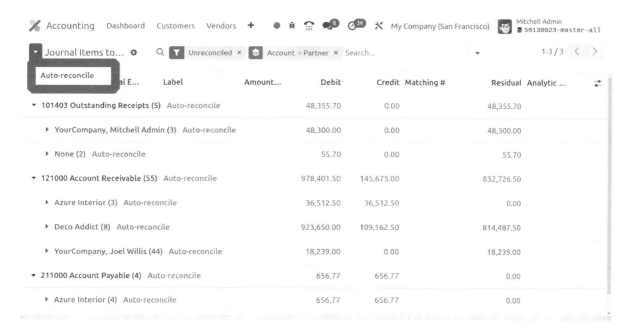

After adding the from and to dates, select the accounts with zero balances or the opposite balances one at a time to reconcile. Include accounts. Next, press the **Launch** button.

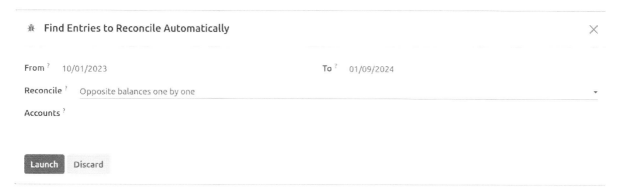

The automatically reconciled entries are then displayed there.

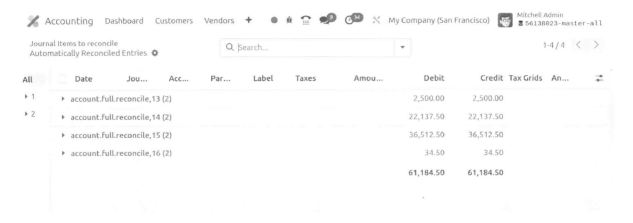

The screenshot below shows the Reconciliation menu of a Chart of Accounts. The Code of Account, Account Name, Type, Group, and Account Currency are all defined here. Additionally, there are reconciling options that may be used to do the reconciliation of the related Chart of Account specified.

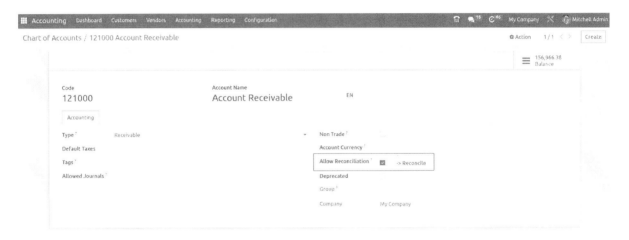

The Reconciliation menu in Odoo 17 Accounting is a useful Action tool for specifying the Financial activities relevant to each of the Chart of Accounts that a firm has set to be running in an orderly manner. Now that we've covered the Reconciliation menu in the Odoo Accounting Action tools, let's move on to the Lock Dates menu in the next section.

Lock Dates

Using the Lock Dates capability in Odoo Accounting, you can configure the activities of the Fiscal Periods of operation for the company operations. This capability will aid company management because they may need to alter the Fiscal Periods based on their demands. The Lock Dates option is located on the Actions tab of the Accounting module. When you choose the menu, a pop-up window will open, as seen in the picture below. You can Lock your Fiscal Period here based on your needs.

In order to set the Journal Entries Lock Date, All Users Lock Date, and Tax Return Lock Date, you must first pick a date from the calendar that appears after choosing a drop-down option. Within the Odoo Accounting module, users in the following categories have varying access rights: Billing, Read-Only, Bookkeeper, Accountant, and Consolidation User.

According to their individual rights, each of them can function in the Accounting module. Similarly, no user can edit the documents until the Lock Date for all users is set. Lock Dates are often specified so that no user may make changes during the company's financial operations auditing period or after the fiscal year ends. Finally, if dates are being defined, you must select the Save option. You may also Discard the Lock Dates whenever you want with the required authority.

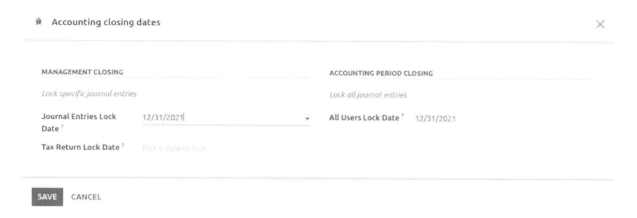

Additionally, if there are specific Unposted entries in the relevant Fiscal Period, the Odoo Warning box will display as a pop-up in your direction, as seen in the picture below. Because the Odoo platform is designed to help the company's financial management operations, alerts are generated automatically. Unposted entries, on the other hand, should be defined before the end of a fiscal quarter. You may prevent the Lock Dates posting from going live by selecting Show Unposted Entries or Cancel.

When you select "Show Unposted Entries," a menu will display all unposted entries corresponding to the financial operations of the relevant fiscal quarter.

Filtering and Group by options will be offered, as with all other Odoo platform menus, allowing us to find the relevant Unposted Entries from the menu being described. Now that we understand the functionality of the Accounting Action tools available in the Odoo Accounting module let's move on to the next part, which discusses Accounting Ledgers.

In conclusion, you may simply do a variety of finance management tasks pertaining to any area of the company by utilizing the accounting management capabilities in the Odoo Accounting module. Furthermore, accounting management solutions provide advanced regulatory features. The following chapter will go through the reporting functionalities of the Odoo Accounting module.

Chapter 6
Insights and Analytics:
Unleashing the Power of Odoo
Accounting Reporting

Insights and Analytics: Unleashing the Power of Odoo Accounting Reporting

Reports are necessary in any organization in order to comprehend the operational stage at which a firm is working. A well-defined report will provide you with an analysis of the business, its phases, and its future features rather than offering a graphical interface of the business activities. Reporting has a significant impact on the control and comprehension of a company's financial activity. A financial report that provides an overview of the company's finances specifies some of the most noteworthy reports and graphs on the company's profit and loss statements and other financial characteristics.

The preceding chapter discussed the Finance management module of Odoo Accounting's Accounting management tools and menus. The numerous menus for the Odoo platform's accounting management operations were completely explored.

In this chapter, we'll focus on the reporting tools provided by the Odoo Accounting module. We will discuss topics such as:
- Statement Reports
- Audit Reports
- Partner Reports
- Management Reports

This chapter will study and demonstrate all of the reporting-related functional menus and capabilities in the Odoo Accounting module.

Statement Reports

The United States Securities and Exchange Commission created the Universally Accepted Accounting Principles (GAAP), often known as. In the event of an overseas transfer, the GAAP standardized the accounting components such as currency rates, interest rates, and tax included in the company's business operations. In addition to import and export taxes, each country has its own national tax. Furthermore, GAAP is a widely accepted standard or procedure for documenting and disseminating accounting-related information inside an organization. A policy board established these guidelines. This standard strategy will ensure that all components of the company's accounting are documented, as well as that paperwork is analyzed and generated. Three fundamental ones are required for the operation of any business.

The GAAP-based report-generating features are provided by default in the Odoo Accounting module since they are needed for any firm operating anywhere in the world. Additionally, under the Odoo Accounting module's unique Reporting page, you will have a new menu that will aid you in preparing and saving all US GAAP reports. In the Odoo

Accounting module, you may automatically generate US GAAP reports like profit and loss statements, balance sheets, executive summaries, cash flow statements, and cheque registers.

In the sections that follow, we'll go through each of the US GAAP reporting options available in the Odoo Accounting module in greater depth.

Balance Sheet

The balance sheet, which provides an in-depth overview of the company's assets, liabilities, and shareholders' equity, is the second most important document in regard to the business's accounting activities. It may also be defined as a balance summary of an individual's, a corporation's, or an organization's financial activity that provides comprehensive information on the total reached as well as transactions and depreciations during a fiscal year of business operations. The balance sheet of an organization is described for each fiscal period as well as whenever necessary. Furthermore, these reports will provide up-to-date information on the company's financial activities and will be critical in directing financial management decisions.

The Odoo platform has a delicate menu that will enable you to prepare financial reports for the organization, including a balance sheet. You may examine the Balance Sheet menu, which is available via the Odoo Accounting module's Reporting menu, as shown in the picture below. The balance sheet's assets, equity, liabilities, and other components are all presented in separate sections here, along with their corresponding quantities and components, such as bank and cash accounts, receivables, and current assets or liabilities. You will have access to filtering, grouping, and comparison capabilities, as with all other report-generating menus in the Odoo Accounting module. Filtering can be done here based on the fiscal year or duration of operation.

Additionally, based on the needs, Journals, Analytical accounting components, Posted and Unposted articles, and others may be selected and aggregated. Furthermore, the Comparison tool allows you to compare the Balance Sheets of one fiscal year with those of another fiscal year, providing you with detailed information on the company's depreciation progress. You won't have any issue comprehending it because they have the same options and procedures. The preceding report described in this chapter contains information on the setup aspects of these Filtering, Grouping, and Comparison tools.

After selecting the drop-down option featured in the detailed entries, you will notice two menu options: General Ledger and Annotate.

Let's start with the General Ledger option, which will display the ledger details of the necessary entry immediately from the Balance sheet, as shown in the image below. Filtering and the Group by option are both accessible here, as they are with all other reporting options on the Odoo platform. You will also have access to a save option, which enables you to save the General Ledger depending on the configuration aspects that are being done, as well as a search option, the ability to examine Print Preview and export the entries, and other features.

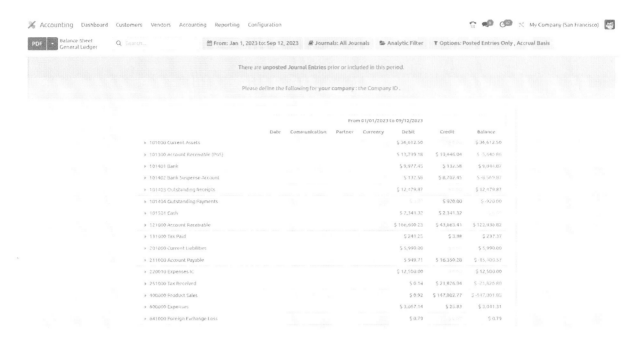

After unfolding, the Journal Items are available from the drop-down menu for each ledger. As seen in the picture above, you will view the journal entries for the appropriate entry. You may also sort the defined components using the Filters and Group by options, which are available by default. Custom entry-based filters and grouping options may also be implemented and saved as favorites for future usage of the same filtration and grouping.

After selecting the Annotate option from the Balance Sheet, you will get a pop-up window similar to the one seen in the picture below. You can provide descriptions for the annotating that has to be done before storing it in this area. Furthermore, the Annotation can be deleted using the given delete option.

The balance sheet of a company accounting is critical to the financial management positions of the business, and you can quickly produce and see the balance sheets of any fiscal users of the company operations using a specialized tool like the Odoo Balance Sheet reporting. Now that we've covered the Odoo Balance Sheet reporting menu's components let's move on to the part where we'll go over the Odoo Profit and Loss reporting menu under the US GAAP Reporting tools.

Profit and Loss Reports

Profit and loss statements are the fundamental US GAAP-based reports that each firm will generate. Profit and loss statements will detail the company's financial activity, as well as whether the firm is profitable or losing money. Profit and loss statements are essential components of every business's accounting activity, and the Odoo platform recognizes this. As a result, the Odoo Accounting module includes a separate menu for creating Profit and Loss Reports. Profit and Loss Reports are accessible from the Odoo Accounting module's reporting menu; choosing them will display the report seen in the following picture.

The report will display all revenue, costs, and the net value of profit or loss, as seen in the screenshot below. Under the Profit aspect, the Gross Profit information, such as Operating Income and cost revenue, will be reviewed. A second section will be included to address the chosen Other Income. Additionally, Expense data such as the company's Expenses and the Depreciation expense-based value will be given. Each Chart of Accounts related to the defined feature will be shown, providing you with further information.

Filtering, grouping, and comparison features will be available in all other Odoo platform reporting menus. Filtering can be done here based on the fiscal year or duration of operation. Furthermore, the Journals, Analytical accounting aspects, and Posted and Unposted items may be selected and categorized based on the requirements. Furthermore, the Comparison tool allows you to compare the Profit and Loss Reports of one fiscal period with those of another, providing you with detailed information on the company's depreciation progress. Research is essential to comprehend the organization's future plan.

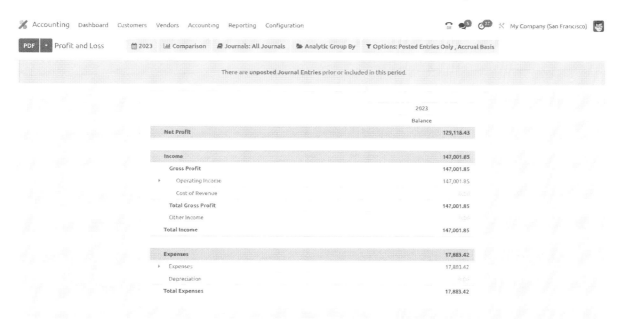

The Profit and Loss Reports of a company play an important role in the financial management operations of the company, providing a clear picture of the company's track record in the past and an insight into the future, allowing you to plan your budget and other financial operations in regards to the company functioning properly. Now that we've covered the Odoo Accounting module's Profit and Loss Reports menu, let's move on to the next part, which covers the Cash Flow Statement reporting features of Odoo Accounting.

Cash Flow Statement

In company operations, you must understand where your money goes and how it is spent. The same is true in your case. The Odoo platform includes a specialized management solution in the Accounting module for managing the business's cash flow. You will be able to grasp the numerous features of cash flow and the channels of your business operations where it has been utilized in this section. There is a specific Cash Flow Statement accessible in Odoo reporting parts of financial operations that will define your company's cash flow activities. The Cash Flow Statement, which is accessible via the Reporting tab of the Odoo Accounting module, will display the features of cash flow (both cash in and cash out of the company) in the form of a report, as depicted in the following screenshot.

The various aspects of the cash flow will be depicted here, such as Cash and cash equivalents, the beginning of the period, Net increase in cash and cash equivalents, and Cash and cash equivalents, closing balance, providing a clearer picture of how the profits, as well as the money involved, is used for the business. These reports will benefit investors since they will be able to grasp all areas of the cash flow firm as needed. Filtering and Grouping capabilities are accessible in the Cash Flow Statement window, as they are in all other Odoo Accounting Reporting menus. Here you may select the Fiscal Periods and Journals that must be presented in the Cash Flow Statement. Furthermore, the Entries may be specified based on both posted and unposted ones using the unique filtering options that are accessible.

Furthermore, the cash Balance associated with each transaction will be defined on the right side of the menu. You will be able to drop down the description of the Cash Flow Statement and view the three menu options available, which are General Ledger, Journal Items, and the Annotate option, which will help you to view the respective menus as available in many of the reporting menus previously discussed in this chapter. Furthermore, if we add a Customer Payment through Accounting Module > Customers > Payments, it will be added to the line Advance Payments received from Customers, and once some amount is matched with invoices, it will be shown under Cash received from operating activities. Similarly, Vendor Payment and bill fall under Advance payments made to suppliers and Cash paid for operating activities, respectively.

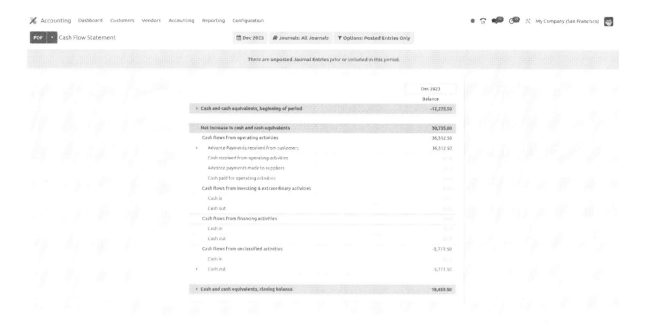

The Odoo Accounting module's Cash Flow Statement Reporting menu is an excellent tool for understanding the cash flow components of your organization as well as the balance amount involved. Now that we understand how the Cash Flow Statement report works, let's move on to the next part, which will discuss the Executive Summary reporting option.

Executive Summary

The Executive Summary of a company's accounting will offer a thorough summary of the company's financial activities for the whole fiscal period. Furthermore, it explains the comprehensive estimate of the minute details of the company's financial activities for executives and investors. The Executive Summary will be utilized to provide a thorough overview of the company's financial management and operational strategy.

The Executive Summary reporting option in the Odoo platform may be accessible from the Reporting tab of the Odoo Accounting module, which will display a report of how the firm runs, as seen in the picture below. The different parts of the company's operations will be explained here, including cash operations, profitability, balance sheet, profitability data, and many more. Furthermore, the structure and subject employed in the Executive Summary may be divided into two categories: performance and position. In the case of performance-based elements, we will have the Gross Profit Margin, which is the total of all direct costs incurred while making a direct sale. The Net Profit Margin is the total of the Gross Profit Margin plus the company's fixed overheads, which include rent, energy, other utilities costs, taxes, and many more in relation to a single transaction. Furthermore, the Return on Investment is the comparable ratio of the Net Profit to the amount as well as the assets used to produce the profit.

Furthermore, the position-based phrases in the Executive summary will offer information on the financial holdings and the status of the sale or the entire firm. The average debtor days is the number of days it takes your customers to make a payment. The Average creditor days will provide the average number of days utilized to credit the amount due for vendor invoices. Furthermore, the Short-term cash prediction is a forecasting tool that provides insight into the monies that will travel in and out of the accounts. Furthermore, the Current assets to liabilities ratio is a ratio of current assets to obligations that may be converted to cash within a year. Additionally, the elements of financial operations related to each of these divisions will be outlined together with the money invested in them.

There are filtering and grouping options available to assist with the sorting out operations of the Executive Summary entries that have been defined. You will be able to group by fiscal periods of operation and posted entries. Furthermore, the available Comparison choices will allow you to compare the Executive Summary information of the company's financial operations from one fiscal period to another, as seen in the image below. There will be several default comparison choices, including the Previous Period and the Same Period Last Year. Furthermore, the Custom Comparison options may be established depending on the situation.

The Executive Summary of a company's financial operations will provide a complete understanding of the company's financial operations and can be used as study material to understand the previous history and current track of operations, which will help management make and take decisions accordingly. Now that we've covered the Executive Summary reporting option on the Odoo platform let's move on to the next section, which will cover the Tax reports.

Tax Report

Taxes and how they are applied in business, which is carried out all over the world, are inescapable factors. As a result, companies like to keep a close eye on how these taxes are applied to their financial operations since governments all around the world falsify records to guarantee that taxes are paid on time and accurately. Section 3.1.2 Configuring Taxes in Chapter 3 of this book gives a thorough description of the Odoo Accounting module's dedicated Tax Management window. You can read the appropriate sections of the book's past to discover how tax management operations for a business in Odoo are carried out.

There is a Tax Report option accessible from the Reporting tab of the Odoo Accounting module for reporting purposes on taxes connected to the financial activities of organizations using Odoo. The screenshot below demonstrates how all financial features in regard to the defined taxes will be shown, along with the operation, the Net worth of money, and the tax amount. There are also buttons for printing reports in PDF and XLSX formats. Another configuration option allows you to store the Consolidated Journals report after the Filtration Group.

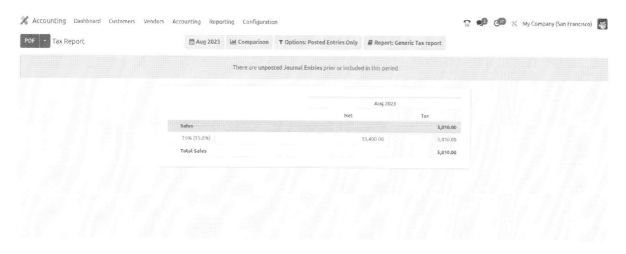

In addition, there is a closing journal entry option that can be used to shut and submit the journal entries linked to tax operations. Additionally, as seen in the following picture, you will have access to filtering and grouping options in the Tax Report menu. Read the sections before this one to understand more about the typical tools available in the reporting menus, such as the Period based Filtering, Comparison filter, and Options filter. There are other options for grouping tax reports that allow you to arrange them as a global summary, a tax group by account, or a tax group by account and tax.

A summary of the tax operations in connection to the company's financial and accounting activities may be found in the Odoo platform's Tax Reporting menu. Let us now go to the part that specifies the EC Sales List Reporting tool.

EC Sales List

The Odoo EC Sales List reporting function is another form of reporting tool that will provide you with a complete insight into the company's financial activity. The EC Sales List reporting, which is based on the sales of goods and services made by VAT-registered firms within the UK to other businesses in the European Union, is one of the instruments that must be submitted to Her Majesty's Revenue and Customs of the UK government. The Odoo Accounting module's Reporting tab leads to the EC Sales List Reporting. Each entry on the EC Sales List will be specified here.

Filtering and grouping tools will be available to help you organize the data according to fiscal years and defined journals. You can refer to the reporting options discussed in the sections preceding this one. There are also buttons for printing reports in PDF and XLSX formats. The SAVE option allows you to save reports to the appropriate workspace in the Documents modules in order to maintain the financial records that are available from the EC Sales List menu and will be important for the financial management operations of the business.

Now that you understand the EC Sales List reporting management menu of the Odoo platform, let's move on to the next step, where the Journal Audits will be set.

Audit Reports

When it comes to business accounting, auditing is a critical component of finance management tasks. This unavoidable component is recognized as a priority throughout the fiscal periods that are now being formed. Furthermore, in compliance with requirements, the entire fiscal year's financial operations are checked, recorded, filed, and audited. This is normally done once every fiscal year. The Accounting module in Odoo provides you with specialized Audit Reporting features to help you manage your company's finances and oversee its accounting operations.

There is a distinct category of Audit Reporting tools available, including General Ledger, Trial Balance, Consolidated Journals, Tax Report, Intrastat Report, EC Sales List, and Journal Audits, all of which are accessible via the Odoo Accounting module's reporting page. Let us now go over each of the Audit reports separately in the next section.

General Ledger

All accounting data related to business operations will be defined in the company's general ledger. Furthermore, filters may be applied to Dynamic reports, and the General ledger displays all business transactions from all Account Ledgers used in the firm. All financial transactions connected to the company's sales, purchases, and other activities will be defined in a unique way here to help the viewer understand those transactions immediately. Furthermore, the well-organized menu may be utilized to study and identify specific information relevant to the company's financial management methods.

You may examine the company's general ledger by selecting the Reporting option in the Accounting module, as illustrated in the following screenshot. All of the financial operations items that have been filtered to appear for the given time will be displayed here. Every journal that has been posted will be explained, along with the invoice and bill details for that journal.

Additionally, you have the option to Print Preview, which will provide a General Ledger Report preview before printing. In addition to exporting General Ledger data, you may export the report in XLSX format for use in other corporate activities by selecting the Export (XLSX) option. The Save option ensures that the set details and filtering parameters are saved in the reporting menu. You may opt to enlarge a Journal, which will display all linked bills and invoices. The Ledger entries in the image below have been filtered to the month of January in the year 2024, and Sample has also been selected as the Journal filter. Furthermore, only the entries that have been uploaded are screened.

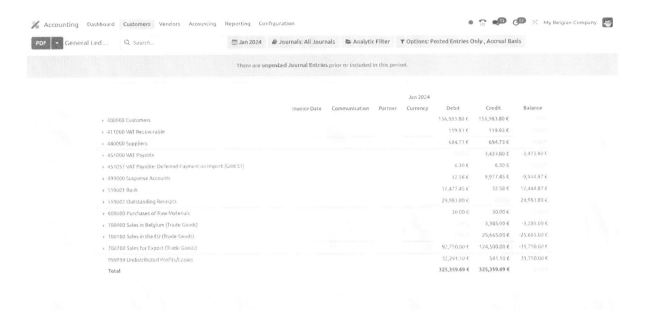

When an account is opened, the impacted journal entries are displayed together with the date, partner information, currency, debit/credit amount, and balance. Additionally, a right-click allows you to see and comment on the Journal Entries (add notes on each entry). The remarks made to the journal entries can be viewed and updated at the bottom of the General Ledger. You may filter the date or month of operations as This Month, This Quarter, This Financial Year, Last Month, Last Quarter, or Last Financial Year if you need to define a custom filter date of operations. The Filtration menu in the General Ledger menu is shown in the screenshot below.

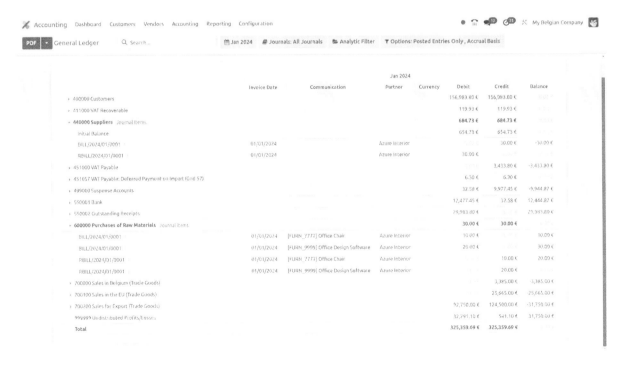

You have a different option to filter the journals where you can pick the particular journals to be filtered as well as the defined journal groupings that may also be selected as the filter.

272

Additionally, using the available Analytic option, the filtration may be done in relation to the Analytical Accounting sections of the firm's financial management. Define the Analytical Accounts and Tags here to filter out General Ledger entries.

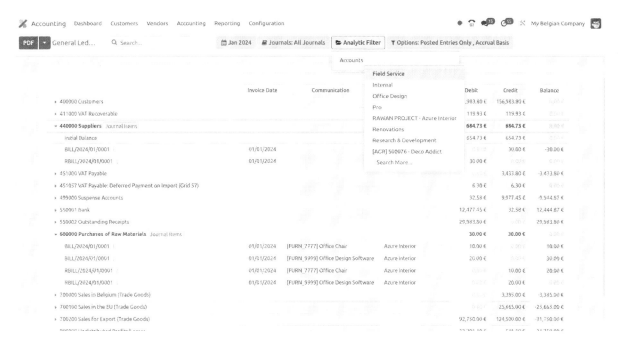

In addition, there is a particular filtering tool provided. This filter contains just Posted Entries by default, but it also offers the choices to Include Unposted Entries, Use Accrual Basis, Unfold All, and Use Cash Basis Method. Using this option, the required General Ledger entries can be defined in operation. There are also buttons that allow you to print reports in PDF and XLSX formats. The Store button saves reports to the proper place in the Documents modules, allowing you to keep financial information.

273

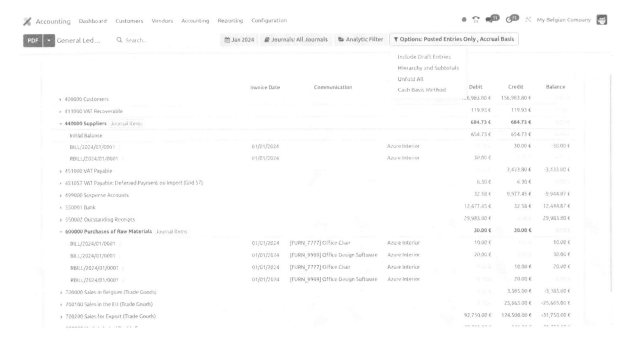

The general ledger is a report that initiates all posted and unposted accounting operations connected to the operation of the firm. In the early days of business, a specialized book known as General Ledger was kept, but with the Odoo Accounting module, all entries will be automatically displayed with regard to the corporate activities of the different Journals. Now that we've covered the Odoo Accounting module's General Ledger reporting menu, let's move on to the next section, which defines the Odoo Accounting module's Trial Balance Report.

Trial Balance

A trial balance is a sort of bookkeeping instrument that describes the balance of each account in credits and debits in terms of the organization's accounting activities. The Odoo Accounting module's specific Trial Balance reporting tool is specified in the module and available via the module's Reporting page. All filtered journals will be displayed in the Trial Balance report option, together with the operations' beginning balance information in the form of a debit and a credit. The Debits for the appropriate time will then be displayed, together with the Credit amounts of the entries, with the Total Debit and Credit Amount stated. You will also be able to search for a certain Account in the Trial Balance report.

There is also a Print Preview option, which displays a preview of the Trial Balance Report before it is printed. In addition to exporting the Trial Balance details, you may export the report in XLSX format for use in other business operations by selecting the Export(XLSX) option. The Save option saves the set details and filtering options in the reporting panel.

274

In terms of the Group by feature, you may define the Trial Balance for This Month, This Quarter, This Financial Year, Last Month, Last Quarter, and Last Financial Year, or add Custom filters as needed. The Group by choice is displayed in the accompanying snapshot, and they may be used to filter the Accounts depending on how long the firm has been in existence.

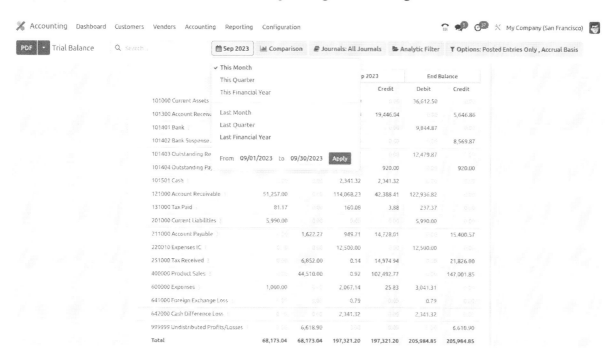

There is also an extra Comparison option that you may use to establish the comparison between the company's Journal entries. The comparison might be with the preceding period, the same period from the previous year, or a bespoke comparison set by the needs. Once the Comparison is created, the Trial Balance Report will specify the two Periods, the current one and the one you need to compare, as seen in the accompanying picture.

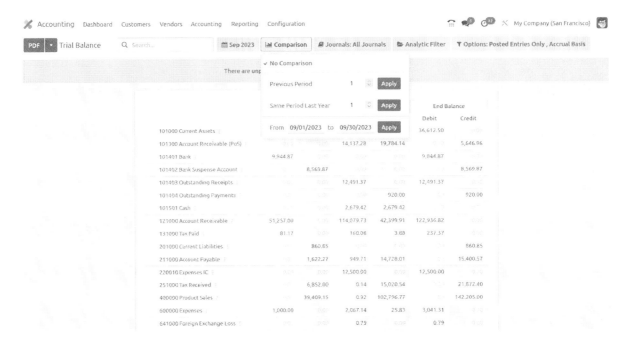

The Journal Groups and particular Journals given can also be used to group the Journals. If you employ this grouping approach, you will have a better understanding of the Trial Balance elements in relation to each of the operational Journals.

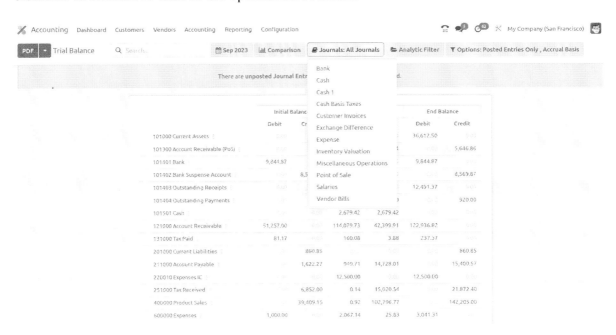

Additionally, the filtration may be done in reference to the Analytical Accounting sections of the company's financial management utilizing the available Analytic option. Define the Analytical Accounts and Tags below to filter the items in the Trial Balance report.

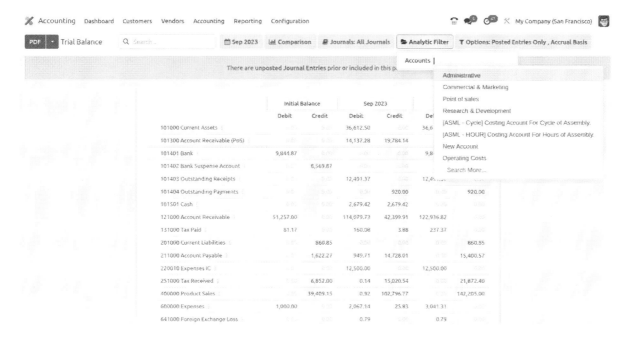

In addition, there is a particular filtering tool provided. This filter contains just Posted Entries by default, but it also offers the choices to Include Unposted Entries, Use Accrual Basis, Unfold All, and Use Cash Basis Method. Using this option, the necessary Trial Balance entries can be defined in operation. There are also buttons that allow you to print reports in PDF and XLSX formats. The Store button saves reports to the proper place in the Documents modules, allowing you to keep financial information.

The Trial Balance report of the company's financial activities will provide detailed information on the Credit and Debit amounts relevant to the organization's operations. The Trial Balance report will also be useful in grasping and gaining an overview of the company's financial activity. Let's move on to the part that defines Journal Reports in Odoo as they relate to the accounting process of the organization.

Journal Report

The journals of your accounting operations that are marked as Consolidated for the operations are defined in the Odoo Accounting module's Journal report menu. All operational Journals and their respective operating months will be presented in the menu. The Consolidated Journals report may also be produced as a preview by selecting Print Preview. Additionally, by selecting the Export(XSLX) option, the Consolidated Journals in the XLSX report may be exported. After filtering and aggregating the Consolidated Journals according to another setting element, you may store them to report using the Store option.

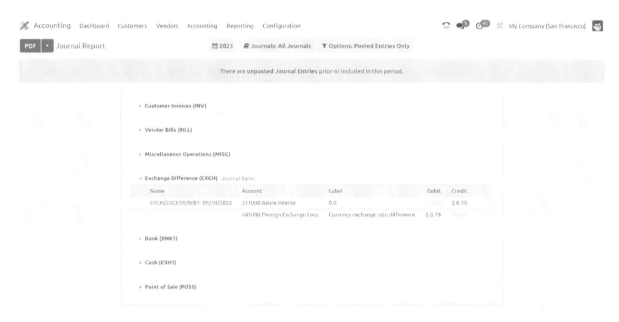

A tax declaration will also be added at the conclusion of the entries for sales and buy journals, as seen in the screenshot.

When it comes to sorting the entire depicted in the Consolidated Journals, you have the option to Group by options based on the period of the operation, as well as filtration options like This Month, This Quarter, This Financial Year, Last Month, Last Quarter, Last Financial Year, or add Custom filters of operations as needed. The Group by options available to you to filter the Accounts based on how long the business has been in operation are given in the screenshot below.

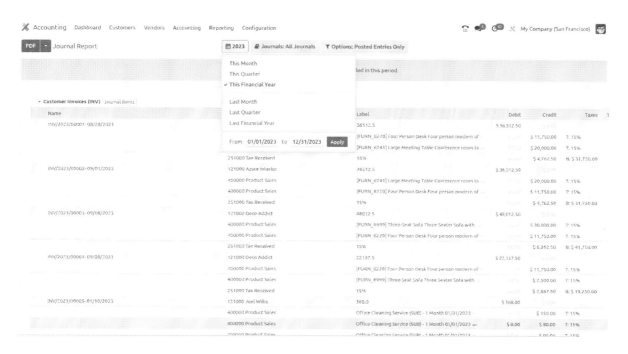

The Journal Groups and particular Journals given can also be used to group the Journals. Using this process of grouping by Journals, you may better understand the Consolidated Journals aspects in connection to each of the operational Journals being built.

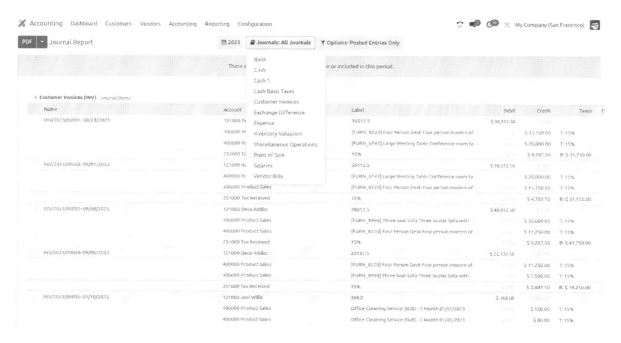

Additionally, the settings tool allows you to filter entries by utilizing the Posted Entries Only, Include Unposted Entries, and Unfold All choices. Thanks to these filtering tools and selections, you will have clearly defined options for excluding and sorting the Consolidated Journals items.

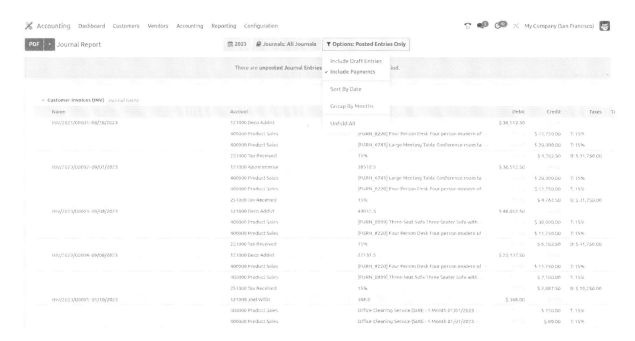

The Consolidated Journals reporting window ensures that the viewer understands all of the financial entries and their allocated components of the company's accounting activities. The Intrastat report, the next reporting tool in the Odoo Accounting module, will be discussed in the following portion of this chapter.

Intrastat Report

The Intrastat Report is one of the more comprehensive reporting options provided by Odoo's Accounting module. The European Union and its member states may track trade and business in a statistical manner owing to the Intrastat reporting mechanism. The Odoo Accounting module's Reporting tab leads to the Intrastat Report menu. This page will display all of the Intrastat Reporting components relating to business operations. There are further options in the menu for Group by and specialized Filtering that can aid in the sorting process.

Filtering tools will aid the Filtering component of the Intrastat Reports in the Odoo platform in relation to the Fiscal Periods of Operations, Journals that have been defined, Types of Journal Entries, and Filtrations depending on the Option as well as the Company in which Business is performed either as Partners, Vendors, or Customers.

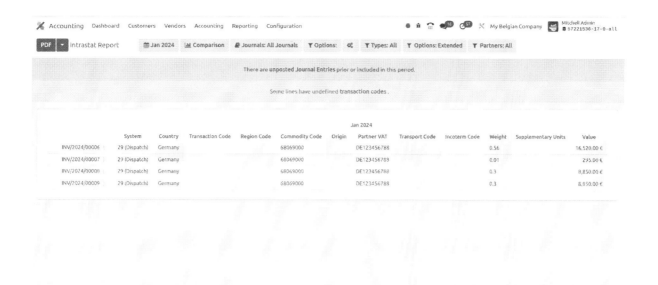

If you want to learn more about the filtration features of the entries mentioned in the report, you may refer to the reporting aspects provided in the preceding sections. There are also buttons that allow you to print reports in PDF and XLSX formats. The Store button saves reports to the proper place in the Documents modules, allowing you to keep financial information. Let us go to the next phase, where we will define the Odoo platform's EC Sales List reporting option.

Check Register

The Check Register option is the last one under the Audit Reporting tools in the Odoo Accounting module, and it will provide you with information about your company's Check Register. A check register will describe every financial transaction linked to the firm's functioning, and the check register report will do so analytically, providing you with a full insight into how everything works.

The Accounts Register report will be illustrated using the numerous working Charts of Accounts that have been established in the platform. Each operational Chart of Accounts, as well as the date of operation, communication information, partner, and currency utilized, will be noted here. Furthermore, the Debit and Credit amounts, as well as the Balance of each of the Charts of Accounts, will be described as shown in the following screenshot.

Filtering and grouping possibilities are accessible, much like any other reporting choices in the Odoo Accounting module. You may use the criteria below to narrow down the information in the cheque register based on fiscal periods, journals, analytical accounting features, and posted and unposted entries. There is also a serving tool that you may use to search the Bill Register entries depending on the data you have. There are also buttons for printing reports in PDF and XLSX formats. The Store button saves reports to the proper location in the Documents modules, allowing you to keep your financial information.

Please define the following for your company : the Company ID .

	Aug 2023					
	Date	Communication	Partner	Currency	Debit	Credit	Balance
101401 Bank					$ 9,977.45	$ 132.58	$ 9,844.87
101402 Bank Suspense Account					$ 132.58	$ 8,702.45	$ -8,569.87
121000 Account Receivable						$ 1,275.00	$ -1,275.00
201000 Current Liabilities					$ 6,309.15	$ 7,170.00	$ -460.35
400000 Product Sales					$ 5,420.00	$ 3,309.15	$ 2,110.85
999999 Undistributed Profits/Losses					$ 1,750.00	$ 3,000.00	$ -1,250.00
Total					$ 23,589.18	$ 23,589.18	

The Check Register reporting menu in Odoo will play an important part in carrying out each operation's elements in terms of the company's financial management and will be a valuable accounting tool. The Bill Register completes the reporting functions of the Odoo Accounting module.

Partner Reports

To manage a business, you will have to interact with a large number of clients and vendors to whom you will sell goods and services and acquire raw materials. All of these tasks are carried out autonomously, with the assistance of remote technology. This is a distinct group of business establishments with whom your firm has cooperated to strive towards a common objective of being the greatest at what you do. Whether owned by the same person or by a separate person, these enterprises will function under an agreement. Products and services will be moved between each other based on the requirements.

In some cases, an organization will work with a different firm dealing in a different field to carry out activities under the partner's name. Both companies will gain from this since it will lower their import and export taxes and broaden their consumer base. Odoo ERP has unique Partner and Partnership management capabilities to support the operations of a business's Partner function. Because of a distinct Ledger and the feature of internal transfer between partners and collective holding, the element of partnership operations may be clearly identified in Odoo operations.

The financial elements of Partner operations are critical for the business as well as the establishment of targeted management strategies. The Odoo Accounting module will help with the financial administration of the Partner activities. Furthermore, the Odoo platform supports the reporting aspects of partner functionality through the Partner-specific reports in the Accounting module's Reporting menu. Thanks to report creation options such as Partner Ledger reporting, Aged Receivable reports, and Aged Payable reporting features, you can be certain that you have a firm understanding and analysis of the financial parts of your business's Partner activities. We'll go through each of these partner report types in further depth in the sections that follow.

Partner Ledger

The Odoo Accounting module's Partner Ledger reporting option provides information on the partners' Ledge data as well as completed entries. In addition, the financial features of each Partner Ledger will be presented. The menu might be caused by the Reporting tab of the Odoo platform's Accounting module. The menu will list all of the Others who work for your firm. You may increase the summary and entries under each Partner by using the drop-down arrow option. This section will describe all Partners, the Transaction Date, Journal Involved, Transaction Account, Transaction Reference Details, and the Transaction Date. Furthermore, the Due Date, Matching Number, Opening Balance, and Amounts of Debit and Credit will be stated.

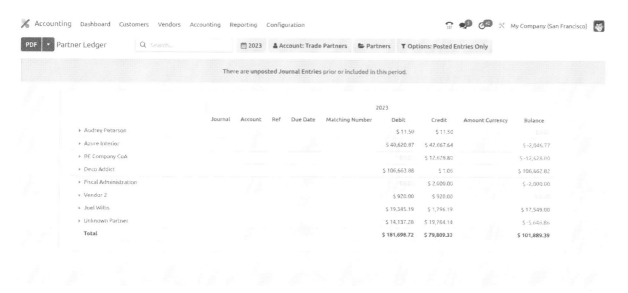

A Search option is available if the entries have been described. This search box may be used to seek up specified Partner items. Additionally, the tools for Distinctive filtering and Group by, which allow you to sort data according to both custom and predefined ones provided by default, will be beneficial. The Partner Ledger entries may be filtered by fiscal period using the Fiscal Period filtering tool, as demonstrated in the pictures below.

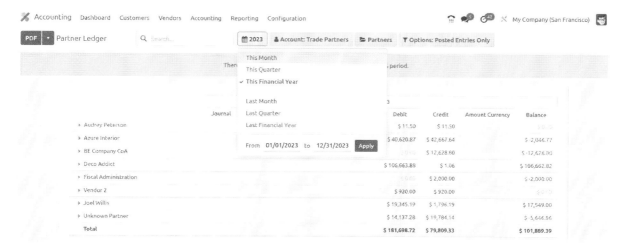

The Partner Ledger entries can also be categorized by the account in which they are specified, whether the Receivables or Payables account. The following screenshot depicts the sorting tool based on the Accounts on which the Partner Ledger entries are defined.

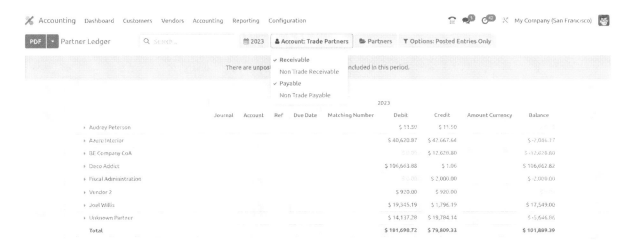

Additionally, you may utilize the Partners filter choices to specify the Partners and Tags by selecting them from the drop-down menu, which will allow you to list out the different Partner Ledger entries. The following screenshot describes the Partner screening tool.

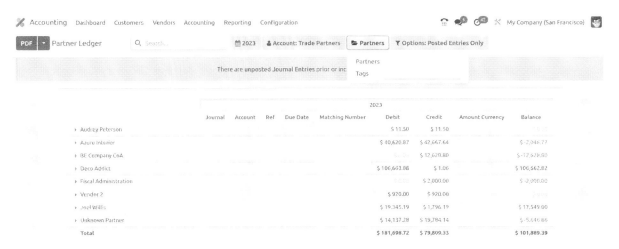

There is also a system for filtering that you can use to categorize the Partner Ledger based on the Posted Data, Include Unposted Entries, Only See Unreconciled Entries, or Unfold All to see all the specified Partner Ledger entries. There are also buttons for printing reports in PDF and XLSX formats. Additionally, after altering the entries, the Partner Ledger report may be saved using the available SAVE option.

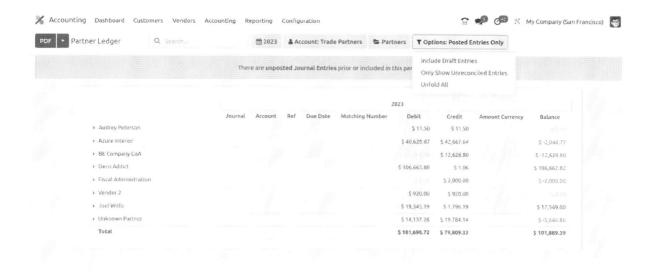

To reconcile the financial entries defined in relation to the partner operations, select one of the Reconcile options under each of the Partners defined in the Partner Ledger. After clicking Reconcile, you will be taken to the Partner's specific Reconcile window, where you can choose whether to reconcile or not.

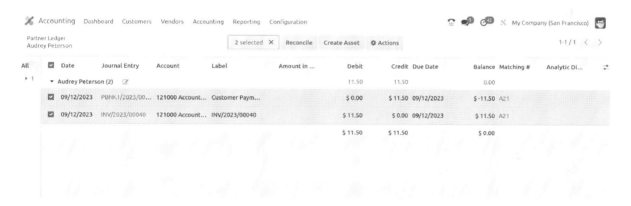

The Odoo Accounting module's Partner Ledger reporting tool will provide you with information on how the financial operations of the Partners compare to those of the firm. Furthermore, you will be able to sort out the essential information by using unique filtering and grouping features, making it an important tool for the organization. Now that we understand how Partner Ledger reports work, let's move on to the next partner-based report type in the Odoo Accounting module, the Aged Receivable reporting menu.

Aged Receivable

When a partner or client fails to pay for products and services, they are classified as old receivable payments by the firm. The Delayed Amount will be classed as an Aged Receivable even after the set payment time has elapsed. Assume that the payment period is 10 days and that the invoice date is December 1st, 2024. As a result, the payment is considered Aged Receivable if the client has not made it by the corresponding payment period, which is 10 December 2024.

As a result, on December 22nd, this sum will be Aged Receivable in 1-30 days. This classification will allow the firm to follow up on the payment, ensuring that you get paid before it is too late. Aged Receivable reporting will be critical to the business in Odoo, where controlling the company's operations is critical. The Aged Receivable reports, which come under the Partner-based reports of the firm utilizing the Odoo Accounting module, will provide you with a better understanding of how the company handles delayed payments that have not yet been received.

The Aged Receivable reports are accessible via the Reporting tab of the Odoo Accounting module. The Aged Receivable entries will be displayed here based on the existing partners and customers. All entries relevant to the partner will be shown and accessible via the various drop-down arrow choices. The partner or customer information will be displayed here, and as the arrow is moved down, the invoice information for each of their aged receivables will be displayed separately. Furthermore, the Report Date, Journal Details, Amount Involved, and Expiration Date are all displayed as 1- 30, 31-60, 61-90, 91-120, and older, respectively, to indicate the amount to be paid if the payment is extended depending on the length. The entire amount owed will also be shown at the conclusion. The screenshot below shows the Aged Receivable reporting option, which defines all Aged Receivable elements.

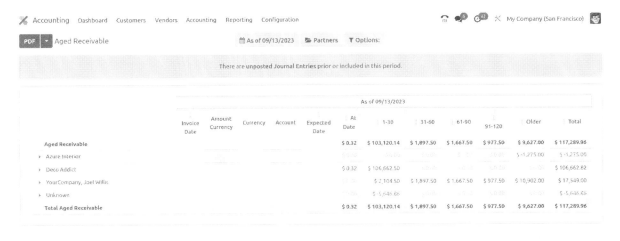

Furthermore, the various filtering and Group by features will aid you in organizing the information according to your requirements. To help in sorting procedures, you may utilize both conventional and accessible custom tools. The fiscal period can be used as the foundation for the initial filtering, as seen in the picture below.

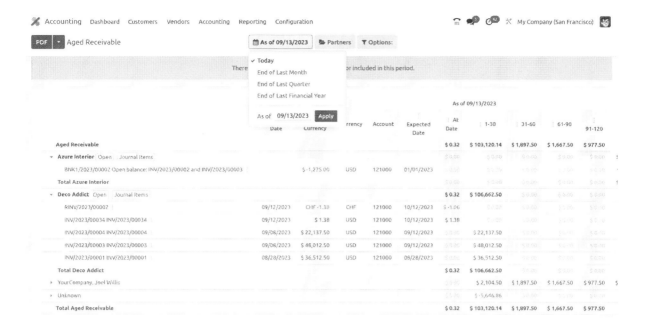

The Partner-based filtering tool will then be displayed, with the Partners and any related tags defined and selectable from a drop-down menu. You will be provided a list of all operating Partners as well as the Tags attached to them, from which you may choose.

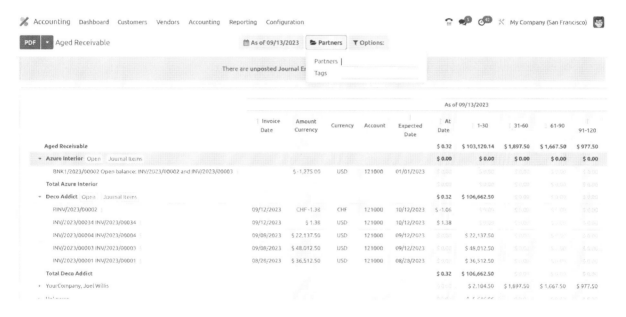

Under the Options tab, you may choose Unfold All Filtering, which will display all items for Aged Receivable. There are also buttons that allow you to print reports in PDF and XLSX formats. The Store button saves reports to the proper place in the Documents modules, allowing you to keep financial information.

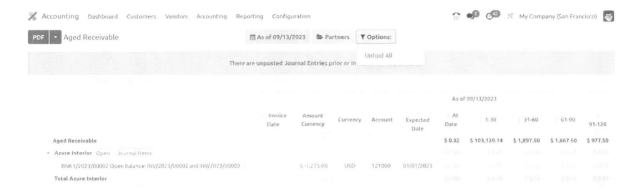

Let's move on to the next step, where the next partner foundation for reporting the Aged Payable reports is created now that we're clear on the Aged Receivable report function, which is available in the Odoo platform's Accounting module.

Aged Payable

Aged Receivable reports in the Odoo Accounting module are the same as the Aged Payable reporting function in Odoo. The report, on the other hand, will be based on the late payment that your company must make to the partner.

With the aid of this reporting capability, you will be able to appreciate the element of the delayed payments that you should have made. The Business Operations Partners or Vendors will be specified, and the Aged Payable entries for each of them will be defined in the Aged Payable reports, exactly as they are in the Aged Receivable reports.

Similarly, the entries in the Aged Payable reports will show the Report Date, Journal details, Amount involved, Expiration date is any depreciation increase the amount as the duration passed will be depicted as 1- 30, 31-60, 61-90, 91-120 and older ones indicating the amount to be paid if the payment is extended based on the duration. The entire amount owed will also be shown at the conclusion. The screenshot below shows the Aged Payable reporting menu, which defines all Aged Receivable elements. Filtering options in the Aged Payable report are equivalent to those in the Aged Receivable reports, as illustrated in the image below.

Let's move on to the next section of the chapter now that we've covered all of the partner-based reporting tools. These are all of the partner-based reporting capabilities available in the Odoo platform's accounting module. The definition of management reports will be supplied in the next section of the chapter.

Management Based Reporting

The essential factor of the company is the management of the financial parts of the operation, and managers are constantly looking for tools and solutions to make the process easier and more efficient. The reporting and report generation features will be utilized as a management tool to evaluate the status of your company's accounting operations. Furthermore, because the reports are real-time, you may rapidly understand how the company's financial operations are developing by taking a fast glance at the accounting-based data.

Odoo, being a sophisticated management tool, provides a number of reporting possibilities as well as report production capabilities for business management and operations. There is a finance management module that provides extensive reporting tools and operating capabilities. In Odoo's Accounting management module, there are various reporting tools for financial operations, as well as reporting tools for Accounting management features such as Invoice Analysis, Analytic Report, Unrealized Currency Gains/Losses, Depreciation Schedule, Budget Analysis, and Product Margins. We will go through each of these components of report production in detail in the sections that follow.

Invoice Analysis

The Invoice Analysis report is the most common sort of accounting management report provided by the Odoo Accounting module. This report will analyze both comprehensive invoices and those that are still in the creation stage of operation. Invoice Analysis reports will include all invoices associated with customer-based activities in the sale of both services and products. View invoice analysis reports using pie, bar, line, and other types of charts. You may see the invoice analysis report based on your requirements by utilizing the filtering and grouping tools featured in the invoice analysis report.

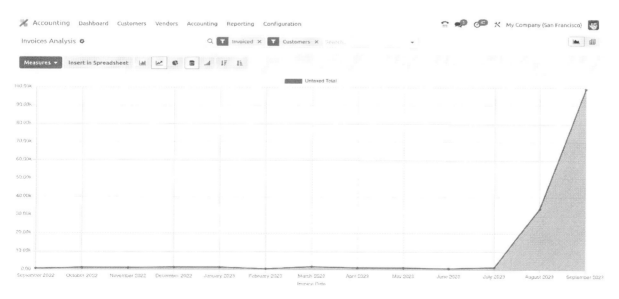

The invoice analysis report bar graphs, which are color-coordinated as appropriate, can be seen in the following screenshot. Filtering and grouping by options help to organize the necessary information about the generated invoices.

In addition, the Kanban view, which is an alternative to the graph view, allows you to produce reports in a different way. Filtering may be done inside the report in the Kanban style, allowing you to display only the essential + and - aspects, as well as expand and depreciate the reporting aspects in respect to the defined entries. You can also use the Filtering and Group by options to generate the report with the available default settings as well as personalized ones. Furthermore, you may establish the measures on which the measurements are based by utilizing the Measures configuration choices, which will assist you in defining the measures on which the Invoice Analysis reporting elements have been defined.

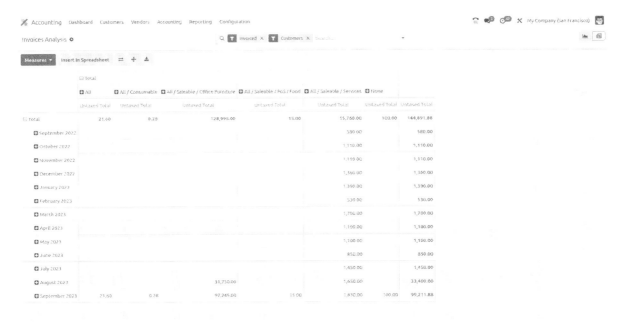

The Invoice Analysis reporting is an exception tool that has been defined for the purposes of the Accounting management alternatives for the business's operations with regard to the invoices that have been created as well as those that are presently in use. Now that we understand the invoice analysis reporting menu in Odoo Accounting, let's move on to the next section, which defines menu for constructing analytical reports.

Analytic Report

With the analytical reporting tool of the Odoo platform, you can define analytical functions related to the accounting components of the organization. In addition, the report provides a quantitative overview of all defined components of the organization's accounting. The available Odoo Analysis Report window is shown in the screenshot. As you can see in the following screenshot, all the components of Odoo's accounting functions are listed here, as well as reference information for the financial functions, the partners involved, and the balance amount.

Additionally, there is a Group by the tool that can help you organize the entries into groups according to the operational, fiscal period, and there is a filter for analytical accounting that can help you filter each of the defined analytical accounts. The different settings may be changed with respect to the Analytical entries to be filtered, which is also possible utilizing a sophisticated filtration tool.

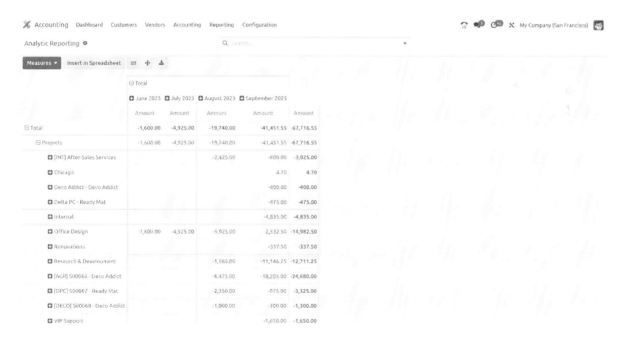

After you choose each entry in the analytical report, you will see all financial operations in connection to the financial elements, as shown in the picture below. We've gone with the Costs & Revenues menu choice here. The menu will define the operations' Date, Description, Analytical Account, and Amount. There are further methods for filtering and grouping available to assist in identifying the relevant entry. By selecting the available Create option, you will also be able to add new entries. Additionally, you may change an entry by choosing the one that has been defined.

By selecting one of the entries, you may read the specifics of that entry, including its description, analytical account, tags assigned, reference information, partner name, and entry date. The level of information, including the amount and quantity allotted to each product, as well as the unit of measurement, will be specified. We will define accounting terms such as Financial Account and Journal Item. You can alter the details that have been defined here as needed by clicking the edit option. The analytical report tool will help you regulate the aspect of the analytical accounting entries by providing you more insight into each activity, making it a vital tool for the company's financial management. Now that we know how the analytical report works, let's move on to the section that covers the reporting requirements for unrealized currency gains and losses in Odoo Accounting.

Unrealized Currency Gains/Losses

The Unrealized Currency Gains/Losses option in the Odoo accounting reporting tools will provide you with information about the company's filtering gains or losses for the selected fiscal quarter. These Gains or Losses are the effect of foreign exchange rates in connection to how the firm is operated. Furthermore, unrealized currency gains and losses are typically connected with multinational enterprises that operate on a worldwide scale or with activities that include many currencies. Because the Odoo platform allows the firm's activities to be conducted in many currencies, this option is accessible in Odoo accounting reporting.

The entries in the Unrealized Currency Gains/Losses reports will be dependent on the filters done for the fiscal periods provided for the report. Furthermore, there are numerous filtering tools that may be utilized to assist with the filtration elements, as well as Custom ones that can be developed based on the requirement. Filtration may be performed using the set conversion rates for the currencies used by your organization and the Odoo platform. With the help of the choices filters, you may sort the data depending on the entries with the Draft entries and the Unposted entries that have been defined.

The entries will comprise Balance in Foreign Currency (the amount taken from the bill in the relevant currency), Balance in Operational Rate (the amount computed at the operation date, or when you received the bill in company currency), and Balance in Current Rate. It is the value in effect at the time the report is submitted or when the corporation is paid. To update your accounting reports with this new information to be specified for the entries to be defined in operation, the Adjustment amount value should also be changed.

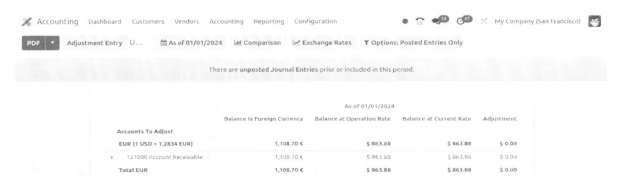

Now that we've covered the Unrealized Currency Gains and Losses reporting tool featured in the Odoo Accounting module, let's move on to the section on Depreciation Schedule-based reporting.

Deferred Expenses

Expenses that have been incurred but are not yet payable are known as deferred expenses. In other words, these are costs that have already been incurred but won't be reimbursed until later. Deferred expenses are crucial because they give firms a mechanism to account for costs associated with assets that will be used over an extended period of time.

Deferred expenses are used in Odoo17 Accounting to manage such expenses. These are intended to specify the framework for the system's handling of postponed expenses. This can be used, for instance, to specify account posting guidelines and the timing of when a cost should be recognized. It can also be applied to create a deferred expense account. Deferred expenses are tracked in this account, which is updated as costs are reimbursed or recognized. This makes it simple for businesses to manage their delayed expenses, maintain tabs on their finances, and control the expense operations of subscription-based products to perfection. The Deferred Expenses take into account costs like;

1. **Prepayment:** In this arrangement, an expense is paid by the business before the product or service is delivered. It is typically used to pay for substantial items like rent, insurance, or subscriptions.
2. **Accrued Expense:** A corporation uses the accrued expense model when an item is incurred but not paid for right away. This might apply to things like unpaid loan interest or staff bonuses.
3. **Depreciation:** When a business buys an asset, it uses this model to expense it throughout the asset's useful life. This might apply to things like structures, machinery, or cars.
4. **Amortization:** When a business pays an expense over time, such loan payments or software license fees, it might use the amortization approach.

The Deferred Expenses are directly related to the subscription-based goods and services that are bought from numerous vendors.

You can navigate to the Accounting module to access the Deferred Expenses pane. You may view the Vendor Bills window here in the Vendor menu, as displayed in the image below.

The Deferred Expenses created in Odoo 17 from the bill like given below;

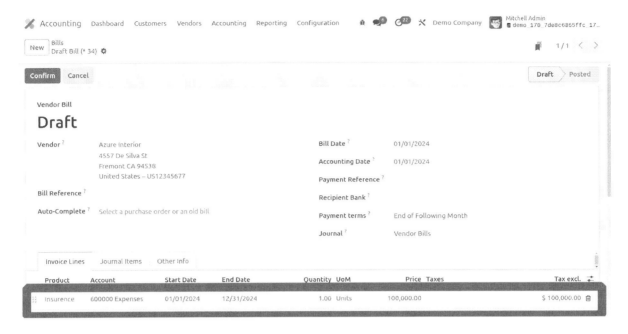

Include the vendor and the product in the vendor bill. The beginning and ending dates of the postponed entries are determined by the start and end dates. Thus, the date the delayed expense begins is the **Start Date**. The deferred expense's expiration date is known as the **End Date**.

To confirm the bill, click the "**Confirm**" button as previously mentioned. Next, a smart tab called "**Deferred Entries**" appears. Users can access the Deferred Expense Entries by activating the Smart Tab.

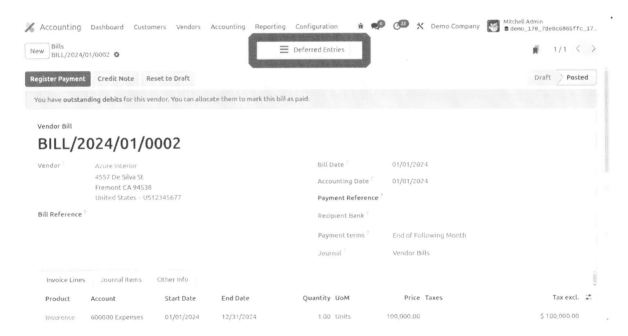

The date, journal entry, account, label, taxes, debit, and credit are all displayed on the entries page.

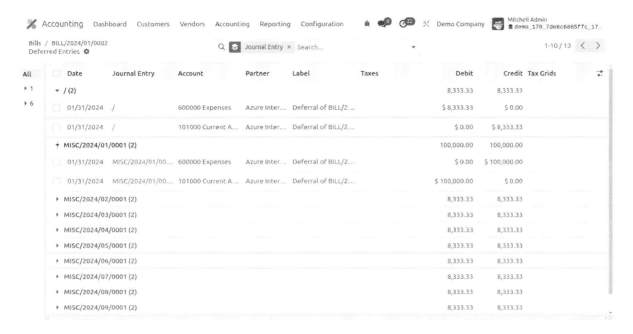

The user has the option to select the accounts for deferred entry posting. There is a mention of these accounts in the settings. The section "Default Accounts" is present. Thus, there is a mention of the default accounts for those entries. There are two ways to generate the deferred expense entries: manually and grouped, or based on the validation of vendor bills. After that, the sum can be calculated using either the equal of all months or the days.

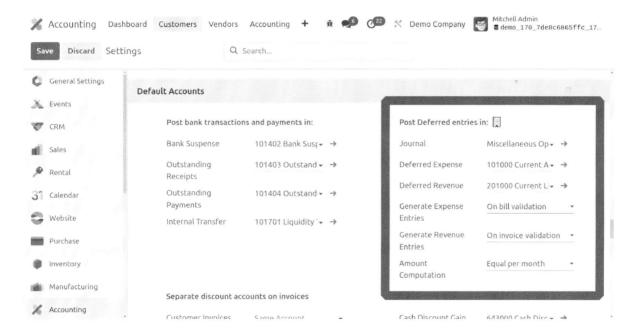

The Deferred Expense Report, located in the Management area, displays each and every deferred expense entry that has been made. The report displays the account, total amount, and depreciation amount.

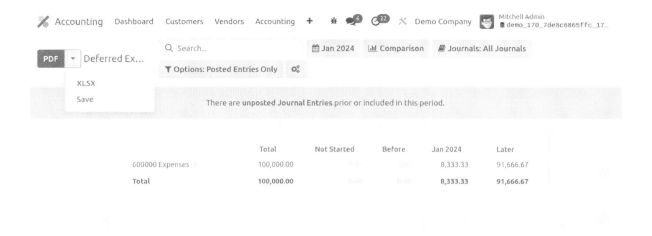

It can be stored on the system as an XLSX or PDF file. Click the Save button to save the report to the Documents module.

Deferred Revenue

The Deferred Revenue feature is especially helpful for businesses that provide subscription services or have a recurring revenue model because it makes it possible for companies to monitor client payments made in advance for goods or services that have not yet been received. The sum is recorded as deferred revenue when a consumer makes an advance payment. When the service or product is supplied, this sum is subsequently recorded as revenue. With the help of this tool, businesses may more easily track their revenue and have more control over their financial statements.

The Odoo 17 Accounting module's Deferred Revenue is simple to set up and utilize. The terms of the deferred revenue agreement, such as the due date, the payment amount, and the delivery date, are readily defined. The money is then recorded as deferred revenue when a customer makes an advance payment, and the revenue is then recognized when the service or product is provided.

It is regarded as a great tool for any companies with recurring revenue models or subscription services. Businesses benefit from safety precautions over the financial records and reliable income tracking. In order to accurately track the organization's present and future liabilities, which will help to ensure that the business can meet its financial responsibilities and continue to be compliant with accounting standards. As a result of knowing when and how much money it expects to get in the future, the company can manage its cash flow more effectively thanks to the deferred revenue model. It is appropriate for services or goods that require upfront payment, such subscriptions or memberships.

For instance, a business might provide a subscription-based service and charge the client before providing the service or commodity. The payment will be represented on the balance sheet as "deferred revenue," indicating that the revenue has not yet been generated.

When the service is rendered, this deferred money will subsequently be recognized as actual revenue.

Let's imagine a business charges $50000 for a year of subscription services. The business adds $50000 in deferred revenue to the balance sheet when the client pays the fee. The business provides the service and generates revenue throughout the year. The corporation will record the deferred revenue as actual revenue at the conclusion of the fiscal year and make the necessary adjustments to the balance sheet.

The organization's Deferred Revenues can be managed through a single invoice in the Odoo17 Accounting module. The invoice, which is located on the Customers menu.

Select the client and the subscription item from within the invoice lines. The invoice line includes additional information such as the account, quantity, and unit price. It also includes the start and finish dates of the service.

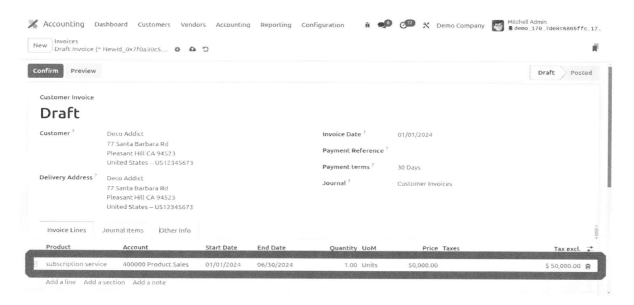

The beginning and ending dates of the postponed entries are determined by the start and end dates. Thus, the date the deferred revenue begins is the **Start Date**. The deferred revenue's end date is known as the **End Date**.

The user can verify the invoice after inputting the necessary information. A new smart tab called **Deferred Entries** will appear after the invoice has been verified.

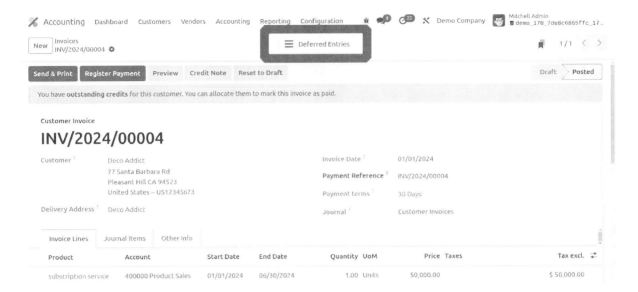

All of the produced entries will be accessible when you open the Deferred Entries smart button. There are several details available, such as the date, journal, account, partner, label, debit, and credit amount.

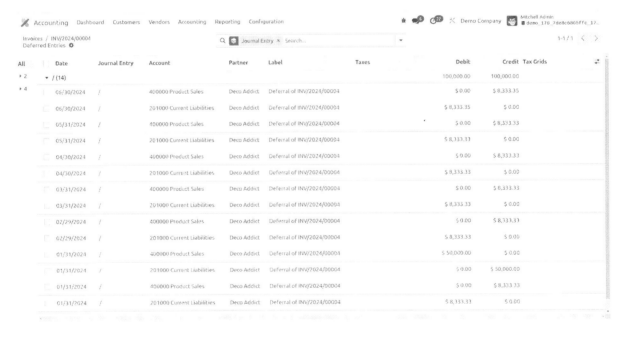

When you click on Settings, you can examine the Default Accounts area where the accounts that are taken are specified.

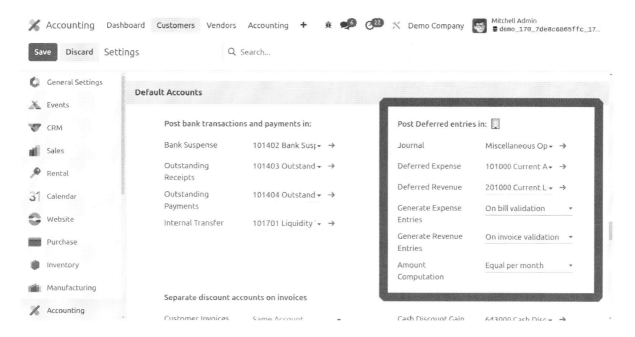

One can set the default Deferred Revenue there. Next, the deferred entries' generation method is determined by the Generate Revenue Entries parameter. Users can select Manually & Grouped or On invoice validation there. To specify how the total money is allocated across the period, there is a money Computation field. It can be divided equally into months or computed using the number of days.

The Deferred Revenue Report, located in the Management section, has the ability to display the entry in the event that one is made. There, you may see the account, total, and monthly depreciation amount.

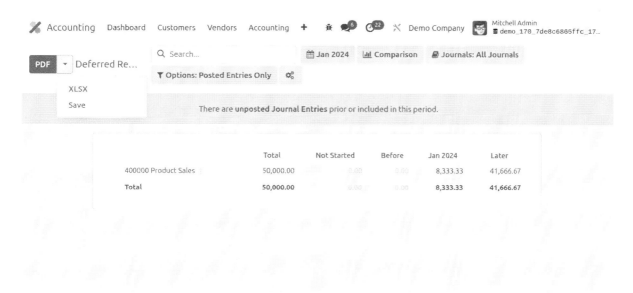

The report is available for download in XLSX and PDF formats to the system. By selecting the Save button, the report can be saved to documents.

Depreciation Schedule

The Depreciation Schedule-based reporting will provide you with information on how rapidly an item selected for usage in your company depreciates. Your company's assets may define the assets you've previously recognized. The Depreciation Schedule reporting option is accessible via the Accounting module's reporting tab. Once you select the choice, the reports on the Depreciation Schedule will be shown, as seen in the image below. The Asset-based Chart of Accounts, as well as any Journals created on it, will be specified by Operations.

In addition, definitions of Characteristics aspects such as Acquisition Date, First Depreciation, Method, and Depreciation Rate will be supplied. The asset's specifications will be stated in terms of months and length of operation. A depiction of the asset's depreciation during the given time period will also be displayed. The book value information for each asset's Depreciation Schedule will also be defined.

Additionally, based on the Fiscal period or the entries, you will have Filtering and Group by tools accessible, exactly like in all other menus on the Odoo platform. These are the usual filtering and grouping choices, and additional ones may be built using the noble tools. These specially specified ones can be saved as Favorites and used in the Depreciation Schedule reporting features filters in the future.

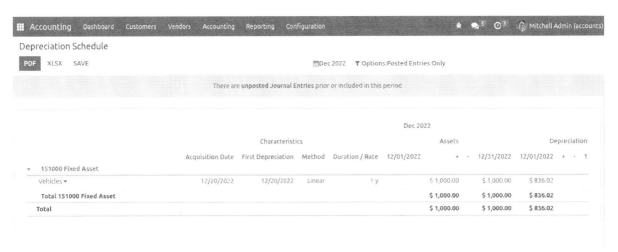

To learn more about the Journal and the entries described in it, choose each entry under the corresponding Chart of Accounts.

To access the asset details, click Open Asset. You can also choose to edit the journal's specifics by using the available Edit option. The MODIFY DEPRECIATION option provides the option to sell, dispose of, re-evaluate, and suspend the asset depreciation. The choices to sell or dispose of the asset are listed under "Sell or Dispose." You can change the depreciation in relation to the asset by choosing the available Re-evaluate option.

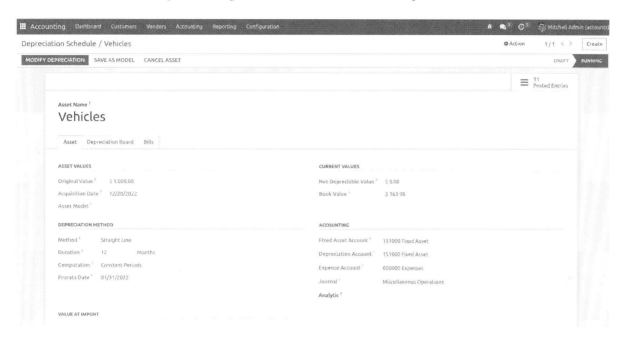

When you select the appropriate Annotate option for the Journal indicated in the Depreciation Schedule, the Annotate window, as shown in the following screenshot, will open. You may add a description to the Annotate actions and save them with the Save option.

The Depreciation Schedule reporting tool, which is accessible on the Odoo platform, will provide you with comprehensive insight into all areas of your company's asset depreciation, as detailed there. Now that we've covered the Depreciation Schedule methods, let's move on to the next part, which will create the Odoo Accounting module's Budget Analysis reports.

Disallowed Expense Report

Disallowed expenses in Odoo 17 Accounting are costs that, in the context of business accounting, are not allowed for reimbursement or deduction, frequently because of internal or regulatory guidelines. The computation of taxable income or reimbursable amounts does not include these expenses.

As a result, these fabricated charges are shown in the Disallowed Expense Report under Management, as may be seen below. Every detail of every Disallowed Expense entry is included in the report. The report displays the total amount, the disallowed rate, and the disallowed amount.

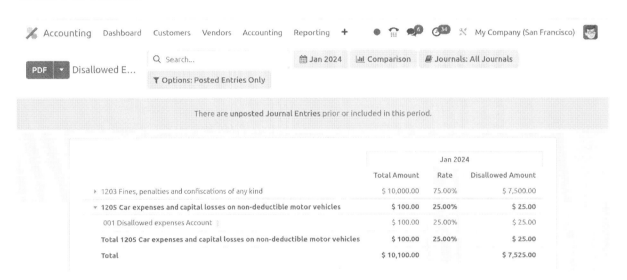

The report is readily available for download to the system in XLSX or PDF format.

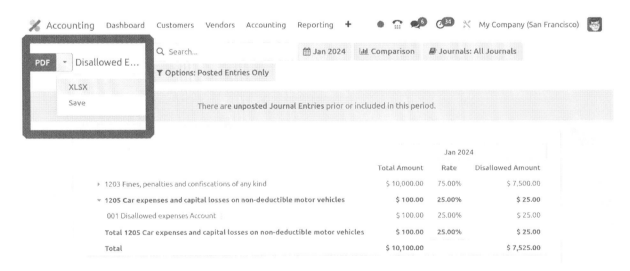

Additionally, by selecting the Save button, the report can be saved to the Documents.

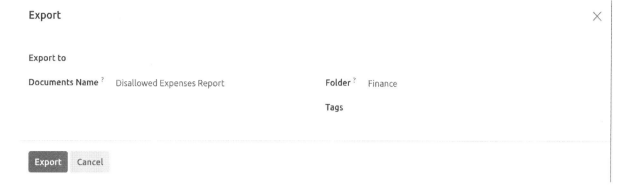

A popup window will appear if the Save button is selected; select the Document Name, Folder, and Tags from there. In order to export this to Documents, click the Export option.

Budget Analysis

The financial planning of a company's business activities for a certain fiscal term or period is primarily reliant on the company's budget. The fiscal department of a corporation will create a single budget as well as several more based on the company's operational and functional requirements. The Odoo platform's Accounting module has a complete Budget Analysis reporting menu where the reporting component of the various budgets can be adjusted. The Budget Analysis Report, which can be accessed via the Accounting module's reporting page, will provide a detailed picture of the business's budgetary activities.

Filtering and grouping by options are available in all Odoo platform menus and may be used to arrange the entries of the Budget Analysis reports in accordance with the needs.

These filtering and grouping options are common, and additional ones may be built using the noble tools. These specially specified ones can be saved as Favorites and used in the Depreciation Schedule reporting features filters in the future. The report will define all budgeted operations from prior fiscal quarters as well as those that are presently ongoing. These sections can easily be expanded to encompass the budget's various financial components.

The budgetary position, analytical account, as well as the Start Date, End Date, Planned Amount, Practical Amount, Theoretical Amount, and Achievement Percentage, will be determined.

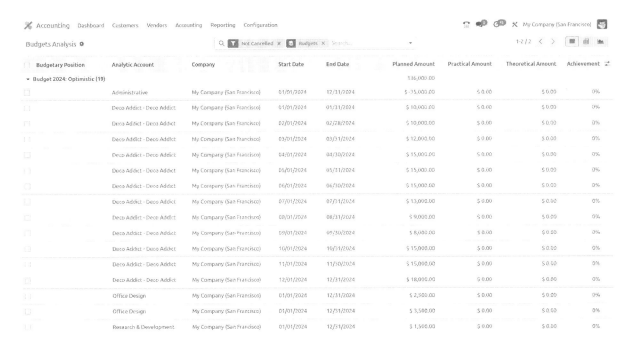

The budget analysis report may be seen in the List view, Pivot view, or Chart view by selecting it from the right-hand menu. The prior pictures showed the list view of the Budget Analysis report. The following screenshot shows the Budget Analysis report's Pivot View. In the pivot view, you may specify the Measures for the aspects that have been created for the different attributes of the entries to be sorted out. By utilizing the + and - signals, you may add the default Measures that have been defined in both axes of the report. You may build and publish reports based on the operational components of the budget using this capability.

Along with the graph view, the budget analysis reports will offer you with a full insight of how your business's budget is running. Furthermore, you will be able to sort out the required entries of each of the reports that have been defined depending on your requirements by using the distinct as well as precise filtering and group by choices that are provided. With Odoo's unique Budget Analysis reporting management solution, you can now grasp the many components of budget management reporting. Let's move on to the part that defines Odoo Accounting's Project Margins reporting.

Product Margins

The product margin is the profit you make from the sale of a thing you manufactured or bought. Product margins and their analysis will provide accurate facts on the products that firms will generate based on product sales. In terms of mathematical operations, the Product Margin is defined as:

Product margin= (selling price – cost of product) / selling price

The product is profitable for the company and the margin percentage is positive if the selling price is higher than the cost price. However, if the selling price is lower than the cost price, the company loses money, and all sales activity results in a negative margin. The Odoo platform is aware of the importance of the production margin in business operations and has created a special reporting function for this purpose in the Odoo accounting module. Product margin reporting, accessible through the Reporting menu in Odoo's accounting module, provides a clear summary of a company's product margin performance.

After selecting the Product Margins option, you will get the pop-up box displayed in the picture below. The General Information data must be configured here, including the From and To choices, which must be further described. You may select Invoice State from the available drop-down menu.

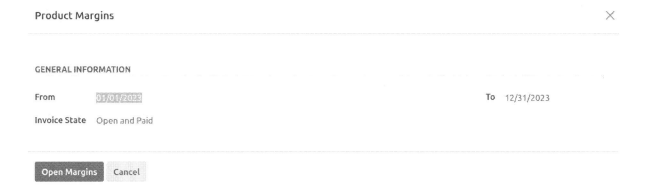

After configuring the operations aspects, select the Open Margins option to show the Product Margins report aspect and the configurations aspect. The product margin reporting will be displayed based on the given settings and the budget analysis. Product names, internal reference information, average sales unit price, invoiced sales amount, turnover, sales gap, total cost, bought amount, total margin, projected margin, total margin rate percentage, and predicted margin percentage are all displayed here.

Furthermore, the Filtering and Group by tools, which are available in all other menus of the Odoo platform, will assist in organizing the Product Margins report inputs according to requirements. These are the usual filtering and grouping choices, and additional ones may be built using the noble tools. Those that are specially tailored to your requirements can be saved as favorites for future use when filtering the Product Margins reporting features.

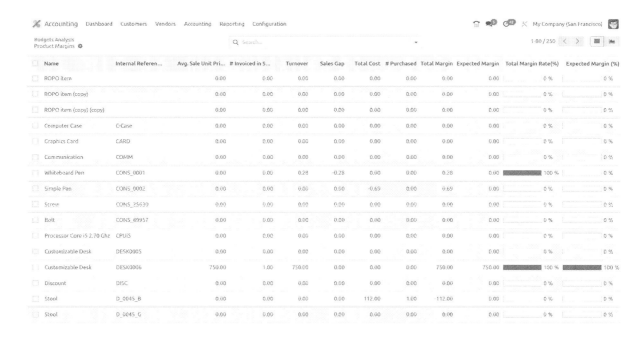

Additionally, you may select from a number of specified Products by using the available Tick box option, which will display the Action option, which will show you the options for Export, Archive, Unarchive, Delete, and the Generate Price List option, as seen in the image below.

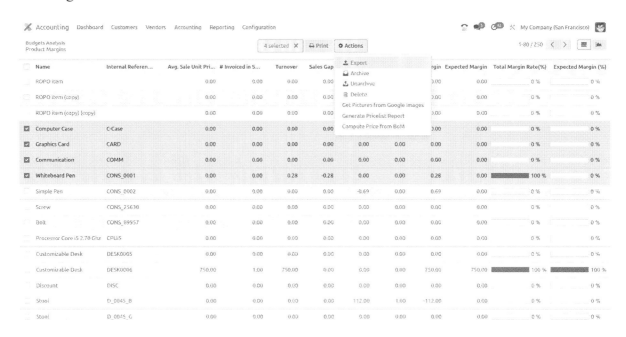

Additionally, the Product Margins reporting menu may be seen in Graph View, which provides a more statistical perspective on the Product Margins. The screenshot below shows the Bar Chart View of the Product Margins reporting. You can also choose whether it should be displayed as a Line or Pie chart based on your needs. There are established grouping options, as well as default and custom filtering tools. The measurements can be defined as needed by selecting from the specified default measures.

The screenshot below displays the Product Margins reporting's Line chart, in which the different attributes of the defined entries are represented by lines.

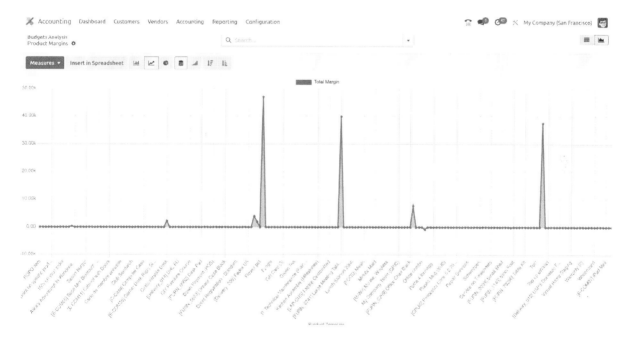

We've been discussing the management-based reporting features of the Odoo Accounting module up to this point.

This chapter focuses entirely on the reporting functions of the Odoo Accounting module and provides a comprehensive description of how they work. We discussed the reporting instruments classified as statement reports, partner reports, audit reports, and management-based reports. The following chapter will focus on configuring Odoo's general settings, which are critical for accounting procedures.

Chapter 7
Mastering Odoo Platform's Configuration Settings

Mastering Odoo Platform's Configuration Settings

The Odoo Admin Settings module provides a variety of configuration options for businesses to customize their Odoo environment. These configuration options enable organizations to customize the Settings to meet their specific needs, such as establishing access privileges, setting up accounting, automating operations, and much more. One of the most important options is the access rights setup, which allows businesses to control who has access to their Odoo environment. This involves creating user groups, roles, and access levels. It also guarantees that only authorized users have access to the platform and its data. Another crucial feature is the Accounting configuration, which enables companies to set up their accounting system and configure account types, tax laws, and other accounting settings to guarantee that the financial information is correct and up to date. Additionally, the module strongly encourages the automation of several procedures, including sales, order management, and billing. By doing this, the time and effort needed to manage the business are reduced.

The Odoo platform controls its configuration settings through the Settings menu. Administrators may change system parameters, control user access levels, set up automatic operations, control email notifications, manage security settings, and more through this menu. These settings may be viewed, changed, and backed up via the Odoo web interface. They are kept in the Odoo database. Users may adapt their Odoo instance to their needs by using the platform's Settings and Configuration features. They offer ways to manage data, configure user access, customize the user interface, and establish automated procedures. The Settings and Configuration choices are intended to make the user experience as efficient and user-friendly as possible while simultaneously offering control over the platform and its components.

In the last chapter, we focused on the reporting features of the Odoo 17 Accounting module and provided appropriate screenshots to illustrate each menu and option. As we all know, the Odoo Admin Settings module is a strong tool that gives administrators the ability to tailor the Odoo system to their organization's particular business requirements. Additionally, it enables administrators to set up and control several features of the Odoo system, including users, modules, businesses, menus, and more. This module provides a considerable level of modification freedom, enabling administrators to modify the system to suit their unique requirements. Additionally, it provides a number of security capabilities to safeguard the system's data as well as a range of analytics tools to provide insight into how the system functions. In this chapter, we will extensively examine the Configuration Settings accessible in the Odoo platform, as well as the tools and capabilities supplied to the Accounting module and its activities. The highlights of this chapter will be the subjects below.

* User settings and
* Translation settings

A thorough explanation of each of these elements will be provided, along with well-equipped screenshots to help you understand each process.

User Settings

The Odoo platform offers a variety of options for setting platform users, their operational potential, and the available authorization. The Odoo system software is regarded as the top business management solution since it opens the way for methodically categorizing people according to their priorities and their permission levels, which is crucial for providing the business management team with superior visibility. Odoo also has a feature that enables users to run their businesses with the appropriate access, flexibility, and freedom and to carry out their duties in line with their respective job roles within the company. In the real-time operation of a firm, it is not reasonable to provide a lower-level employee total authority and authorization to control all elements of the organization, since this would introduce complexity and challenges in operational practice.

Realizing this, the founders of Odoo and its engineers created a hierarchical authorization level for users in the functioning, which would aid in efficient administration. Three different sorts of users will be available through this platform for the system's functioning. which are

- Internal User
- Public User
- Portal user.

Internal users in Odoo are employees of corporations. It might be admin users with full access to the ERP or regular workers who work in various departments within the organization and only have access to those sections. Additionally, department leaders who have full access to their specific department's activities but do not have full access privileges to the organization are also regarded as internal users. Therefore, both workers with restricted access permissions and admin users with full access are included in this internal user group. In the first case, someone with full access to the Odoo system is considered the highest level user in the system and can perform any action, such as creating other users, configuring views and menus, changing system configuration, assigning privileges, and performing other administrative tasks. All remaining users are under their control because they have administrator capabilities on their superuser account and a knack for administering. The team leads, and business managers often come under this type of authorization.

Additionally, the Odoo platform allows for the operation of several Admin users, each of whom receives a separate authorization to fall under this category in line with the requirements. This will ensure that the associated Admin user has safe and secure management control over the team or department. Only the admin user has the ability to add new modules or update current ones. Users who are employed by the firm, excluding managers and management teams, make up the second type of internal users. These are likely to be the executives and other workers who report to the manager. The Odoo system provides a different login and log-out code of operation for these sorts of users, and it will acquire insight into each employee's performance and functioning. The same operational features for logging in and out may be used to record attendance, take time off, and understand how an employee's timesheet of operations relates to organizational functionality.

The second category of users is the Public Users, who are website visitors. Users of the portal are the third sort of user, distinct from the other user types, and are often used to grant consumers access to the Odoo portal. Portal users have restricted access to Odoo's backend. Since they normally do not have access to the back end of Odoo, they may access some sections like the customer portal, website, or other places that are visible to the public. Portal users are often used for customers, vendors, and other external entities. Without having full access to the system, they grant consumers or suppliers access to the Odoo platform. This user may access documents and do operations like as placing orders and confirming quotations, checking the supply of certain items, service availability, and so on. Additionally, the organization's responsible authority can determine what level of access should be provided to these portal users.

The three categories that were just discussed are the three types of fundamental users that Odoo enables you to administer inside the platform for carrying out different organizational functions. With its most extensive User setup options and the accessible Management menu, the Odoo platform handles all of these users quite fluidly. Now that we've covered the Users on the Odoo platform, let's go through the User menu and its many setup options in detail.

User Menu

In Odoo, the User menu allows users to customize their user interface with their own preferences and settings. It offers access to a number of customizing choices and is situated in the interface's upper right corner. The Users & Companies page found in the Settings module also provides access to the Users menu.

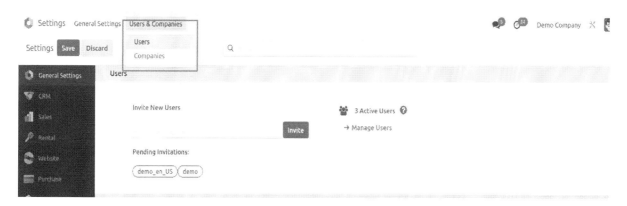

It allows the user to choose their language, theme, company, notification choices, and more. Additionally, it gives access to the user's settings, favorites list, and profile. You may create the Users menu displayed in the picture above by using the specialized Users management menu in the Odoo system's General Settings and the Dashboard. To obtain extra features, functions, and operational elements, you may enable the Odoo Developer mode from Odoo Settings, where you will have access to more complex functional tools and capabilities that will be useful in platform setup.

As seen in the picture below, you may access the Developer mode from the General Settings option found in the Developer tools.

In addition, the Odoo platform's dashboard will have a Debugging option that may be selected to enable developer mode. Similar to this, there are extensions and other programs for Chrome, Firefox, and other top browsers that will enable you to quickly activate or disable the Developer and Debugging modes of the Odoo platform.

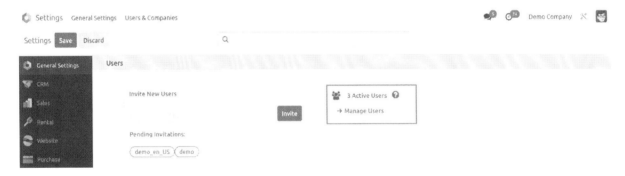

When you select the User option, you will be sent to a new window where you can examine all of the users that have been specified in the platform. The window will display the user's key information, such as the User Name and Login ID, the Company and Language of operation data, and the Most Recent Authentication details.

314

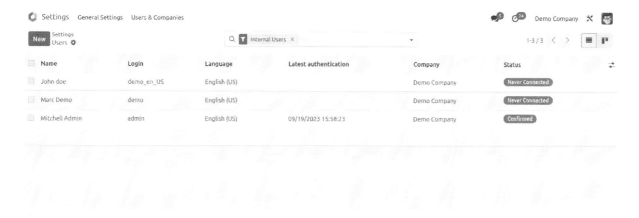

The preview of the Users' information may be expanded by clicking on the corresponding line and seen in full, as well as edited if necessary. Using the CREATE button on this window, you may create additional Users.

Furthermore, the different sorting functions available at the top of the window will be highly beneficial for filtering, grouping, and searching for needed information. The Filters tab provides a variety of preset and configurable filtering options to help you discover your urgent record quickly. Internal Users, Portal Users, Inactive Users, Two-factor authentication enabled, Two-factor authentication disabled, and, of course the Add Custom Filter option are the pre-selected filters shown under the Filters tab.

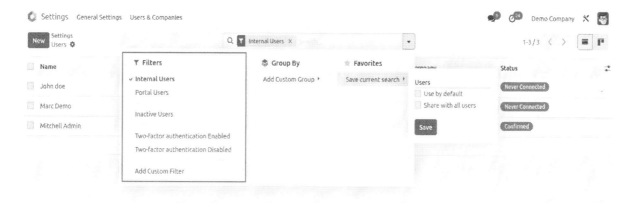

The Favourites tab includes choices such as Save current search as seen in the figure below.

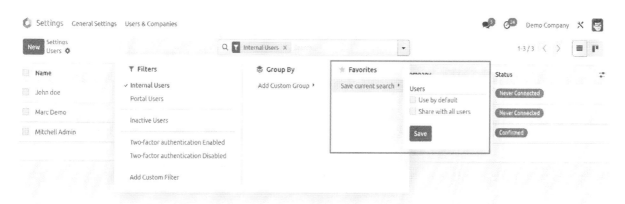

The Group By option allows you to Add a Custom Group to sort the user according to the group of users.

Furthermore, Odoo allows you to pick a previously added user by selecting the checkbox option, which is present in each user record. When you activate it, the system will manage a top Action and Print button, as seen in the picture below. Under the Action button, you may conduct the following actions: Export, Archive, Unarchive, Delete, Change Password, Disable two-factor authentication, Send Password Reset Instructions, and Invite to use two-factor authentication.

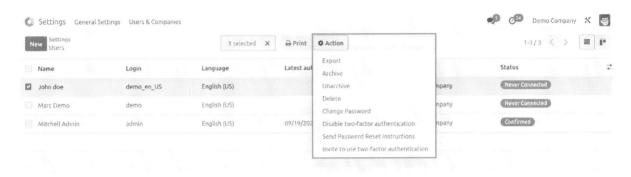

The user has the option to export the fields in CSV or XLSX format when they select the Export button. Additionally, users may select which fields to export before clicking the **Export** button to start exporting their data.

The **Archive** and **Unarchive** buttons allow you to archive and unarchive the specified record. And possible to delete the selected users simply by pressing the **Delete** button. Click the **Change Password** option to modify the user's password. A new window will then emerge with the updated password, as seen below.

316

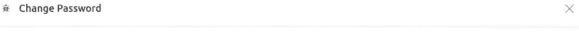

User	User Login	New Password
	lauriepoiret	

Change Password   Cancel

The Print Labels option, which is also accessible through the Print button, is particularly helpful for printing. Additionally, you may access the User window in Kanban format by selecting the Kanban view menu button in the upper right corner. From there, you can view the user's profile information and picture, as demonstrated below.

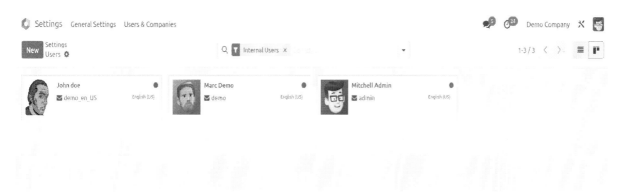

Viewing this window will clearly show if the users are online or offline, with a green indicator on the top right corner of each user record.

The Odoo platform's proprietary User menu provides a comprehensive view of your Odoo system's users and provides maximum administrative functionality. Now that we have a good picture of the Odoo platform's User administration menu let us move on to the details of new user creation.

Creation of a New User

As we said in the previous part, we can create new users by using the CREATE button. A single click on the CREATE button opens the creation form, which contains all of the data needed to set up a new Odoo user. You may set up as many users as you need for your business operation using this creation form. Check out the creation window first.

Settings General Settings Users & Companies Translations Technical Demo Company Mitchell Admin demo_saas-163_aaabd8b728..

New Users
New Groups 69 Access Rights 1,152 Record Rules 195

Never Connected Confirmed

Name

e.g. John Doe

Email Address

e.g. email@yourcompany.com

Access Rights Preferences

MULTI COMPANIES

Allowed Companies Demo Company X

Default Company Demo Company

USER TYPE

User types ○ Internal User
○ Portal
○ Public

Settings General Settings Users & Companies Translations Technical Demo Company Mitchell Admin demo_saas-163_aaabd8b728..

New Users
New Groups 69 Access Rights 1,152 Record Rules 195

SALES		SERVICES	
Sales	Administrator	Field Service	Administrator
Point of Sale	Administrator	Project	Administrator
Sign	Administrator	Timesheets	Administrator
		Helpdesk	Administrator

ACCOUNTING		INVENTORY	
Accounting	Accountant	Inventory	Administrator
Bank		Purchase	Administrator

MANUFACTURING		WEBSITE	
Manufacturing	Administrator	Website	Editor and Designer

MARKETING		HUMAN RESOURCES	
Online Appointment	Administrator	Planning	Administrator
Events	Administrator	Employees	Administrator
Email Marketing	User	Contracts	Administrator
Email Marketing	User	Contracts	Administrator
		Time Off	Administrator
		Recruitment	Administrator
		Expenses	Administrator

PRODUCTIVITY		ADMINISTRATION	
Documents	Administrator	Administration	

TECHNICAL

A warning can be set on a partner (Account)	☐	A warning can be set on a partner (Stock)	☐
A warning can be set on a product or a customer (Purchase)	☐	A warning can be set on a product or a customer (Sale)	☐
Access to Private Addresses	☑	Access to export feature	☑
Advanced Pricelists	☐	Allow the cash rounding management	☐
Allow to define fiscal years of more or less than a year	☐	Analytic Accounting	☐

318

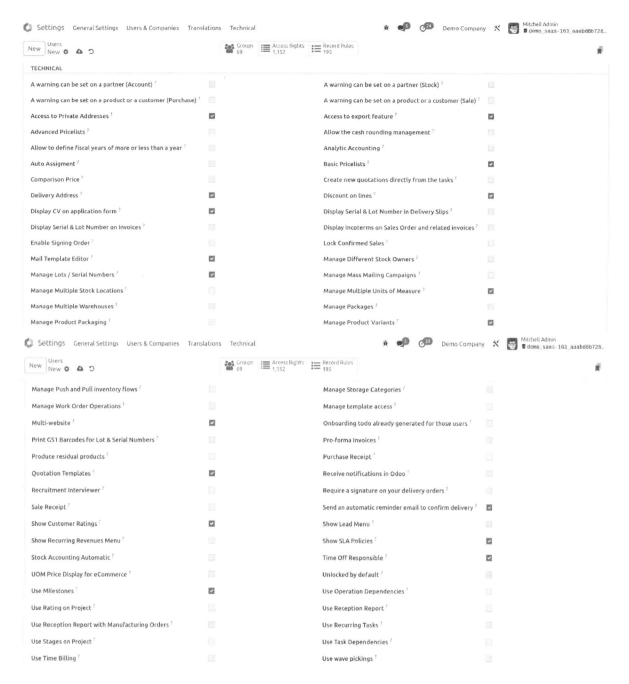

You can first enter the user's name in the Name box of this User Creation form. The user's email address can then be entered in the corresponding field. Additionally, you may upload the user's photo in the area given. After completing these basic setups, you may customize the user's preferences and access rights under the Preferences and Access Rights tabs, respectively. Let's talk about each tab below.

Access Right Configuration

The Access Rights tab in the Users setup form allows you to define the user's access rights-related information. There are various fields on the Access Rights tab. First of all, you can describe the Multi companies' associated information, such as Allowed Companies and Default Company. In the Allowed Companies section, you may specify which companies the user has access to if the system is multi-company. The Default Company option allows the user to specify their default company. Next, under the User types area, the platform offers three options: Internal User, Portal, and Public, from which you may choose the most appropriate. Then you may talk about the user's potential for sales. In the Sales area, there is a dropdown menu with three options: User: Own Documents Only, User: All Documents, and Administrator. If you choose the first option, the user will be able to view his personal data in the Sales application. In the second scenario, the user will have access to every user's sales application record. In the case of the Administrator, the user will have access to the sales configuration as well as statistics information.

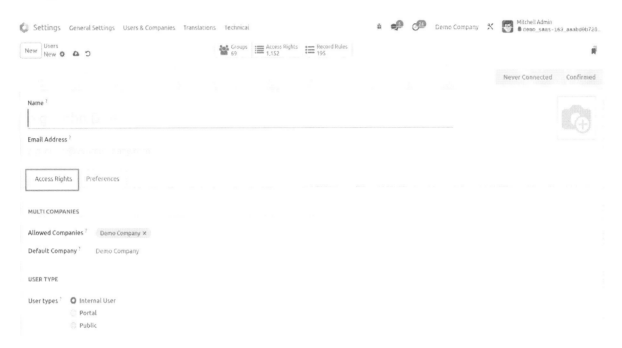

Furthermore, in the Point of Sale field, there are User and Administrator choices in the dropdown menu. Setting a good one right now on the spot enables you to get the most out of your point of sale through quick sale encoding, streamlined payment mode encoding, automatic pricing list production, and other features. Similar to this, the Sign field makes it simple for you to sign and finish your papers by allowing you to select the best option from the choice of "User Own Templates or Administrator."

Following that, you may describe the Accounting-related components, making it easier to manage accounting demands. You have a variety of options here, including Billing, Read-only, Bookkeeper, and Accountant, which we will go into more depth about later. Likewise, the user's manufacturing characteristics might be classified as either Administrator or User in the respective field.

Then, under the Services area, you may define the Field Services, Project, Timesheet, and Helpdesk. Additionally, the Inventory and Purchase sections allow you to choose either Administrator or User depending on the relevant user and are used to control inventory operations and stock activities. The Live Chat, eLearning, and Website fields are then found in the Website section. The user will have the ability to remove assistance channels if the Live Chat box is set to Administrator. The user will have the authority to remove the support channel

320

if it is designated to be a User. Similar to this, you may designate the user as an Officer or Manager in the eLearning field. In the Website area, you can select 'Restricted Editor' or 'Editor and Designer'.

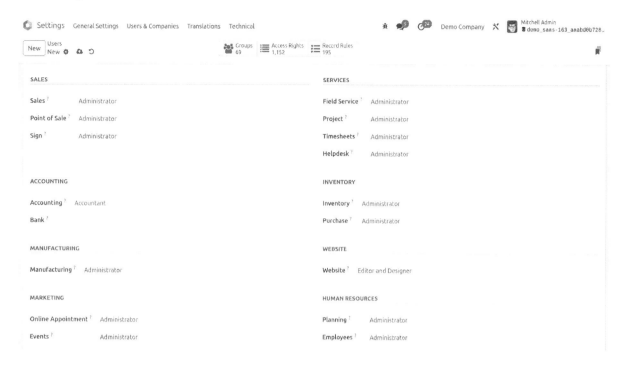

Furthermore, in the Marketing area, you may describe the essential features using the Online Appointment, Social Marketing, Marketing Automation, Events, Email Marketing, and Surveys sections.

Then, under the Human Resources area, you can see several fields like Fleet, `Lunch, Planning, Employees, Approvals, Contracts, Time Off, Recruitment, and Expenses. Furthermore, the Administration option allows you to specify whether the user has 'Access

Rights' or 'Settings' access. Similar to this, an appropriate selection from the dropdown menu may be entered in the Documents box found under Productivity.

Boolean fields are now available in the Technical area, and they can be activated or disabled depending on the user. A warning can be put on a partner (Account), a product or a client (Purchase), and several other variables. Private Addresses Access, Modern pricelists, Permit fiscal years to be defined that are longer or shorter than a year, Basic Pricelists, immediate creation of a new quote from the chores, reduction on lines, delivery slips, show the serial and lot numbers. On the Sales Order and any related invoices, display the Incoterms, Lock Confirmed Sales, Control Access to Templates, Control Multiple Units of Measure, Control Multiple Stock Owners, Control Mass Mailing Campaigns, Control Packages, Control Product Variants, Control Storage Categories Print GS1 Barcodes for Serial Numbers and Lots, create leftover items, Templates for quotes, the reward for referrals, responsible user Purchase Receipt, Display Customer Reviews, Display Recurring Revenues, B2B tax display, Time Off Responsible, Default Unlocked, Operation Dependencies are useful. Use recurring tasks, use subtasks, and the reception report Utilize time billing A warning can be put on a partner (stock), a product, or a customer (sale), among other things. access to the export function Allows cash management, Analytic Accounting, Price comparison, shipping address, display of a resume on an application, and Clearly showing serial and lot numbers on invoices.

Activate the signing order Editor for Mail Templates, Manage Product Packaging, Push and Pull Inventory Flows, Multiple Stock Locations, Multiple Warehouses, Manage Lots/ Serial Numbers, Manage Work Order Operations Pro-forma invoices, several websites, Order Receipt, the interviewer for a job, ask for a signature on your delivery orders, Send an automated email reminder to verify delivery. Display Lead Menu SLA Policies, please UOM Price Display for eCommerce, Tax Display B2C Use benchmarks, Use the Project rating Use Manufacturing Orders and Reception Report, Project Stages are used, Use wave pickings and task dependencies. The other rights areas, such as Contact Creation and Multi Currencies, can likewise be activated or removed in a similar manner. The appropriate user will be helped by the setting of the Technical and Access Rights elements to manage all of these actions on your platform. Furthermore, all of these configuration elements will simply aid you with the permission part of the respective user in your Odoo platform.

So far, we have discussed the operations and maintenance of the User's Access Rights description, and now we can go on to the following part, which will cover the Preference choices configuration.

Preference Options Configuration

Now that we've covered the choices accessible on the Access Rights page of the Users creation window, let's move on to the Preferences tab, where you can see the options indicated in the picture below.

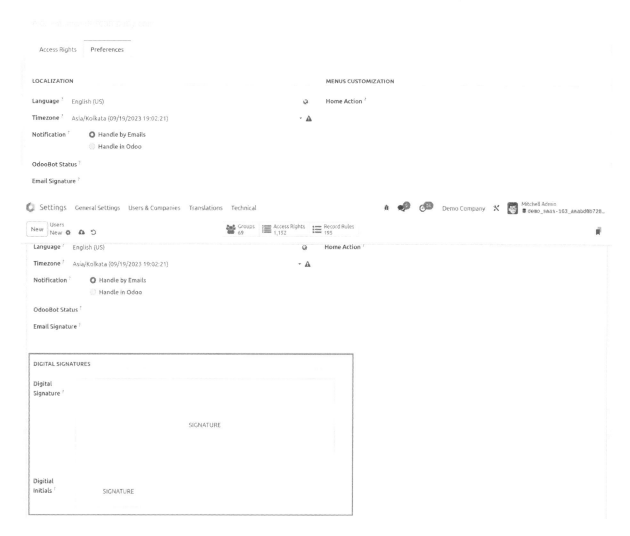

You can adjust the Preferences characteristics of the corresponding user on this Preferences tab. Initially, you can assign the Localization information in the LOCALIZATION section. There are several fields here. You can choose your chosen language first by entering it in the Language area. for the purpose of having all emails and documents sent to this contact translated into the chosen language. After that, the Time zone may be selected using the dropdown menu. Additionally, you may define the protocol for handling Chatter alerts. Therefore, the handling of notifications for user operations may be either handled via emails or handled in Odoo. By selecting emails (Handle by Emails), notifications will be sent to your (the user) email address, which means that enabling this option will notify the user of the corresponding email IDs, which is useful for users who log into the Odoo platform infrequently as they operate in the organization without major benefit from the Odoo platform. The alerts will show up in your Odoo mailbox in the second scenario (Handle in Odoo).

Furthermore, you (administrators) can indicate the state of the particular user's OdooBoot account. It may be configured in a variety of ways, and you'll show all the options in the dropdown menu.

- Not Initialized
- Onboarding emoji
- Onboarding Attachment

- Onboarding command
- Onboarding ping
- Idle
- Disabled
- Onboarding Canned

Additionally, you may establish an email signature in the Email Signature box, where you can enter a command by typing "/" in this area. The system will then provide a drop-down menu from which you may choose from a variety of Structures, Formats, Images, Navigation, Widgets, Basic blocks, and other options. You may add text, photos, and many other components to the email signature using these choices.

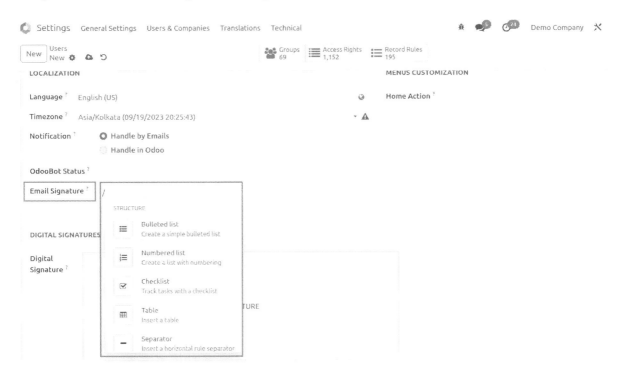

You also have the 'Karma' field. In this section, you may specify a numerical number that indicates how active a user is on the Odoo platform. The user's interactions with other users, such as comments and postings, as well as their work on tasks, projects, and documents, are taken into account while calculating it. The more engaged a user is, the higher their karma worth.

Similar to this, Home Action's MENU CUSTOMIZATION features may be selected from a drop-down menu within the field, and you can even create a new one based on your needs. This option allows you (administrators) to choose an action that users will see initially, in addition to the regular menu, when they log in. Similarly, the DIGITAL SIGNATURES field can be configured to include a digital signature. You may add your signature in a new window by clicking the Signature description box.

Depending on your choices, you may either Draw or Load signatures here. The Digital Initials field may be used in the same way. Finally, the Live chat Username box is where the Live Chat features may be obtained.

It became clear that the configuration aspects of the user preference management that can be configured in the Odoo platform, and the following section will focus on the specific types of users and the functional aspects they are offered in conjunction with the Accounting management of the company operations.

Access Rights for Users in Odoo Accounting

Providing authorization-based degrees of operation among a company's personnel is critical not only for its smooth operation but also for securing sensitive data, restricting access to particular portions of the system, and avoiding unauthorized publication of confidential information. It also helps to guarantee that staff only have access to the information they require to accomplish their jobs, which can lessen the risk of hacking.

Furthermore, limiting access to certain regions can aid in the prevention of harmful ensure and ensuring that only authorized individuals have access to the system. Similar to this, the authorization-based levels of operation will show who has the power and is in charge of what aspects of the organization's operation. The advanced Odoo platform supports hierarchical processes by developing default user options in the platform. You have the option to define the default user options that may be selected to designate the associated user's authority in this feature.

When setting up new users, the Odoo 17 platform allows you to assign the user a Billing, Read-only, Bookkeeper, or Accountant in terms of the company's financial activities.

Access privileges are assigned to users in Odoo Accounting using access control lists. Access permissions can be issued, updated, or withdrawn for certain users based on their function in the organization. The Accounting module's access privileges can range from read-only access to total control. It is also used to restrict access to certain financial data and transactions, ensuring that only authorized individuals may see and change financial data.

According to the hierarchy, the Consolidated user will be given the greatest honor of control over your company's financial management activities. Then comes the accountant. While the Bookkeeper and Billing are beneath them, Read-only employees are at a lower level and have less access to organizational resources. This is so because they work in the customer-facing area of the company, where their primary responsibilities include talking with clients, making sales, and doing billing desk duties.

Now is allowed to validate the trusted bank accounts only by the person who has access to them. Under the accounting section, 'Bank' can either be left empty or choose "validate bank account".

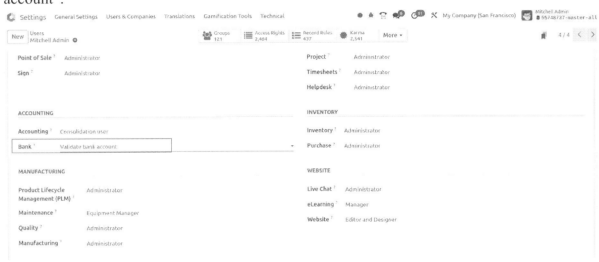

The Accountant of an organization is in charge of filing the accounting elements and organizing them in an orderly manner in accordance with the rules and laws. The Accountant fills up each bill and invoice, and they are all controlled in operation as needed. Additionally, an accountant will be in charge of disbursing funds in relation to the purchase operations carried out and the requirements and prerequisites of the business's operation. The Accountant in Odoo will be in charge of managing all areas of the administration of the financial operation, including the Chart of Accounts, Ledgers, and Journal entries.

The second level of hierarchy for Odoo users determines the Bookkeeper's access privileges. A user with bookkeeper access permissions will be in charge of managing customers and vendors and having access to the accounting dashboard. Accounting features of journal entry production and asset deferred revenue/expense management tool, as well as reporting components.

Users with access rights Billing will not have access to the accounting dashboard, but it will be able to create invoices, bills, and payments as well as some management reports, such as invoicing analysis, depreciation schedules, and unrealized currency gain/loss reports, among others.

The next level of the hierarchy specifies the Read-only access right, which allows Odoo users to view the accounting dashboard in read-only mode. It will be able to create partner bills and invoices while having read-only access to all other accounting and administration functions, such as managing assets, deferred revenue/expense, reporting, and partner payments.

The Odoo platform is quite effective for this. For the appropriate operation of the business, you should offer distinct power and accessibility to every single employee in accordance with the person's talents, skills, and designations.

Furthermore, the platform's cutting-edge tools and features will serve as a full solution for seamless and successful company management. The software allows you to continually monitor if workers have the correct access and opportunities, and whether they are not misrepresenting the company's operations.

Now it is clear that the various sorts of users mentioned in Odoo with the Accounting activity. It will be extremely satisfying and beneficial to each member to be given the appropriate power. Let us now proceed to explore the setup components of the Companies and the accompanying Settings choices.

Company Settings

Switching to better technologies and systems is essential for any organization or business that wants to ride the wave of rapid development in the business environment and boost its business structure. A strong ERP system not only cuts costs but also simplifies corporate activities. As we previously stated, compared to other ERP systems, Odoo ERP is more simple to set up and operate. Odoo ERP is a fully integrated software system that can be installed for any type and size of business. After successfully implementing Odoo for your business's seamless management, you will initially need to set up the firm and the accompanying information needed for Odoo to perform all of your business's necessary duties. It is necessary to outline every aspect of the company's and business's operations and activities. Odoo has a strong and specialized Settings menu that may help you properly design its configuration features. This menu is used to control all of these characteristics. The Odoo system's General parameters page has a special Companies management menu, which allows you to effectively create different company-related parameters. With the help of this menu, you can easily create the firm and set up the necessary activities for it.

Additionally, you will be able to set up several operating companies, each of which may be run from a single platform and consist of both parent and child firms. Odoo's multi-company operation support allows you to set up and manage many businesses from a single database. This functionality is important if you have several businesses that need to be managed from a single platform. With Odoo, you can quickly create and manage various companies, assign users to various companies, and securely handle the data of each firm. Additionally, you may transfer data between firms using Odoo's multi-company capability, including information about goods, clients, and accounting. This will be beneficial in terms of saving time and resources while managing many enterprises.

A firm can now establish many branches. It implies that managing the company's branches is now quite simple. And it's also possible to add multiple branches to the parent company. Odoo's multi-company configuration makes it easy to share sales and buy procedures between firms in the same Odoo database. It is also suitable for invoicing between organizations involved in inter-company activities. In the next part, we will gain a thorough grasp of the many aspects of the Odoo platform's Company administration settings and configurations.

Creation of a Company

On the Odoo 17 platform, finding and managing the company's menu is rather simple. As seen in the picture below, you may access the Manage Companies option as well as other company-related features by going to the Settings module, where you will find the menu. There, you will also find a clearly marked Companies tab.

The companies tab in Odoo 17's General Settings window is seen above, and it allows you to modify the businesses and their associated settings. It gives you a summary of every company in your Odoo instance and allows you to modify, delete, and create new businesses. The tab also allows you to view the company's settings, which include its name, currency, timezone, and logo, as well as its address, contact information, and other pertinent information. It also gives access to the company's security options, including passwords, roles, and user access levels.

The Companies window, as seen in the picture below, will appear when you click on the Manage Companies arrow under the Companies.

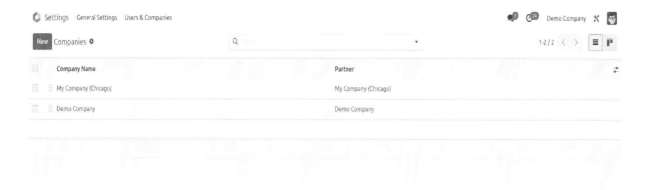

You can see that two businesses are already set up on this platform, and the specifics are shown here. Similar to that, all the configured firms' information will be presented in this window. By switching the corresponding menu icon that is visible in the upper right corner, you may access and examine this information in either list format or kanban format. The window will display the Company Name as well as the Partner details. The Filters, Group By, and Search features will be incredibly helpful for quickly locating and classifying businesses while managing so many businesses on one platform. The sorting features can be adjusted based on your preferences. The Favourites tab has helpful options to carry out a variety of tasks, which is crucial for the efficient administration of your company and business. In the menus, there are options to Save Current Search, Import Records, Link Menu in Spreadsheet, and Insert List in Spreadsheet. The Export All button, which is located next to the CREATE button, makes it easy to swiftly export information into an Excel file. Additionally, you may pick a specific firm record. To do this, simply tick the box next to the appropriate business. As illustrated below, the system will now provide an Action button with the Export, Archive, Unarchive, and Delete choices. The Print option is also visible in the Action menu on the left.

As shown in the picture above, the Print menu features sub-menus such as Preview Internal Report, Preview External Report, and Report Layout Preview. The company window's Kanban view will appear as in the below-displayed illustration.

The Kanban view will show the company name, email address, and phone number, as well as additional keys and options.

The **New** button makes it simple to create a new company record in your Odoo platform. As seen in the screenshot below, the New button directs you to the Company configuration form.

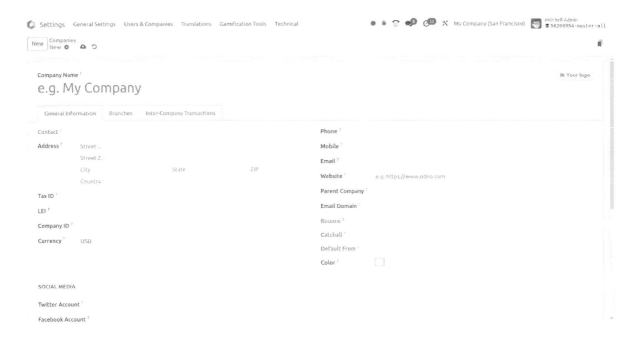

First and foremost, the organization Name section on the formation form requires you to provide the name of your organization. In the next step, you may add your company's logo to the designated area. This is crucial for clearly distinguishing your business from that of other businesses. You may upload your logo from the system by choosing the Your logo option and choosing to attach it. You may customize the general information and the VAT Units data under the corresponding tabs after specifying these two pieces of information.

Under the General Information tab, you may describe the company's address in the Address area. Here, you must include details like your street address, city, state, zip code, and country of business. Then there's the Tax ID box, which allows you to control the firm's tax identification number, which will be used to identify the company in tax processes and legal documents. When the firm is liable to government taxes, this area must be filled out. The company's register number can then be assigned in the Company ID box. It serves as the business's unique internal ID for Odoo. Then, in the Currency area, you may specify the correct currency.

In addition, the Phone number, Mobile number, Email Address, Website information, and Parent Company can be mentioned in the available area. Additionally, you must mention the Company Favicon, which is used to configure the favicon or logo that is displayed next to the company name in the web browser's title bar while the firm's website is open. It is quite helpful for rapidly locating the business and website that is connected to it.

Following that, in specific fields, social media information such as Twitter Account, Facebook Account, GitHub Account, LinkedIn Account, YouTube Account, and Instagram Account may be defined.

Users can use the Add a Line option on the Branches page to list the parent company's branches. A new window will open as you click the Add a Line button. As seen in the figure below, the branch company will be listed inside the Branches tab when it has been added. Any number of branches that the parent firm has can be listed there by just selecting the Add a line option.

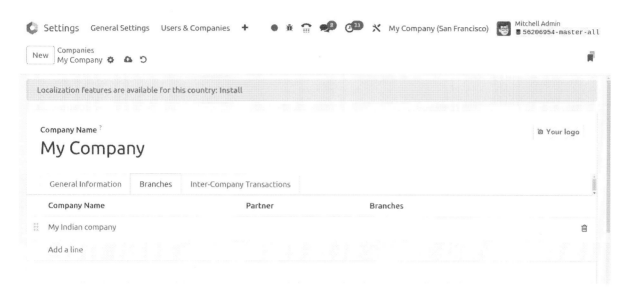

This is the Inter-Company Transaction tab. This gives users the option to choose the rule that will synchronize the Purchase and sales processes.

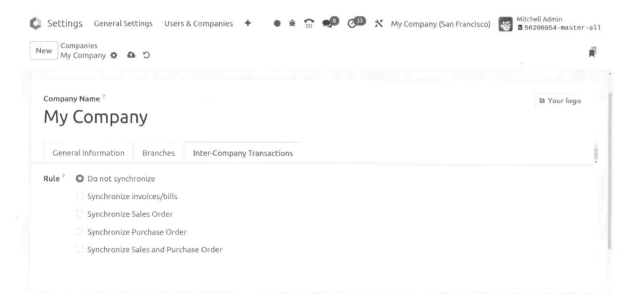

All of the information you enter into the system is immediately stored and may be changed later if necessary.

When we create a database in the Odoo platform with a defined country, the system will automatically install the accounting localization packages for that specific country when we install the Accounting module. By doing this, the company's currency and tax elements will be completed in compliance with the laws and regulations of the relevant jurisdiction.

Furthermore, if it is necessary to establish a new business on a multi-company structure in a nation other than the one previously indicated, the localization features required for managing the new company will be different. Therefore, in these situations, before adopting any accounting entries, we must apply the necessary localization capabilities in the Configuration Settings of the Accounting module.

The Company menu on the Odoo platform may be used to configure a variety of businesses. Now that it is clear how to establish a new business in Odoo, let's look at how to manage several companies' activities in Odoo in the next part.

Multi-Company Operations in Odoo

For enterprises with several companies, Odoo 17 allows you to set up multi-company operations. This enables businesses to handle many organizations, accounts, and financial activities from a single installation. It may also be used for the management of resources that are shared, including customers, partners, and users. Businesses are now able to see every aspect of their operations across all of their subsidiaries thanks to this functionality. In one location, you can access both the individual data of each company and their combined data. Data sharing between businesses is possible when they are connected to one another. This will help them to precisely record transactions and manage their books and accounts in separate ledgers.

From the main platform, you can effortlessly oversee the activities of several firms. These companies could be the partners or the subsidiaries of the primary business, and all of these models can be effectively run from a single platform. It is also possible to create an eCommerce website and a business website for each of the firms, which can be managed independently using the same Odoo system. Businesses operating in the present environment will benefit greatly from this capability. Let's discuss a few advantages of the multi-company business.

- Improved efficiency and cost savings are made possible by multi-company operations, which assist firms to standardize and simplify their processes across many enterprises.
- Centralized data management makes it simpler to access, exchange, and analyze data from any firm throughout the organization by managing data from all companies in a single, centralized system.
- Improved cooperation and communication: A centralized system makes it easier for managers and workers to communicate and collaborate across organizations.
- Improved customer service: Multi-company operations can assist in enhancing customer service by allowing consumers to access all of the company's services and products in one location.
- Simplified financial reporting: With multi-company operations, financial reporting is sped up by the ability to combine financial information from various businesses into a single report.
- Share resources across several businesses to better utilize them.
- Improved visibility of performance and financials across many firms.
- Automatically update and synchronize data across numerous firms.

- Increase security by allowing several degrees of user access and management.

In addition to all these benefits, you can effectively identify and sell the items you set up in one business in others by configuring the product to be available on the websites of all other companies as well as on your own. This feature is available for all product kinds, including services, subscription-based items, rental products, and others. Similarly, as previously said, this functionality allows you to produce distinct reports and synchronized reports with Odoo in line with each of the corporate operations and requirements. In addition to accounting aspects, appropriate oversight of each company with full access to financial management is also available. The system will enable different authorizations for each employee and user of this platform depending on their affiliated firm. This would be highly efficient in guaranteeing that every single task in the business is carried out by the accountable staff members or users of the Odoo platform.

If you've set up many businesses of operations in your Odoo system, you may quickly access them all from the dashboard itself, as the following picture demonstrates.

When you click on the Company name displayed on the main dashboard, a menu will appear displaying all the firms you defined using this platform. You may easily go from one firm to the next by simply clicking on the appropriate company once. This simplest technique will assist in quickly managing the operations of numerous firms, and all responsible users and management may migrate to another company by selecting the appropriate one, and they can function in real-time.

So far, we've spoken about Multi-company management, one of the important operational tools offered by the Odoo platform. We may now move on to the activities of intercompany transfers and their administration in Odoo in the next section.

In the next section, you will learn how to properly handle Intercompany Transfer procedures within partner organizations using Odoo.

Intercompany Transfers

Intercompany Transfer operations may be successfully coordinated among partner organizations using the same Odoo system. In most cases, the element of many companies is directly tied to the operations of the partnership firms, and the normal management team or the manager is responsible for ensuring that the operations run smoothly. The likelihood of running out of goods increases while the affiliated firms are in operation. Because of this, the management or other accountable party will keep the stock from the affiliated firm to get the goods as quickly as feasible. You can manage all the transfer procedures easily with the aid of the Odoo system, and it also makes sure that both organizations have enough inventory. All of these transfers take place within the parameters of very specific contract procedures.

The Odoo platform has a well-designed menu in its Inventory management module, and the module includes extensive capabilities for handling all transfer activities. You can utilize this functionality to function correctly when a product moves from one company's storage site to another's warehouse. In certain cases, having the same warehouse of operations means the goods are directly added to the company's inventory and withdrawn from the other inventory rather than being relocated to the company's warehouses. The intercompany transfer option in Odoo will handle all of the information, and it will be beneficial for future reference.

When discussing the Accounting perspective in relation to the transfer operations of products and services from one company to another, all financial documents and accounting operations should be uniform and in operation in accordance with the requirements set. The Odoo Accounting module aids in your ability to check that all activities are carried out in a highly developed and suitably organized way with regard to the company's operations and future requirements. All descriptions and procedures required for smooth functioning are well established. Let's use an example to help illustrate the points. Suppose there are two companies named B and C that work together to handle the same product. When a product is moved from B to C due to internal requirements, an invoice is created from B to C. Similarly, when a transfer is made from B to C, C creates a purchase bill and sends it to B. This happens in the other direction and between each of the operating firms.

The Odoo platform's invoice generation and Purchase Bills functionalities will ensure that the accounting-related processes in both businesses regarding the transfer of operations are precise. Similar to this, the Odoo platform facilitates both the efficient management of partner businesses and the movement of payments between enterprises via banks. These are all Odoo activities for the internal transfer of products and services in Odoo. Let's now talk in depth about the Translation Settings in Odoo.

Creation of Branches

The process of creating several business records in Odoo 17, each of which represents a different branch, streamlines the management of corporate branches. Independent financial and operational management is made possible by the ease of branch navigation and switching. While preserving branch autonomy, Odoo's centralized configuration guarantees effective communication and data sharing.

Thus, adding branches to a business is quite easy. After choosing the firm's option from the Users & Companies menu, click the New button to add a new firm. The creation form is identical to the one we covered previously. Nonetheless, the General Information tab contains a field called Parent Company. Users are able to specify which corporate branch has been established here.

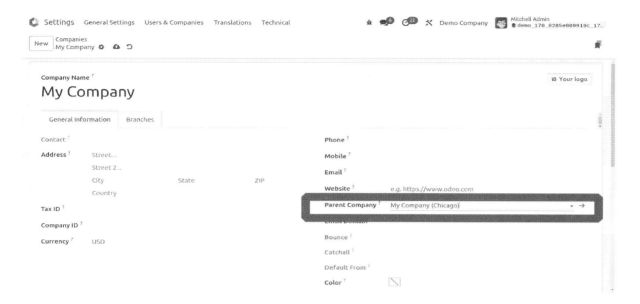

In this case, My Company (Chicago) is designated as its parent company. Thus, My Company is a branch of My Company (Chicago). While you pursued the list of businesses, it depicts the recently established My Company as a branch of My Company (Chicago). In the branch concept, they are using the same chart of accounts.

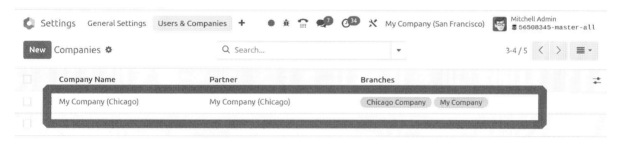

Then, as seen in the picture below, My Company was also added to the Branches page of the parent company My Company (Chicago).

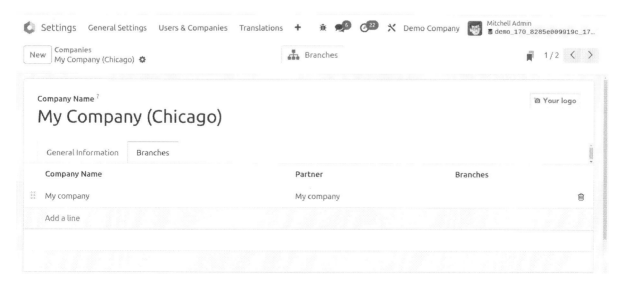

As seen in the figure below, consumers can then navigate to the Branch company with ease.

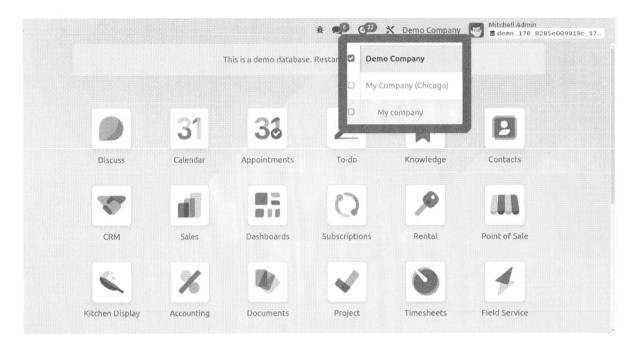

Translation Settings

The Translation Settings function in a business program is a vital tool for multinational enterprises. It enables companies to simply convert their information into a wide range of languages, allowing them to reach a wider audience. By using this functionality, businesses will be able to focus their operations and messaging to customers from other nations and take into account local laws and regulations, improving the user experience. Additionally, it may assist organizations in more effectively communicating complicated information and comprehending the ways in which their company operations work.

In today's business world, all organizations operate on a global scale and in several nations. Additionally, employees are hired from other nations. The management team must be vigilant about the necessity of setting up several languages since the eCommerce website or the corporate website of the organization is seen abroad. It is crucial to provide business management the freedom to function in a multilingual environment, thus, the system has to be able to translate its processes into many languages. The Odoo platform provides it with a localization capability and gives users the option to select the operating language of their choice.

The Translation Settings in Odoo 17 are used to customize an Odoo instance's language and regional settings. The Odoo interface and content may be made to be localized for a particular language, nation, or location using translation options. This makes it easier to design an interface that meets the individual requirements of users in a given location. Additionally, the translation settings enable clients to tailor reports and other materials to their preferred language and geographical location.

The Translation Settings in Odoo 17 allow you to customize your Odoo instance's language settings and make it multilingual. You can manage languages, customize translations, and more with the help of this function, which also allows you to import and export translations in other languages. The Translation Settings are crucial for Odoo 17 because they provide multilingual functionality, making their Odoo instance more accessible to more people. Additionally, it aids in ensuring that the material supplied to various users is in the tongue in which they feel most at ease. The users may access the material in their native tongue thanks to this functionality. Odoo provides descriptions of nearly all languages and enables you to do business globally. You may also download the languages you need based on your needs. In the following section, we can examine the Language configuration tool available in the Odoo platform in detail.

Language Configuration

Odoo's Language Configuration function allows users to choose a default language, set up language preferences, install additional languages, and customize language-specific parameters. The Translation tab of the Odoo Settings module's Odoo Settings module is where you'll find the Language setup menu.

Or else, you can access it from the Settings page under the Languages section.

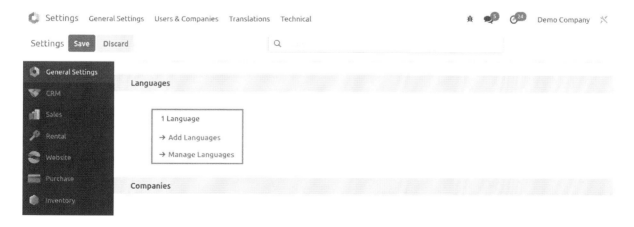

You can see the Add Languages and Manage Languages options here, which will help you complete the appropriate tasks. It will appear in the snapshot of the Languages window below.

The Language window will display in a list style all of the previously specified language information. You may see each language's Locale Code, ISO Code, URL Code, Direction, and a boolean field to determine if it should be active by browsing this window itself. Additionally, you may browse the Update, Disable, and Activate choices based on the active and inactive languages. To enable that specific language, you can tick the boolean column. Similarly, the Filters, Group By, Search, and Favourites tab, which is present in practically all windows of the Odoo platform, is also available here in the window. You can set various filters and grouping options to sort and categorize the list of languages defined according to your business functions and requirements. The Favorites tab has the Save Current Search option as shown below.

The customized one may be saved and put to the favorites list for future reference. Additionally, any language record shown in the menu may be chosen, inspected in depth, and given the option to change some elements if necessary. The establish button is located in the upper left corner of the window and may be used if you need to establish a new language for your company. The following screenshot shows the creation form that will now be displayed by the system.

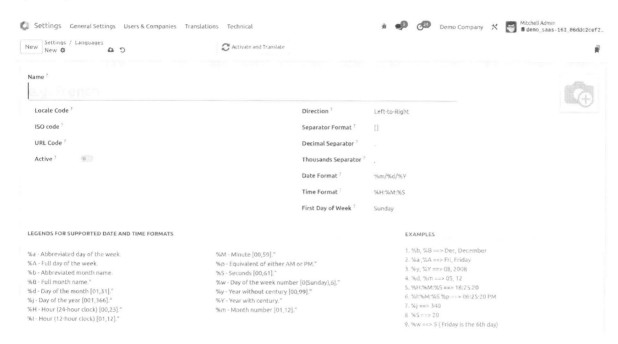

The first item you need to configure in the Language configuration box is the Name field, where you may enter the name of the language. Following that, you must enter the language's locale code in the designated box. Then you must provide the ISO Code where you may assign the names of po files to be used for translations. The URL Code, which will be the language code displayed in the URL, can then be described. The Active field, a boolean field that may be engaged to make the language active, is visible after this field. You can also see the Direction box, where you may select between two options: Right-to-Left and Left-to-Right, where you can choose the suitable one. Then you can mention the Separator Format. Additionally, you can select an appropriate alternative to fill in the Decimal Separator and Thousands Separator sections. The Date Format can then be mentioned in the area given. The Time Format and the First Day of the Week can also be assigned to the field. You have a photo upload area in the window's top right corner where, with the aid of the Edit option, you may upload an image associated with the language. In addition to all of these choices, the window has a separate area where you can examine Legends for the various date and time formats and examples linked to the operations, which will help you understand how the language operates.

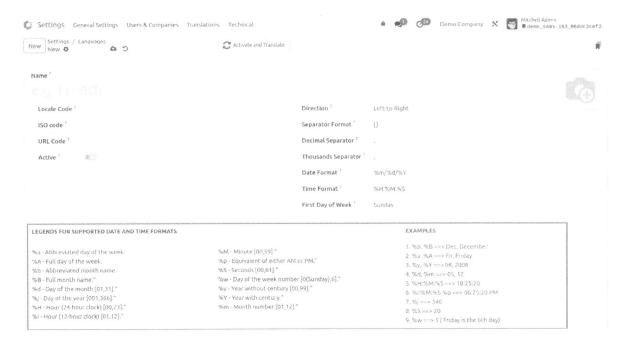

In addition to these options, you can see a smart button labelled 'Activate And Translate,' which is positioned in the upper right corner, as shown in the image below.

This smart button may be used to swiftly activate and translate a language. You may then begin translating the information and activate language with the aid of this. You may swiftly switch between languages with it. When you click the button, the system displays a new pop-up window with a few fields, as seen below.

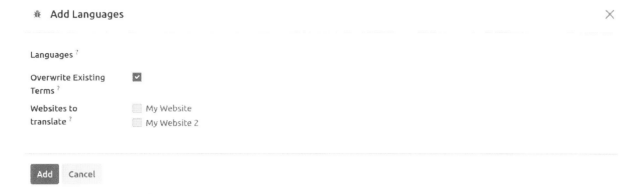

By utilizing this window to add a language, you will be able to rapidly activate and translate into this language and its related documents in the system. As a result, you may use the dropdown menu to select the languages you want to add. The Overwrite Existing Terms box is next. Depending on the user's choices, this field can either be ticked or unchecked. When you enable this feature, you will be able to override existing words in the languages they are translating. This option is helpful if a user wishes to add new translations or update ones that are already there. This implies that the official translations will take precedence over your customized translations. Then, by activating the button, you can select which websites you wish to translate.

Now, the Odoo system will instantly download and install the chosen language, along with all of its translations for all of the system's documents. In their options, users can select their preferred language. In a multilingual setting, this facilitates and expedites language switching.

So far, we have discussed the characteristics of Language configuration in the Odoo platform, and now we may explore the platform's Sequence Number Modification operations in the Accounting activities in the next part.

Sequence Number Modification Operations

Sequence Numbers are used to track and organize data in a business environment. They are used for a variety of purposes, such as tracking purchases, invoices, shipments, inventory, and customer orders. They also help to ensure accuracy and consistency in data entry. Sequence Numbers are also used to help enforce security measures, as they can be used to uniquely identify individual records or transactions. It also helps businesses to identify data that has been changed or added, helping to ensure that data integrity is maintained.

The Odoo ERP encourages Sequence number operations which will result in the better management of every significant document in the business operations. These Sequence Numbers are vitally important in everyday business operations and provide insight into the kind of document operations where the sequence numbers are described. This will perform as an identification tool which will be very useful for collaborative business functioning.

As we said, the Sequence Number Modification in the Odoo Accounting module is an automated process that helps in modifying the already existing sequence numbers in the system. The Sequence numbers are automatically generated in Odoo for various documents such as Sales orders, Invoices, Purchase orders, Journal entries, and other documents. These sequence numbers are very important in maintaining the accounting data in an organized manner.

You can quickly modify the sequence number operations in accordance with the functional requirements in the operations of your business. The option for Sequence Number modification will only be available when you activate the developer mode of the Odoo system. To do so, you can get into the General Settings tab, where when you scroll down, you will find the Activate developer mode option.

Once you activate the Developer mode of the Odoo platform, you will get more options and tools for advanced operations. Now in the Settings module, under the Technical tab, you will find the Sequences menu in the Sequences & Identifiers section, as highlighted in the screenshot below.

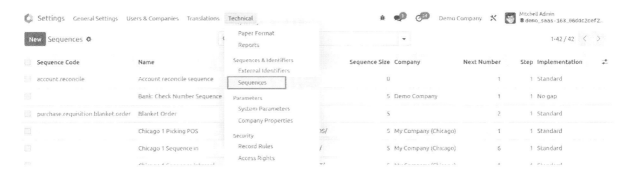

A smart click on the menu will take you to the Sequences window, where you can manage the sequences, as shown below.

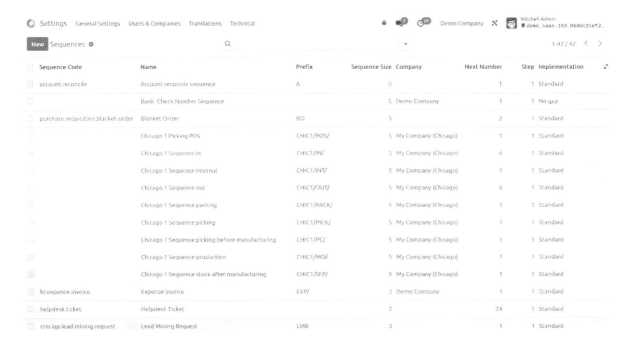

The Sequences window will depict the preview of all already defined sequences along with the Sequence Code, Name, Prefix, Sequence Size, Company, Next Number, Step, and Implementation aspects. This window also furnishes various kinds of sorting functionalities, as we can see in every window of the Odoo platform. The default and customizable filtering options available under the Filters tab are convenient for filtering out the required sequences from the whole list. In addition, you can categorize and group the sequences in various terms based on the needs using the Group By option available. The Favourites tab consists of the Save current search, Import records, Link menu in spreadsheet, Link list in spreadsheet options which will be depicted in the dropdown when you click on the Favourites button. Likewise, you can export all the details of the window to an excel sheet by choosing the 'Export All' button. Using the Search bar, you can easily search the required Sequences that you defined in the platform.

Every single record that is already configured in the platform can be selected and viewed in detail. Also, you can edit the existing details of the sequence, and it is also possible to perform various actions with the help of the Action button. The Action button existing on the top right will consist of the Archive, Duplicate, and Delete buttons which can be applied to performing corresponding actions.

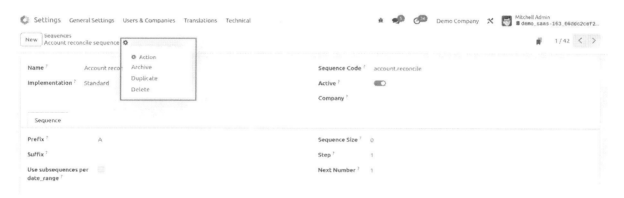

The CREATE button situated on the top left corner of the Sequences window paves you the way to create new sequences. The new creation window will look like in the image given below.

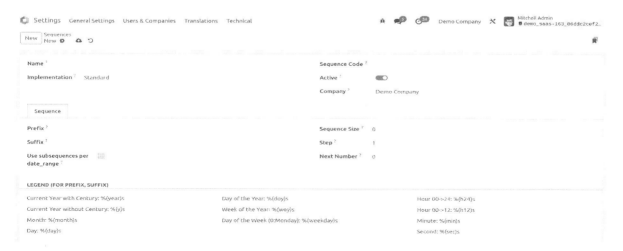

Here, first of all, you can allocate the name of the Sequence in the Name field. Then you can set the Implementation detail as 'Standard' or 'No gap' from the dropdown menu. These options are useful for deciding whether or not a gap should be left between the numbers of two consecutive sequence numbers. (While assigning a sequence number to a record, the "No Gap" sequence implementation ensures that each previous sequence number has been assigned already. While this sequence implementation will not skip any sequence number upon assignment, there can still be gaps in the sequence if record is deleted. The 'No gap' implementation is slower than the standard one. After defining this field, you can set the Sequence Code. the Active field can be enabled or disabled based on your preferences. If you want to make this respective sequence active, you can activate this boolean field. The Company associated with this operation will be auto-depicted in the Company field, and this field is very useful for managing multiple companies of operation.

Under the **Sequence** tab, you can define the sequence configuration aspects where the Prefix field allows you to set the prefix value of the record for the sequence. Similarly, the Suffix field can be filled with the suffix value of the record for the respective sequence. Further, the Sequence Size will be automatically defined as zero so that the Odoo will automatically add up 'zero' on the left of the 'Next Number' to get the required padding size. Also, the Step of operation can be described based on your preferences in the corresponding field. As a result, the next number of the sequence will be incremented by this number.

Next, you can see the 'Use subsequences per date range' field which can be activated for configuring the respective subsequence operation details. When you activate this option, you will depict the extra lines to add the details, as shown in the screenshot below.

By clicking on the Add a line, you can add the details. For adding the details, the system will depict the calendar pop-up in the 'From' and 'To' fields. Using this calendar pop-up, the dates of the sequence operation can be effortlessly configured by defining the From, To dates along with the Next Number of sequences. In each of the lines, you can view the delete option, which can be used to remove the respective sequence operation if required. The operational aspects of the prefix and the suffix are there under the LEGEND (FOR PREFIX, SUFFIX) section, as shown in the screenshot below.

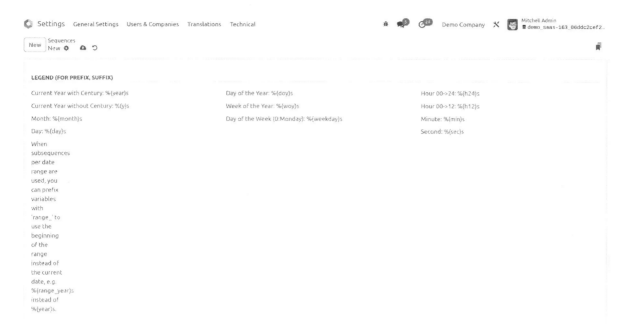

With the help of this feature in Odoo, the sequence operations associated with the functioning of the different documents and businesses in your organization can be systematized. Using this particular menu, Odoo allows the required modifications with respect to the business functioning.

By referring to this chapter, you will get complete knowledge about the aspects of the configurations of Admin Settings using the Odoo platform and its benefits. The Odoo 17 is a highly improved version of Odoo, and it helps you to configure the platform in accordance with the requirements of the business. We had a detailed analysis of the User Settings, Company Settings, Translation Settings, and other aspects available in the Odoo instance. In the next chapter, we can have an exclusive view of - Storno Accounting - a new accounting feature introduced in the Odoo 17 platform, which is the feature that allows you to make corrections to incorrect financial transactions by reversing the incorrect transactions and recording a new, corrected transaction. This helps to ensure that your book remains accurate and up to date. Storno Accounting also simplifies the process of reconciling your accounts and simplifies the process of making corrections to incorrect transactions. The chapter also takes a look at the Accounting firms mode introduced in the 17 version of Odoo.

Chapter 8
Unlocking the Power of Odoo 17 Storno Accounting

Unlocking the Power of Odoo 17 Storno Accounting

Storno accounting in Odoo17 is described as the process of undoing initial journal account entries by using negative values. Storno Accounting is a prevalent business practice in Eastern European nations. Storno Accounting is required in several nations, such as:

- Bosnia and Herzegovina
- China
- Czech Republic
- Croatia
- Poland
- Romania
- Russia
- Serbia
- Slovakia
- Slovenia
- Ukraine

They view storno accounting as the ideal method for reversing journal entries with negative debits and credits so that the accounting system won't have duplicate figures. The reversal can occur for a variety of reasons, such as when errors occur in the initial transaction or, when a refund must be made for the return of merchandise, etc. This accounting approach is also known as Red Storno since bookkeepers commonly write Storno entries in red ink. The accounting reports will display all such items in red.

To use these functionalities, turn on "Storno Accounting" in the Odoo 17 Accounting Module's Configuration Settings.

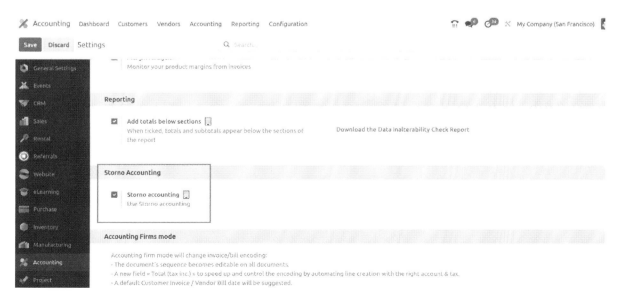

In general, when a transaction takes place, let's say an invoice is generated, certain ledger accounts will be impacted. Generally, when an invoice is paid, the Income Accounts are credited, and the Account Receivable is debited. If this transaction is reversed, normally, what will happen is the Income Account will be debited, and the Account Receivable will be credited. However, for Storno accounting, the Account Receivable will be a "-ve" Debit and the Income Account a "-ve" Credit for the reverse entry.

Consider the Invoice that has been added in the screenshot below.

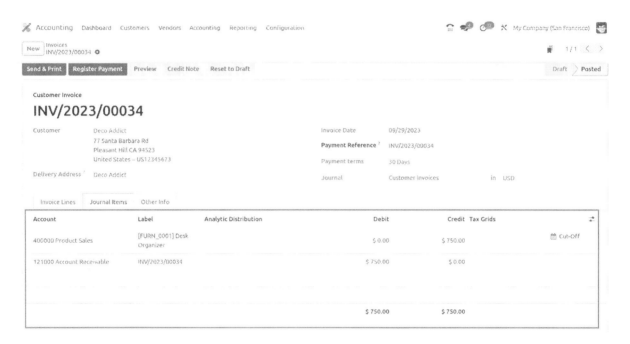

And for some reason, if this invoice is reversed, a credit note is made, posted, and recorded. Let's examine the journal entry now and how it affects each ledger.

When creating an invoice, the Income Account is Credited and the Account Receivable is Debited; however, when creating a reverse invoice or credit note, the Income Account is established as the opposite entry and is Debited and the Account Receivable is Credited.

When Storno accounting is enabled, the Debits and Credits for reversed journal entries are negative. For the invoice, make an invoice and a credit note accordingly. Viewing the ledger posting in Storno Accounting is next.

In the case of invoicing, the Income Account is first credited, the Tax Account is credited, and the Account Receivable is debited. When a journal entry is reversed, the Income Account and Tax Account are credited with a negative value, while the Account Receivable is debited with a negative figure. In a nutshell, the table below displays the posting to both the regular ledger and the Storno ledger.

		General		Storno	
		Debit	Credit	Debit	Credit
Invoice	Income Account		147.00		147.00
	Tax Account		22.05		22.05
	Account Receivable	169.05		169.05	
Reverse Invoice	Income Account	147.00			-147.00
	Tax account	22.05			-22.05
	Account Receivable		169.05	−169.05	

Accounting Firm Mode

Accounting Firm Mode, another feature of Odoo 17, alters the invoice/bill encoding. Depending on the encoding, a defined sequence of documents is decided whether or not it is editable. The accounting module's configuration settings allow you to set the accounting firm mode. The document can be encoded under the Accounting Firm Mode section. 'Customer Invoices,' 'Vendor Bills', or 'Customer Invoices plus Vendor Bills' are all acceptable options.

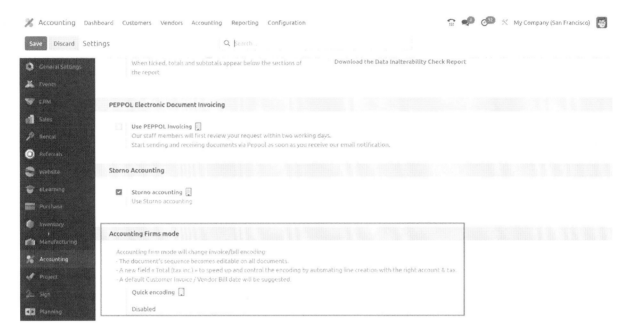

Once the encoding document has been selected, save the modifications. Accounting firm mode will change the encoding of bills and invoices. The sequence of the document is now customizable on all invoices and bills.

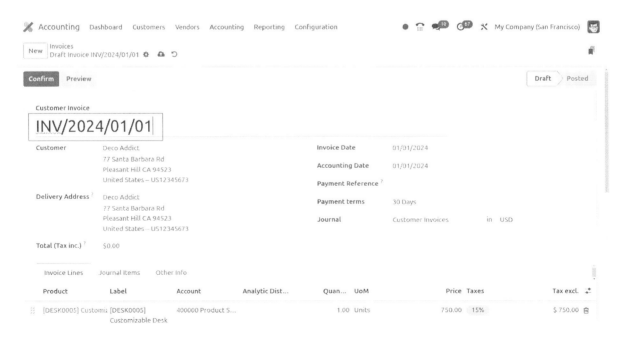

The new field "Total (tax inc.)" on the invoices and bills will appear in the document with the appropriate account and tax, speeding, and managing the encoding.

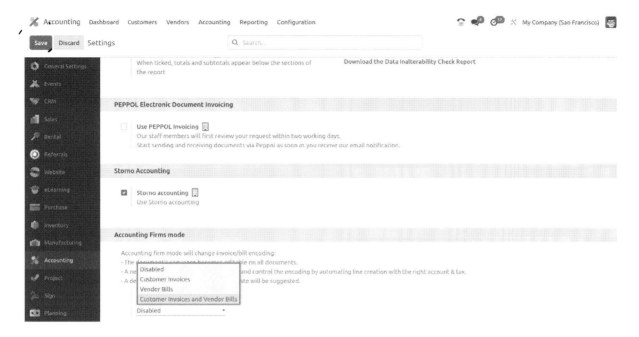

If 'Customer Invoices and Bills' is selected as the quick encoding, the sequence of these documents is customizable. It is also possible to determine the gap between the invoices/bills. So, while creating an invoice, the sequence number can be changed, and a new field, Total (tax inc), needs to be added.

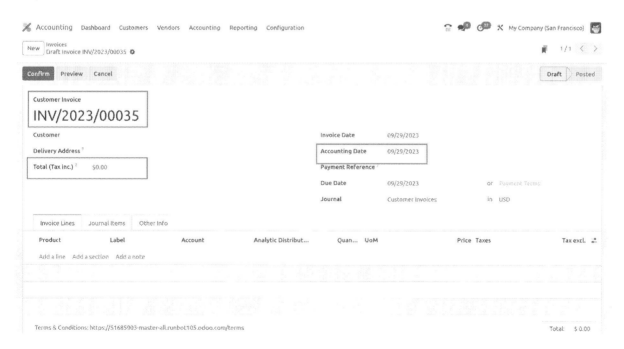

The field 'Total (tax inc)' is used to encode the invoice's total amount. Odoo will automatically generate a single invoice line with matching default values. Also, the invoice date is predicted automatically.

Consider changing the invoice number in the screenshot below to INV/2023/00035 and the 'Total (tax inc)' field to $400, even if the customer hasn't been specified. The price, including taxes, is $400. As a result, a line is automatically inserted under the bills line even though there is no product present; instead, the untaxed value is 347.83, and a 15% tax is applied for a total of $400.

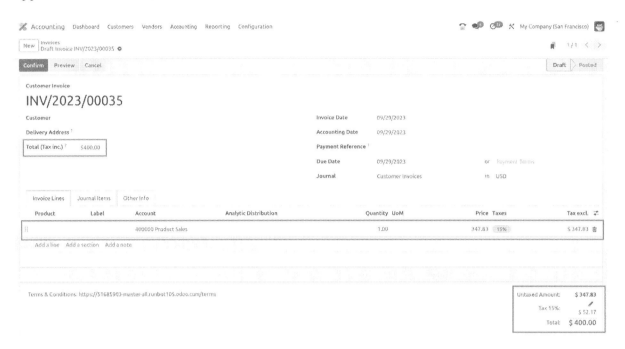

Since quick encoding documents have been selected as 'Customer Invoices and Vendor Bills' in the accounting setup settings, this will also be accessible for vendor bills. The accounting dashboard for the relevant journal will indicate any gaps in the invoice or bill sequence.

The invoices with sequence gaps will be shown in red color in the list view.

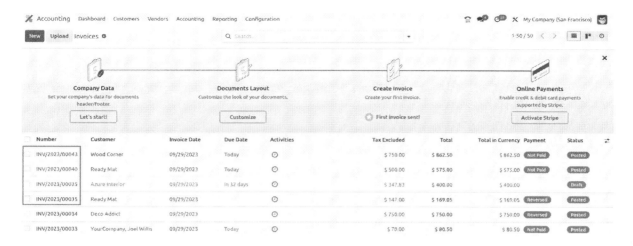

If needed, the invoice/bill number can be resequenced. Select the records whose sequence has to be changed, and the 'Resequence' option will appear in the actions menu.

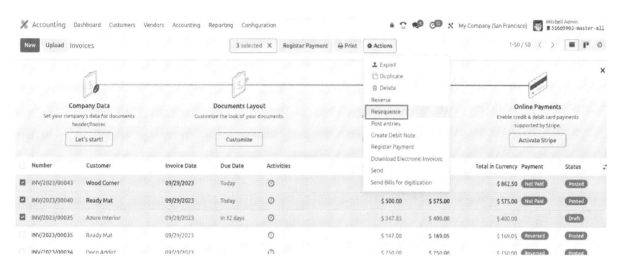

When you click 'Resequence,' a pop-up window displays where you may provide information for requesting the data. In the screenshot above, the invoice number 'INV/2023/00035' is followed by 'INV/2023/00040' and then 'INV/2023/00043'. Therefore, we can resequence to fill in this gap.

Resequence   ✕

| Ordering ? | ● Keep current order | First New Sequence ? | INV/2023/00035 |
| | ○ Reorder by accounting date | | |

Preview Modifications ?

Date	Before	After
09/29/2023	INV/2023/00043	INV/2023/00037
09/29/2023	INV/2023/00040	INV/2023/00036
09/29/2023	INV/2023/00035	INV/2023/00035

Confirm Cancel

We will be able to include the next sequence number in the pop-up, and so the records following the INV/2023/00035 will be modified from INV/2023/00036 onwards. Additionally, you have the option to reorder documents using the "Keep Current Order" or "Reorder By Accounting Date" criteria.

When the sequence is confirmed to be in sequential order, the accounting dashboard's sequence gap alert is also eliminated.

Audit Trails

Accounting audit trails are an essential instrument for preserving accountability and openness in financial operations. They give auditors a thorough, chronological record of all financial transactions, making it possible for them to follow and confirm the accuracy of entries. This supports financial integrity and regulatory compliance by identifying mistakes, fraud, or disparities. Furthermore, by offering a thorough record of all operations that can be examined and adjusted as needed, audit trails improve the accuracy of financial statements. In the end, accounting's use of audit trails guarantees a solid framework that inspires confidence in stakeholders and promotes efficient financial management.

Thus, the accounting module in Odoo 17's Settings displays an option named Audit Trail. Give the audit trail activation option a go.

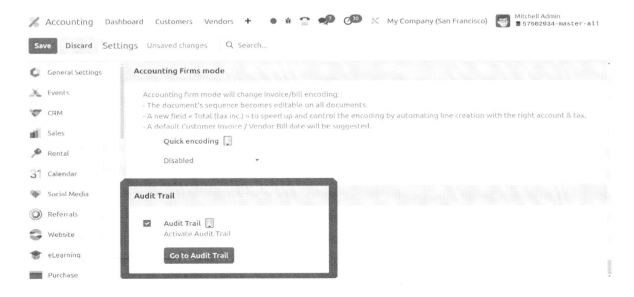

User modifications to an invoice will all be recorded in this audit trail. In order for the auditor to easily comprehend the modifications and revisions made to each invoice. This can be accessed by selecting the **Go to Audit Trail** option.

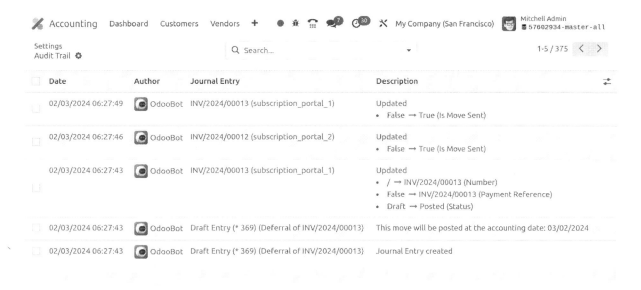

As seen in the image above, the date, author, journal entry, and description are accessible here.

The Odoo Accounting module will operate as the solution provider for the business operations management activities of an Organization, starting with specialized tools and solution providers that will pave the way for the company's efficiency in finance management. The Odoo Accounting book gives you a thorough understanding of the accounting management processes used by your company. In the book, we first covered an overview of Odoo. Then, we moved on to the Configuration choices and tools available in the Odoo Accounting module, which will serve as the foundation for operations and management.

In the following chapter, we focused on the Configuration tools in the Accounting module, where all of the configuration options, such as Accounting configurations, Payment Options, Management Options, Analytical Accounting, Configuring Invoicing, and Configuring Bank Payments, provide insight into how the Configuration tools in Odoo can be configured to meet the best of needs. We concentrated on the financial management elements of suppliers and customers with Odoo Accounting in the fourth chapter. The Accounting Module Dashboard, Customer Finance management with the Odoo Accounting module, and Odoo Accounting module Vendor management procedures were all discussed.

The fifth chapter of the book focuses on the accounting management tools in the Odoo Accounting module and includes detailed descriptions of the accounting management tools, accounting management actions, accounting ledgers, journal management, and administration of other miscellaneous entities. Additionally, in the sixth chapter, we discussed reporting, which is the best aspect of Odoo Accounting. In this chapter, we went into detail about topics like audit reports, management-based reporting, partner reports, and US GAAP reports, and provided examples of the Odoo platform.

In the seventh chapter of the Odoo Accounting book, we concentrated on the Configurations of Admin settings of the Odoo platform. In this chapter, the functions of the Odoo platform's User settings, Company settings, and Translation settings were thoroughly explained. Finally, the new accounting practice Strono Accounting and Accounting firms mode introduced in Odoo 17 is defined in this chapter.

In general, the Odoo Accounting module addressed a gap in the Odoo resource in terms of the demand for Functional reference materials for the Odoo Accounting module.

Conclusion

Odoo 17's Accounting module represents a significant step forward in empowering businesses to streamline their financial operations, improve efficiency, and make informed decisions. With its streamlined user interface, enhanced automation capabilities, advanced reporting tools, seamless integration with other modules, and improved multi-currency support, Odoo 17 is poised to revolutionize the way businesses manage their accounting processes. Whether you're a small startup or a large enterprise, embracing Odoo 17's Accounting module can unlock new levels of efficiency and productivity in your organization's financial management practices.

From the foundational understanding provided in the introductory chapters to the advanced techniques explored in later sections, we've witnessed firsthand the transformative power of Odoo in revolutionizing financial management for businesses of all scales. One of the standout features of Odoo 17 is its commitment to user empowerment through intuitive configuration tools. Whether it's tailoring settings to match specific business requirements or seamlessly integrating with existing workflows, Odoo empowers users to take control of their financial processes with ease and efficiency.

Moreover, the comprehensive suite of features for financial management with customers and vendors underscores Odoo's dedication to streamlining interactions across the entire supply chain. From invoicing and payments to vendor management and reconciliation, Odoo offers a holistic solution that fosters stronger relationships and smoother transactions.

As we delved deeper into Odoo 17's Accounting Management capabilities, we discovered a wealth of tools and functionalities designed to optimize every aspect of financial tracking and reporting. From automated journal entries to real-time analytics, Odoo equips users with the insights needed to make informed decisions and drive business growth.

Furthermore, the reporting capabilities of Odoo Accounting are unparalleled, offering customizable dashboards and reports that provide actionable insights at a glance. With Odoo, users can unlock the power of data-driven decision-making, gaining a competitive edge in today's dynamic business landscape.

Beyond its core accounting features, Odoo 17 shines in its platform-wide configuration settings, offering endless possibilities for customization and scalability. Whether it's adapting to changing regulatory requirements or scaling operations to meet growing demand, Odoo provides the flexibility needed to thrive in any environment.

Finally, the introduction of Storno Accounting in Odoo 17 represents a significant milestone in financial management, simplifying the process of correcting errors and ensuring data accuracy with minimal effort.

In essence, Odoo 17's Accounting Module stands as a testament to the platform's commitment to innovation, usability, and efficiency. By harnessing the power of Odoo, businesses can elevate their financial management practices to new heights, driving success and sustainability in an ever-evolving marketplace.

We hope this book has served as a valuable resource in unlocking the full potential of Odoo 17's Accounting Module, empowering you to navigate the complexities of modern finance with confidence and clarity. As you embark on your journey with Odoo, may you continue to explore, innovate, and thrive in pursuit of your financial goals.

Made in United States
Orlando, FL
11 May 2025

61197672R00199